Network Analyzers
Computer Network Security

Contents

Chapter 1

Accelops

AccelOps provides a unified network analytics platform via a software virtual appliance for security information and event management (SIEM) and performance, availability, and change monitoring of Data Center Infrastructure from network devices, environmental equipment such as UPS, servers, storage, hypervisors, and applications.

1.1 Description

AccelOps offers an integrated, unified and service-oriented platform for monitoring, alerting, analyzing and reporting across performance, availability, security and change management for IT service management.

1.1.1 Details

AccelOps' data center and IT service management platform, presented through a Web 2.0 GUI using Adobe Flex, provides operational data collection, monitoring, predictive alerting, root-cause analysis and detailed reporting on all IT event log and performance data acrossnetwork management, systems management, applications, virtualization, vendors and technology systems.

Integrated datacenter monitoring functionality includes:

- Performance and availability monitoring

- Security Information and Event Management

- Configuration Management Database (CMDB) and change management

- Compliance automation

- Network visualization and enterprise search

- Identity and location management

AccelOps software is deployed on-premises as a "virtual appliance" on VMware with no agents required.[1] As of December 2012, AccelOps claimed it was used to monitor 350 datacenters.[2]

1.1.2 History

AccelOps is short for Accelerate Operations.[3] The Silicon Valley-based company is privately held, venture-backed and led by the team that created the Cisco Security Monitoring, Analysis, and Response System (CS-MARS) security appliance. Imin Lee and Partha Bhattacharya left Cisco Systems in 2007 and founded the company.[4] By 2009 the company had $8 million in funding and 48 employees.[3]

1.1.3 Recognition

The product was described as the "best integrated security" in a marketing research report in 2012.[5] AccelOps was selected by Gartner Group as one of the "Cool Vendors in IT Operations Management" for 2012.[6]

1.2 See also

- Comparison of network monitoring systems

- List of systems management systems

1.3 References

[1] Joan Goodchild. "Network and Security Operations Convergence: A Mini-Case Study". *CSO Magazine*. Retrieved May 28, 2013.

[2] AccelOps (November 29, 2012). "AccelOps Doubles Customers, Revenues for Its Integrated SIEM, Performance and Availability Software in FY 2012". *News release*. Retrieved May 28, 2013.

[3] "AccelOps solves problems by looking at whole data center". *San Jose Business Journal.* November 15, 2009. Retrieved May 28, 2013.

[4] Ellen Messmer (June 4, 2010). "California Casualty ditches Cisco security box". *Network World.* Retrieved May 28, 2013.

[5] Dennis Drogseth (December 2012). "Enterprise Management Associates Radar for Advanced Performance Analytics Use Cases: Q4 2012" (PDF). Retrieved May 28, 2013.

[6] Milind Govekar, Ronni J. Colville and Ian Head (April 11, 2012). "Cool Vendors in IT Operations Management, 2012". Gartner.

1.4   External links

- Website

- Computer Technology Review of AccelOps v1.5.1

- Enterprise Management Associates Report

- Frost and Sullivan Report

- Redmonk Research Review

- CIO Magazine: High-Powered Data-Center Management Tools Come Down Market

Chapter 2

Aircrack-ng

Aircrack-ng is a network software suite consisting of a detector, packet sniffer, WEP and WPA/WPA2-PSK cracker and analysis tool for 802.11 wireless LANs. It works with any wireless network interface controller whose driver supports raw monitoring mode and can sniff 802.11a, 802.11b and 802.11g traffic. The program runs under Linux and Windows; the Linux version is packaged for OpenWrt and has also been ported to the Android, Zaurus and Maemo platforms; and a proof of concept port has been made to the iPhone.

In April 2007 a team at the Darmstadt University of Technology in Germany developed a new attack method based on a paper released on the RC4 cipher by Adi Shamir. This new attack, named 'PTW', decreases the number of initialization vectors or IVs needed to decrypt a WEP key and has been included in the aircrack-ng suite since the 0.9 release.

Aircrack-ng is a fork of the original Aircrack project.

2.1 Features

The aircrack-ng software suite includes:

2.2 See also

- Packet sniffer

- SpoonWEP/WPA

- AirSnort

- Kali Linux

- BackTrack

- TCP sequence prediction attack

2.3 References

[1] "Aircrack-ng 1.2 Release Candidate 2". *Aircrack-ng - Official Aircrack-ng blog* (Blog). 2015-04-10. Retrieved 2015-04-28.

2.4 External links

- Official website

- Aircrack airodump and aireplay tutorial

- Aircrack-ng (WEP, WPA-PSK crack) on openSUSE10.1 at the Wayback Machine (archived August 5, 2012)

- Aircrack-2.3 on Windows (Wireless WEP crack) at the Wayback Machine (archived June 19, 2012)

- Aircrack-ng on BackTrack

Chapter 3

AirSnort

AirSnort is a Linux and Microsoft Windows utility (using GTK+) for decrypting WEP encryption on an 802.11b network. Distributed under the GNU General Public License,[1] AirSnort is free software. It is no longer maintained or supported.

3.1 See also

- Aircrack-ng
- SpoonWEP/WPA

3.2 References

[1] "source code: /AirSnort/COPYING".

3.3 External links

- AirSnort Homepage

Chapter 4

Argus - Audit Record Generation and Utilization System

Argus – the Audit Record Generation and Utilization System is the first implementation of network flow monitoring, and is an ongoing open source network flow monitor project. Started by Carter Bullard in 1984 at Georgia Tech, and developed for cyber security at Carnegie Mellon University in the early 1990s, Argus has been an important contributor to Internet cyber security technology over its 30 years.[1] .

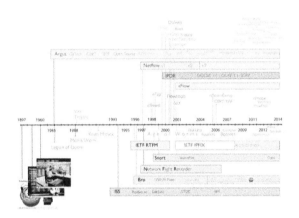

Network Flow Monitoring Timeline

The Argus Project is focused on developing all aspects of large scale network situational awareness and network audit trail establishment in support of Network Operations (NetOps), Performance and Security Management. Motivated by the telco Call detail record (CDR), Argus attempts to generate network metadata that can be used to perform a large number of network management tasks. Argus is used by many universities, corporations and government entities including US DISA, DoD, DHS, FFRDCs, GLORIAD and is a Top 100 Internet Security Tool.[2] Argus is designed to be a real-time situational awareness system, and its data can be used to track, alarm and alert on wire-line network

conditions. The data can also be used to establish a comprehensive audit of all network traffic, as described in the Red Book, US DoD NCSC-TG-005,[3] supplementing traditional Intrusion detection system (IDS) based network security.[4] The audit trail is traditionally used as historical network traffic measurement data for network forensics[5] and Network Behavior Anomaly Detection (NBAD).[6] Argus has been used extensively in cybersecurity, end-to-end performance analysis, and more recently, software-defined networking (SDN) research.[7] Argus has also been a topic in network management standards development. RMON (1995) [8] and IPFIX (2001).[9]

Argus is composed of an advanced comprehensive network flow data generator, the Argus monitor, which processes packets (either capture files or live packet data) and generates detailed network traffic flow status reports of all the flows in the packet stream. Argus monitors all network traffic, data plane, control plane and management plane, not just Internet Protocol (IP) traffic. Argus captures much of the packet dynamics and semantics of each flow, with a great deal of data reduction, so you can store, process, inspect and analyze large amounts of network data efficiently. Argus provides reachability, availability, connectivity, duration, rate, load, good-put, loss, jitter, retransmission (data networks), and delay metrics for all network flows, and captures most attributes that are available from the packet contents, such as Layer 2 addresses, tunnel identifiers (MPLS, GRE, IPsec, etc...), protocol ids, SAP's, hop-count, options, L4 transport identification (RTP detection), host flow control indications, etc... Argus has implemented a number of packet dynamics metrics specifically designed for cyber security. Argus detects human typing behavior in any flow, but of particular interest is key-stroke detection in encrypted SSH tunnels.[10] and Argus generates the Producer Consumer Ratio (PCR) which indicates whether a network entity is a data producer and/or consumer,[11] an important property when evaluating the potential for a node to be involved in an Advanced persistent threat (APT) mediated exfiltration.

Argus is an Open Source (GPL) project, owned and managed by QoSient, LLC, and has been ported to most operating systems and many hardware accelerated platforms, such as Bivio, Pluribus, Arista, and Tilera. The software should be portable to many other environments with little or no modifications. Performance is such that auditing an entire enterprise's Internet activity can be accomplished using modest computing resources.

4.1   Supported platforms

- Linux: Unix operating system running the Linux kernel

- Solaris: Unix operating system developed by Sun Microsystems

- BSD: Unix operating system family (FreeBSD, NetBSD, OpenBSD)

- OS X: Unix operating system developed by Apple Inc.

- IRIX: Unix operating system developed by Silicon Graphics

- AIX, Unix operating system developed by IBM

- Windows, (under Cygwin) operating system developed by Microsoft

- OpenWrt: Unix operation system running the Linux kernel on embedded devices

4.2   References

[1] http://www.qosient.com/argus/publications.shtml

[2] http://sectools.org

[3] http://csrc.nist.gov/publications/secpubs/rainbow/tg005.txt

[4] R. Bejtlich, The Tao of Network Security Monitoring: Beyond Intrusion Detection , New York:Addison-Wesley, 2004.

[5] Emmanuel S. Pilli, R. C. Joshi, and Rajdeep Niyogi. 2010. Network forensic frameworks: Survey and research challenges. Digit. Investig. 7, 1–2 (October 2010), 14–27. DOI=10.1016/j.diin.2010.02.003 http://dx.doi.org/10.1016/j.diin.2010.02.00

[6] G. Nychis, V. Sekar, D Andersen, H Kim, H Zhang, An empirical evaluation of entropy-based traffic anomaly detection, Proceedings of the 8th ACM SIGCOMM conference on Internet measurement, pp 151–156, October 20–22, 2008, Vouliagmeni, Greece

[7] J. Naous, D. Ericson, A. Covington, G Appenzeller, N. McKeown, Implementing an OpenFlow switch on the NetF-PGA platform, Symposium On Architecture For Networking And Communications Systems, pp. 1–9, 2008, San Jose, CA

[8] ftp://ietf.org/ietf/rmonmib/rmonmib-minutes-94dec.txt

[9] http://www.ietf.org/proceedings/51/slides/ipfx-2/sld001.htm

[10] Saptarshi Guha, Paul Kidwell, Asgrith Barthur, William S Cleveland, John Gerth, and Carter Bullard. 2011. SSH Keystroke Packet Detection, ICS-2011—Monterey, California, Jan 9–11.

[11] http://www.qosient.com/argus/presentations/Argus.FloCon.2014.PCR.Presentation.pdf

4.3   External links

- Argus website

Chapter 5

ArpON

ArpON (**ARP handler inspection**)[1] is a computer software project to improve network security.[2] It has attracted interest among network managers[3][4][5][6][7][8][9] and academic researchers[10][11][12][13][14][15] and is frequently cited as a significant means of protecting against ARP-based attacks.[16][17][18][19][20]

5.1 Motivation

The Address Resolution Protocol (ARP) has security issues. These include the Man In The Middle (MITM) attack through ARP Spoofing, ARP Cache Poisoning or ARP Poison Routing (APR) attacks. ArpON also blocks derived attacks including Sniffing, Hijacking, Injection, Filtering attacks and complex derived attacks, as: DNS Spoofing, WEB Spoofing, Session Hijacking and SSL/TLS Hijacking attacks.

This is possible using three kinds of anti ARP Spoofing techniques. ArpON requires a daemon in every host to be authenticated. It does not modify the classic ARP standard base protocol defined by IETF, but rather sets precise policies for static networks, dynamic networks and hybrid networks.

ArpON does not use a centralized server or encryption. It uses a cooperative authentication between the hosts based on the policies that all hosts with ArpON must respect. These policies allow exactly total protection by these attacks for all hosts that use ArpON.

5.2 Features

Some of ArpON's features are:

- Support for interfaces: Ethernet, Wireless

- Manages the network interface with: Unplug iface, Boot OS, Hibernation OS, Suspension OS

- Proactive based solution for connections: Point-to-Point, Point-to-Multipoint, Multipoint

- Type of authentication for host: Cooperative between the hosts

- Support for networks: Statically, Dynamically (DHCP), Hybrid network that is statically and dynamically

- Retro compatible with: Classic ARP standard base protocol by IETF

- Support of Gratuitous ARP request and reply for: Failover Cluster, Cluster with load-balancing, High-Availability (HA) Cluster

- Blocks the Man In The Middle (MITM) attack through: ARP Spoofing, ARP Cache Poisoning, ARP Poison Routing (APR)

- Three kinds of anti ARP Spoofing techniques: SARPI or Static ARP Inspection, DARPI or Dynamic ARP Inspection, HARPI or Hybrid ARP Inspection

- Blocks the derived attacks: Sniffing, Hijacking, Injection, Filtering and co attacks

- Blocks the complex derived attacks: DNS Spoofing, WEB Spoofing, Session Hijacking, SSL/TLS Hijacking and co attacks

- Tested against: Ettercap, Cain and Abel, DSniff, Yersinia, scapy, netcut, Metasploit, arpspoof, sslsniff, sslstrip and co tools

5.3 Algorithms

ArpON detects and blocks man-in-the-middle attack (MITM) through ARP spoofing, ARP cache poisoning, ARP poison routing (APR) attacks and it is countermeasure against these attacks and the derived attacks by it, which sniffing, hijacking, injection, filtering & co attacks for more complex derived attacks, as: DNS spoofing, WEB spoofing, session hijacking and SSL/TLS hijacking attacks.

- SARPI (Static ARP Inspection) manages a list with static entries, for statically configured networks without DHCP.

- DARPI (Dynamic ARP Inspection) manages uniquely a list with dynamic entries so can be used in dynamically configured networks having DHCP.

- HARPI (Hybrid ARP Inspection) manages both kinds of lists simultaneously.

5.4   See also

- Arpwatch

- Arping

5.5   References

[1] "ArpON(8) manual page".

[2] "ArpON - Google books".

[3] Kaspersky lab. "Storage Cloud Infrastructures - Detection and Mitigation of MITM Attacks" (PDF).

[4] Prowell, Stacy; et al. *Seven Deadliest Network Attacks*. p. 135.

[5] Gary Bahadur, Jason Inasi; et al. *Securing the Clicks Network Security in the Age of Social Media*. p. 96.

[6] Roebuck, Kevin. *IT Security Threats: High-impact Strategies - What You Need to Know*. p. 517.

[7] Wason, Rohan. *A Professional guide to Ethical Hacking: All about Hacking*.

[8] Prowse, David L. *CompTIA Security+ SY0-401 Cert Guide, Academic Edition*.

[9] Roebuck, Kevin. *Network Security: High-impact Strategies - What You Need to Know*. p. 17.

[10] Stanford University. "An Introduction to Computer Networks" (PDF).

[11] Martin Zaefferer, Yavuz Selim Inanir; et al. "Intrusion Detection: Case Study" (PDF).

[12] Jaroslaw Paduch, Jamie Levy; et al. "Using a Secure Permutational Covert Channel to Detect Local and Wide Area Interposition Attacks" (PDF).

[13] Xiaohong Yuan, David Matthews; et al. "Laboratory Exercises for Wireless Network Attacks and Defenses" (PDF).

[14] Hofbauer, Stefan. "A privacy conserving approach for the development of Sip security services to prevent certain types of MITM and Toll fraud attacks in VOIP systems" (PDF).

[15] D. M. de Castro, E. Lin; et al. "Typhoid Adware" (PDF).

[16] Jing (Dave) Tian, Kevin R. B. Butler; et al. "Securing ARP From the Ground Up" (PDF).

[17] Jyotinder Kaur, Sandeep Kaur Dhanda. "An Analysis of Local Area Network ARP Spoofing" (PDF). International Journal of Latest Trends in Engineering and Technology (IJLTET).

[18] Palm, Patrik. "ARP Spoofing" (PDF).

[19] S.Venkatramulu, Guru Rao. "Various Solutions for Address Resolution Protocol Spoofing Attacks" (PDF). International Journal of Scientific and Research Publications, Volume 3, Issue 7, July 2013 ISSN 2250-3153.

[20] T. Mirzoev, J. S. White. "The role of client isolation in protecting Wi-Fi users from ARP Spoofing attacks" (PDF).

5.6   External links

- Official website

Chapter 6

Burp suite

Burp Suite is a Java application that can be used to secure or penetrate web applications.[1] The suite consists of different tools, such as a proxy server, a web spider, intruder and repeater.

6.1 Proxy server

When Burp Suite is used as a proxy server, it allows the user to manipulate the traffic that passes through it, i.e. between the web browser i.e. client and the web server. This is typically referred to as a Man-in-the-middle (MITM) type attack architecture. Burp employs tables--a user-friendly method of making changes to web traffic--to manipulate data before it is sent to the web server. With this functionality, exception situations can be reproduced, allowing any bugs and vulnerabilities present on the web server to be accurately pinpointed.

6.2 Spider

The Burp suite spider tool examines cookies and initiates connections with web applications, enumerating and mapping out the various pages and parameters of a website.

6.3 Intruder

Burp Suite's intruder tool can perform automated attacks on web applications. The pen tester must already have detailed knowledge of the application and HTTP protocol to be attacked. The tool offers a configurable algorithm that can generate malicious HTTP requests. The intruder tool can test and detect SQL injections, cross-site scripting, parameter manipulation and vulnerability for brute-force attacks.

6.4 Repeater

The repeater is a simple tool that can be used to manually test an application. A pen tester can use it to modify requests to the server, resend them, and observe the results.

6.5 See also

- Penetration test
- Web Application Security Scanner
- Fiddler (software)

6.6 References

[1] "Burp Suite". *PortSwigger Web Security*. PortSwigger Ltd. 2014. Retrieved 2014-09-13.

6.7 External links

- Burp Suite

Chapter 7

Cain and Abel (software)

Cain and Abel (often abbreviated to **Cain**) is a password recovery tool for Microsoft Windows. It can recover many kinds of passwords using methods such as network packet sniffing, cracking various password hashes by using methods such as dictionary attacks, brute force and cryptanalysis attacks. Cryptanalysis attacks are done via rainbow tables which can be generated with the winrtgen.exe program provided with Cain and Abel. Cain and Abel is maintained by Massimiliano Montoro and Sean Babcock.

7.1 Features

- WEP cracking
- Speeding up packet capture speed by wireless packet injection
- Ability to record VoIP conversations
- Decoding scrambled passwords
- Calculating hashes
- Traceroute
- Revealing password boxes
- Uncovering cached passwords
- Dumping protected storage passwords
- ARP spoofing
- IP to MAC Address resolver
- Network Password Sniffer
- LSA secret dumper
- Ability to crack:
  - LM & NTLM hashes
  - NTLMv2 hashes
  - Microsoft Cache hashes

- Microsoft Windows PWL files
- Cisco IOS - MD5 hashes
- Cisco PIX - MD5 hashes
- APOP - MD5 hashes
- CRAM-MD5 MD5 hashes
- OSPF - MD5 hashes
- RIPv2 MD5 hashes
- VRRP - HMAC hashes
- Virtual Network Computing (VNC) Triple DES
- MD2 hashes
- MD4 hashes
- MD5 hashes
- SHA-1 hashes
- SHA-2 hashes
- RIPEMD-160 hashes
- Kerberos 5 hashes
- RADIUS shared key hashes
- IKE PSK hashes
- MSSQL hashes
- MySQL hashes
- Oracle and SIP hashes

7.2 Status with virus scanners

Some virus scanners (and browsers, e.g. Chrome 20.0.1132.47) detect Cain and Abel as malware.

Avast! detects it as "Win32:Cain-B [Tool]" and classifies it as "Other potentially dangerous program", while Microsoft Security Essentials detects it as "Win32/Cain!4_9_14" and classifies it as "Tool: This program has potentially unwanted behavior." Even if Cain's install directory, as well as the word "Cain", are added to Avast's exclude list, the real-time scanner has been known to stop Cain from functioning. However, the latest version of Avast no longer blocks Cain.

7.3 See also

- Black-hat hacker

- White-hat hacker

- Hacker (computer security)

- Password cracking

7.4 External links

- Official homepage

- Interview with Massimiliano Montoro, creator of Cain & Abel

Chapter 8

Capsa

This article is about the line of network analyzers from Colasoft. For other uses, see Capsa (disambiguation).

Capsa is the name for a family of packet analyzer developed by Colasoft for network administrators to monitor, troubleshoot and analyze wired & wireless networks. Currently, there are three editions available: **Capsa Enterprise Edition**, **Capsa Professional Edition**, and **Capsa Free Edition**.

8.1   Functionality

- Wired & wireless network real-time packet capturing -- (Packets never lies)

- Traffic & bandwidth monitoring -- (Which machines are downloading or watching online videos?)

- Advanced protocol analysis -- (What network protocols are used in your network? HTTP - web browsing, MSN - chatting.)

- Multiple network behavior monitoring -- (What the users are doing: web browsing, chatting?)

- Expert network diagnosis -- (Are there any attacks and problems in my network?)

- Network activity logging -- (Who and when visited which website/chatted with whom/sent email to whom?)

- Email contents preservation -- (Need to save a copy of all emails' contents sent/received by your employee in your network as evidence?)

- Quick & intuitive reports -- (Need rich charts and graphs in your presentations and reports?)

- In-depth packet decoding -- (What is the original information in network communications?)

8.2   Advance Features

- Captures packets from a single or multiple network adapters

- Analyzes the header & contents of each packet

- Provides statistics on MAC & IP address

- Analyze Protocol (Data link -> Application Layer)

- Diagnoses 40 kinds of network problems

- Presents statistics in graphs

- Alerts Computer network anomalies

- Outputs packets & logs to files

- Logs DNS, web browsing, Email, FTP & IM services

8.3   Capsa Enterprise Edition

Capsa Enterprise Edition is the flagship of Colasoft Capsa packet analyzer family, it supports both Ethernet and WLAN networks. It performs real-time packet capturing and analysis as well as supporting past-events analysis. It is marketed as a tool for enterprise network administrator to help them deal with daily network work, various kinds of network problem and maintain a productive enterprise network.

8.4   Capsa Professional Edition

Capsa Professional Edition is an Ethernet packet analyzer designed for networking professionals or small business network administrators. It is marketed as a network tool for network monitoring, troubleshooting and analyzing purposes.

8.5 Capsa Free Edition

Capsa Free Edition is a freeware Ethernet packet analyzer designed by Colasoft for personal use. It is marketed as a tool for network geeks to learn protocols, packets, and other networking related knowledge, and it is free of charge for personal or family users' network monitoring or troubleshooting needs. Anyone can download Capsa Free Edition at Colasoft website for any legal noncommercial use.

8.6 Comparison of editions

*Wireless traffic analysis is not supported on this OS version

Source:[1]

8.7 References

[1] "Capsa - Compare Editions". Colasoft. Retrieved November 25, 2012.

8.8 External links

- Colasoft Official website

- Colasoft Official Blog

- Colasoft Capsa FAQ

- Techrepublic, July, 19,2009,Review:Test-drive: Colasoft Capsa network analyzer, by Rick Vanover

- CrunchGear, Aug,3,2009, Review: Colasoft Capsa Network Analyzer, by Scott Merrill.

- PCWorld, Dec, 1,2009, Review: Capsa Keeps Tabs on Your SMB Network, by Ian, Harac.

- WindowsITPro, June,1,2010, Review: Colasoft Capsa 7.1, by Michael Dragone.

- Firewall.cx, July 3, 2010, Review: Colasoft Capsa 7.2, by Chris Partsenidis.

- ITWire, July 26,2010, Review: Colasoft Capsa , by David M Williams.

- PCWorld, Sept,13,2010, Review: Capsa Free Gives You the Skinny on Your Network-for Free, by Ian, Harac.

- IT Wired, April 03,2011, Review: Colasoft Capsa 7 WiFi, by David Williams.

- Firewall.cx, October 1st, 2012, Review: Colasoft Capsa Enterprise 7, by Chris Partsenidis

Chapter 9

Carnivore (software)

Carnivore, later renamed **DCS1000**, was a system implemented by the Federal Bureau of Investigation that was designed to monitor email and electronic communications. It used a customizable packet sniffer that can monitor all of a target user's Internet traffic. Carnivore was implemented in October 1997. By 2005 it had been replaced with improved commercial software such as NarusInsight.[1]

9.1 Development

Carnivore grew out of an earlier FBI project called "Omnivore", which itself replaced an older surveillance tool migrated from the US Navy by FBI Director of Integrity and Compliance,[2] Patrick W. Kelley, which had a still undisclosed name. In September 1998, the FBI's Data Intercept Technology Unit (DITU) in Quantico, Virginia, launched a project to migrate Omnivore from Sun's Solaris operating system to a Windows NT platform. This was done to facilitate the miniaturization of the system and support a wider range of personal computer (PC) equipment. The migration project was called "Phiple Troenix" and the resulting system was named "Carnivore."[3]

9.2 Configuration

The Carnivore system was a Microsoft Windows-based workstation with packet-sniffing software and a removable Jaz disk drive.[4] This computer must be physically installed at an Internet service provider (ISP) or other location where it can "sniff" traffic on a LAN segment to look for email messages in transit. The technology itself was not highly advanced — it used a standard packet sniffer and straightforward filtering. The critical components of the operation were the filtering criteria. To accurately match the appropriate subject, an elaborate content model was developed.[5] An independent technical review of Carnivore for the Justice Department was prepared in 2000.[6]

9.3 Controversy

Several groups expressed concern regarding the implementation, usage, and possible abuses of Carnivore. In July 2000, the Electronic Frontier Foundation submitted a statement to the Subcommittee on the Constitution of the Committee on the Judiciary in the United States House of Representatives detailing the dangers of such a system.[7] The Electronic Privacy Information Center also made several releases dealing with it.[8]

The FBI countered these concerns with statements highlighting the target-able nature of Carnivore. Assistant FBI Director Donald Kerr was quoted as saying:

> The Carnivore device works much like commercial "sniffers" and other network diagnostic tools used by ISPs every day, except that it provides the FBI with a unique ability to distinguish between communications which may be lawfully intercepted and those which may not. For example, if a court order provides for the lawful interception of one type of communication (e.g., e-mail), but excludes all other communications (e.g., online shopping) the Carnivore tool can be configured to intercept only those e-mails being transmitted either to or from the named subject.
>
> ... [it] is a very specialized network analyzer or "sniffer" which runs as an application program on a normal personal computer under the Microsoft Windows operating system. It works by "sniffing" the proper portions of network packets and copying and storing only those packets which match a finely defined filter set programmed in conformity with the court order. This filter set can be extremely complex, and this provides the FBI with an ability to collect transmissions which comply with pen register court orders, trap & trace court orders, Title III interception orders, etc....
>
> ...It is important to distinguish now what is

meant by "sniffing." The problem of discriminating between users' messages on the Internet is a complex one. However, this is exactly what Carnivore does. It does NOT search through the contents of every message and collect those that contain certain key words like "bomb" or "drugs." It selects messages based on criteria expressly set out in the court order, for example, messages transmitted to or from a particular account or to or from a particular user.[9]

After prolonged negative coverage in the press, the FBI changed the name of its system from "Carnivore" to the more benign-sounding "**DCS1000**." DCS is reported to stand for "Digital Collection System"; the system has the same functions as before.

9.4 Successor

The *Associated Press* reported in mid-January 2005 that the FBI essentially abandoned the use of Carnivore in 2001, in favor of commercially available software, such as NarusInsight, a mass surveillance system.[1] A report in 2007 described the successor system as being located "inside an Internet provider's network at the junction point of a router or network switch" and capable of indiscriminately storing data flowing through the provider's network.[10]

9.5 See also

- Communications Assistance For Law Enforcement Act
- DITU
- Total Information Awareness
- Surveillance
- COINTELPRO
- DCSNet
- Echelon NSA worldwide digital interception program
- Room 641A NSA interception program (started circa 2003, but first reported in 2006)
- Policeware

9.6 References

[1] "FBI Ditches Carnivore Surveillance System". Foxnews.com. Associated Press. 2005-01-18. Retrieved 2008-10-29.

[2] http://fbi.gov/about-us/executives/kelley

[3] EPIC Obtains First Set of FBI Carnivore Documents, October 12, 2000

[4] "How Carnivore Email Surveillance Worked". *about.com*. Retrieved 2008-10-29.

[5] Kevin Poulsen (October 4, 2000). "Carnivore Details Emerge". *SecurityFocus*.

[6] Independent Technical Review of the Carnivore System, 8 December 2000

[7] https://www.eff.org/Privacy/Surveillance/Carnivore[]

[8] Electronic Privacy Information Center: Carnivore FOIA Documents

[9] "Internet and Data Interception Capabilities Developed by the FBI, Statement for the Record, U.S. House of Representatives, the Committee on the Judiciary, Subcommittee on the Constitution, 07/24/2000, Laboratory Division Assistant Director Dr. Donald M. Kerr".

[10] "FBI turns to broad new wiretap method". *CNET News*. January 30, 2007.

9.7 External links

- EPIC collection of documents on Carnivore
- Carnivore Software Official Website

Chapter 10

Clarified Networks

Clarified Networks is a company that is headquartered in Oulu, Finland. The company was acquired by Codenomicon in 2011, but continues to operate as a separate company under the Codenomicon Group.[1]

The company is most famous for producing visualizations of security incidents, for example the patching of DNS cache poisoning attacks[2] and Botnet[3] traffic.

Since 2006 Clarified Networks has in particular concentrated in developing the collaborative focus in their products and currently refers to itself as a provider of Collaborative Network Analysis tools. Practical applications for Clarified Networks' tools are for example Traffic Auditing, troubleshooting and malware analysis.

10.1 Products

Clarified Networks provides a wide set of different situation awareness tools,[4] including:

Virtual Situation Room (VSRoom) provides unified, real-time views to the information provided by your monitoring systems. With VSRoom you will be able to collect, visualize and share monitoring data collected from your critical infrastructure. It provides beautiful situation overviews of complex data for decision makers and first line operation centers.

AbuseHelper is an open framework for collecting and sharing intelligence on suspected malicious activity. Clarified Networks is the lead developer and community contributor of AbuseHelper.

Network Analyzer is the tool of choice for collaborative analysis and visualization of complex networks. The analyzer helps you in collaborative troubleshooting, traffic audits and network documentation based on real traffic.

10.2 History

The research and development for Clarified Networks' tools began in 2002 and continued for four years in the Oulu University Secure Programming Group (OUSPG) before Clarified Networks spun off from the research group in 2006.

The company entered the Venture Cup competition that year, and was one of the finalists.[5]

In 2007, the founders of Clarified Networks also were awarded for their VMware Applicance called HowNetWorks.[6][7]

In 2011, Company was acquired by Codenomicon.

10.3 References

[1] Financial Tech Spotlight. Codenomicon Acquires Clarified Networks

[2] O'Reilly Radar. Kaminsky DNS Patch Visualization.

[3] Clarified Networks Tia - Botnet analysis (YouTube)

[4] "Clarified Networks: Products". Clarified Networks. 2011-05-23. Retrieved 2012-06-08.

[5] Venture Cup Finland, Greatest Hits

[6] Shields, Greg. "Greg Shields - HowNetWorks: An Interview with its designers at Clarified Networks". Archived from the original on 10 November 2007.

[7] News on Finnish Newspaper on the 100.000 USD prize from VMware Ultimate Virtual Appliance Challenge

10.4 External links

- https://www.clarifiednetworks.com/
- http://www.youtube.com/user/clarifiednetworks

Chapter 11

CommView

CommView is an application for network monitoring, packet analysis, and decoding. There are two editions of CommView: the standard edition for Ethernet networks and the wireless edition for 802.11 networks named **CommView for WiFi**.[1][2] The application runs on Microsoft Windows. It is developed by TamoSoft, a privately held New Zealand company founded in 1998.

11.1 Functionality

CommView puts the network adapter into promiscuous mode and captures network traffic.[3] It also supports capturing packets from dial-up and virtual adapters (e.g. ADSL or 3G modems), as well as capturing loopback traffic. Captured traffic is then analyzed and the application displays network statistics and individual packets. Packets are decoded using a protocol decoder. CommView for WiFi puts Wi-Fi adapters into monitor mode, providing the functionality and user experience similar to that of CommView, with the addition of WLAN-specific features, such as displaying and decoding of management and control frames, indication of signal and noise level, and per-node and per-channel statistics.[4][5][6][7]

11.2 Features

- Protocols distribution, bandwidth utilization, and network nodes charts and tables.[8]

- Detailed IP connections statistics: IP addresses, ports, sessions, etc.

- VoIP analysis: H.323 and SIP (TMC'S Internet Telephony Magazine product of the year award[9])

- WEP and WPA2-PSK decryption (wireless edition only)[10]

- Multi-channel capturing using several USB adapters (wireless edition only)

- Packet injection using a packet generator

- User-defined packet filters and alarms[10]

- TCP and UDP stream reconstruction[11]

- Packet-to-application mapping

- Reporting

- Capture log file import and export

11.3 References

[1] "Wireless LAN Tools: Analyze This". 2004-06-20.

[2] "Commercial WLAN Analyzers". 2004-06-20.

[3] "Home Office: Software Rx for a Healthier Windows". Retrieved 2012-01-20.

[4] "TamoSoft's CommView offers ease of use". Retrieved 2012-01-20.

[5] Devin Akin; Jim Geier (2004). *Certified Wireless Analysis Professional Official Study Guide*. McGraw-Hill. pp. 303, 329, 331, 397. ISBN 0-07-225585-4.

[6] David D. Coleman; David A. Westcott (2006). *Certified Wireless Network Administrator Study Guide*. John Wiley & Sons. pp. 239–243. ISBN 978-0-471-78952-9.

[7] Robert J. Bartz (2009). *Certified Wireless Technology Specialist Official Study Guide*. John Wiley & Sons. pp. 313–317. ISBN 978-0-470-43889-3.

[8] "7 Things Hackers Hope You Don't Know". 2010-07-07.

[9] "TMC'S INTERNET TELEPHONY Magazine Announces 12th Annual Product of the Year Award Winners". 2010-02-15.

[10] M.L.Shannon; Steve Uhrig (2005). *Electronic Surveillance and Wireless Network Hacking*. Paladin Press. pp. 118–123. ISBN 1-58160-475-0.

[11] Matthew Strebe; Charles Arthur Perkins (2002). *Firewalls 24seven*. Sybex Inc. p. 352. ISBN 0-7821-4054-8.

11.4   External links

- Official CommView Product Page

- Official CommView for WiFi Product Page

Chapter 12

Comparison of packet analyzers

The following tables compare general and technical information for several packet analyzer software utilities. Please see the individual products' articles for further information.

12.1   General information

Basic general information about the software—creator/company, license/price, etc.

12.2   Operating system support

The utilities can run on these operating systems.

Chapter 13

Debookee

Debookee is a packet analyzer for OS X which has the ability to intercept network traffic through a Man-in-the-middle attack. This interception feature allows the user to analyze easily network traffic of non-desktop devices like mobiles, phones, tablets, printers...

13.1 Features

- Scan and discover all devices currently active on a network

- Intercept traffic from any device on your network through MITM

- Real-time packet capture analysis of following protocols
  - HTTP
  - HTTPS (no decryption)
  - DNS
  - TCP
  - DHCP
  - SIP

- Displays Wifi connection details: channel, signal strength, MAC address of the Access Point (BSSID) ...

13.2 System requirements

- OS X 10.8 or higher (64-bit)

13.3 See also

- Ettercap - An open source network security tool for man-in-the-middle attacks on LAN.

- Cain and Abel - A password recovery tool for Microsoft Windows which also uses MITM for traffic interception.

- Wireshark - A Mac OS X tool for wireless networks assessment, scanning and surveys.

13.4 External links

- Official website

Chapter 14

DRDO NETRA

For the unmanned aerial vehicle by DRDO, see DRDO Netra.

NETRA (NEtwork TRaffic Analysis) is a software network developed by India's Centre for Artificial Intelligence and Robotics (CAIR), a Defence Research and Development Organisation (DRDO) laboratory, and is used by the Intelligence Bureau, India's domestic intelligence agency,[1] and the Research and Analysis Wing (RAW), the country's external intelligence agency to intercept and analyse internet traffic using pre-defined filters.[2][3] The program was tested at smaller scales by various national security agencies, and is reported to be deployed nationwide soon, as of January 2014.[1][4]

14.1 Development history

Security agencies were looking to build a system that could monitor Internet traffic on a real time basis due to the rapidly escalating threat posed by terrorist and criminal elements using data communication, which had brought service providers like BlackBerry, Skype and Gmail into the focus of law enforcement agencies.[5]

Two such systems were designed, one by DRDO's Centre for Artificial Intelligence and Robotics, and the other by the National Technical Research Organisation (NTRO), which is India's technical intelligence agency. An inter-ministerial committee staffed by members from Ministry of Home Affairs, Intelligence Bureau, Department of Telecom, Department of IT, and National Investigation Agency was formed to evaluate both systems and to select one internet monitoring system.[5]

NTRO's system was designed with the help of Paladion, an international private company and NETRA was designed by a team of 40 scientists from CAIR. The committee selected CAIR's NETRA as it had multiple issues with NTRO's system. It had serious security reservations about involvement of an international private company in such a sensitive

project, and had doubts about NTRO's ability to operate, maintain and upgrade their system independently. Also, RAW, which tested NTRO's system was not happy with the NTRO solution and reported that it crashed frequently. The committee favoured NETRA as it was an indigenous solution involving government scientists and personnel and no component of solution had been outsourced to an outside agency. The agency testing NETRA, the IB, was also pleased with its performance. The committee further observed that CAIR has been continuously investing in R&D to keep up with the fast-changing web technologies, unlike NTRO.[3][5] The system was first demonstrated at the premises of Sify Technologies to capture the entire internet traffic passing through its probes.[3]

14.2 Capabilities

NETRA can analyse voice traffic passing through software such as Skype and Google Talk, and intercept messages with keywords such as 'attack', 'bomb', 'blast' or 'kill' in real-time[5] from the enormous number of tweets, status updates, emails, instant messaging transcripts, internet calls, blogs, forums and even images generated on the internet to obtain the desired intelligence. The system with RAW analyses large amount of international data which crosses through the internet networks in India.[1][2][3] Three security agencies, which include the IB and RAW, have each been allotted a maximum of 300 Gigabytes (GB) per node totaling more than 1000 nodes for storing intercepted internet traffic(o, there are 1000 nodes x 300GB = 300,000GB of total space is initially decided to set up.), and an extra 100 GB per node is assigned to the remaining law enforcement agencies.[1][4]

14.3 Users

The *Internet Scanning and Coordination Centre* will use this system to monitor the Internet,[3] similar to the ones used by USA, UK, China, Iran and many other nations.[1][5] Initially, RAW was the only current user of this monitoring system, but in 2013, the Ministry of Home Affairs recommended the use of a second NETRA system by domestic law enforcement agencies. This was done as the intelligence gathered by the external intelligence agency were largely irrelevant for the use by law enforcement agencies, and could not handle more data.[2] A note from the Department of Telecommunications (DOT) stated that the system can provide access to multiple security agencies.[1]

Netra's deployment was discussed in 2013 by an apex inter-ministerial group headed by DoT, and included representative from the Cabinet Secretariat, Ministry of Home Affairs, DRDO, CAIR, Intelligence Bureau, C-DoT and Computer Emergency Response Team (CERT-In).[1]

14.4   Awards and recognition

DRDO Scientist Dr. G. Athithan of CAIR and his team were awarded the 'Agni award for excellence in self-reliance 2008' for developing NETRA. The team comprised scientists from Indian Institute of Science, G.Ravindra and Rahul M. Kharge.[6][7]

14.5   See also

- Mass surveillance in India
- NATGRID, the Indian national intelligence grid.
- Central Monitoring System
- Telecom Enforcement Resource and Monitoring
- National Internet Exchange of India

14.6   References

[1] "Government to launch 'Netra' for internet surveillance". *The Economic Times.* 16 December 2013. Retrieved 16 December 2013.

[2] "Home seeks system to intercept Net chatter". *The Indian Express.* 23 June 2013. Retrieved 23 June 2013.

[3] "Govt holds contest between two Internet spy systems". *The Economic Times.* Retrieved August 17, 2012.

[4] "Govt to launch internet spy system 'Netra' soon". *The Times of India.* 7 January 2014. Retrieved 7 January 2014.

[5] "Panel slams roping in of private firm for Net snooping". *The Hindu Business Line.* Retrieved August 17, 2012.

[6] "CAIR team gets Agni award". *The Hindu.* Retrieved August 17, 2012.

[7] "Agni awards announced". *The Deccan Herald.* Retrieved August 17, 2012.

Chapter 15

dSniff

Dsniff is a set of password sniffing and network traffic analysis tools written by security researcher and startup founder Dug Song to parse different application protocols and extract relevant information. dsniff, filesnarf, mailsnarf, msgsnarf, urlsnarf, and webspy passively monitor a network for interesting data (passwords, e-mail, files, etc.). arpspoof, dnsspoof, and macof facilitate the interception of network traffic normally unavailable to an attacker (e.g., due to layer-2 switching). sshmitm and webmitm implement active man-in-the-middle attacks against redirected SSH and HTTPS sessions by exploiting weak bindings in ad-hoc PKI.[2] [3]

15.1 Overview

The applications sniff usernames and passwords, web pages being visited, contents of email etc. Dsniff, as the name implies, it is a network sniffer, but it can also be used to disrupt the normal behavior of switched networks and cause network traffic from other hosts on the same network segment to be visible, not just traffic involving the host dsniff is running on.

It handles FTP, Telnet, SMTP, HTTP, POP, poppass, NNTP, IMAP, SNMP, LDAP, Rlogin, RIP, OSPF, PPTP MS-CHAP, NFS, VRRP, YP/NIS, SOCKS, X11, CVS, IRC, AIM, ICQ, Napster, PostgreSQL, Meeting Maker, Citrix ICA, Symantec pc Anywhere, NAI Sniffer, Microsoft SMB, Oracle SQL*Net, Sybase and Microsoft SQL protocols.

The name "dsniff" refers both to the package as well as an included tool. "dsniff" the tool decodes passwords sent in cleartext across a switched or unswitched Ethernet network. Its man page explains that Song wrote dsniff with "honest intentions - to audit my own network, and to demonstrate the insecurity of cleartext network protocols." He then requests, "Please do not abuse this software."

These are the files that are configured in dsniff folder **/etc/dsniff/**

/etc/dsniff/dnsspoof.hosts --> Sample hosts file.[4] If no hostfile is specified, replies will be forged for all address queries on the LAN with an answer of the local machine's IP address.

/etc/dsniff/dsniff.magic --> Network protocol magic

/etc/dsniff/dsniff.services --> Default trigger table

The man page for dsniff explains all the flags. To learn more about using dsniff you can explore the Linux man page.[5]

This is a list of descriptions for the various dsniff programs. This text belong to the dsniff "README" written by the author Dug Song.

See also: filesnarf,[3] macof,[3] mailsnarf,[3] msgsnarf,[3] sshmitm,[3] tcpnice,[3] urlsnarf,[3]webmitm,[3] webspy.[3]

Other tools included with the package include:

- "webspy", a program which intercepts URLs sent by a specific IP address and directs your web browser to connect to the same URL. This results in your browser opening up the same web pages as the target being sniffed.

- "sshmitm" and "webmitm", programs designed to intercept SSH version 1 communications and web traffic respectively with a man-in-the-middle attack

- "msgsnarf", a program designed to intercept Instant Messenger and IRC conversations

- "macof", a program designed to break poorly designed Ethernet switches by flooding them with packets with bogus MAC addresses (MAC flooding).

15.2 References

[1] LICENSE file in the tarball

[2] dsniff

[3] Christopher R. Russel. "Penetration Testing with dsniff".

[4] dnsspoof(8) - Linux man page

[5] dsniff(8): password sniffer - Linux man page

15.3   External links

- Official website
- dsniff FAQ

15.4   See also

- Comparison of packet analyzers
- Network tap
- tcpdump, a packet analyzer
- Packetsquare, a protocol field (pcap) editor and replay tool
- Tcptrace, a tool for analyzing the logs produced by tcpdump
- EtherApe, a network mapping tool that relies on sniffing traffic
- Ngrep, a tool that can match regular expressions within the network packet payloads
- netsniff-ng, a free Linux networking toolkit
- Wireshark, a GUI based alternative to tcpdump

- Song, Dug. "dsniff." http://www.monkey.org/~{}dugsong/dsniff/
- Dsniff - Linux man page, http://linux.die.net/man/8/dsniff
- Dsniff most recent version 2.3, http://dsniff.darwinports.com/
- Dunston, Duane, Linuxsecurity.com, "And away we spoof!!!" http://www.linuxsecurity.com/docs/PDF/dsniff-n-mirror.pdf

Chapter 16

Ettercap (software)

Ettercap is a free and open source network security tool for man-in-the-middle attacks on LAN. It can be used for computer network protocol analysis and security auditing. It runs on various Unix-like operating systems including Linux, Mac OS X, BSD and Solaris, and on Microsoft Windows. It is capable of intercepting traffic on a network segment, capturing passwords, and conducting active eavesdropping against a number of common protocols.

16.1 Functionality

Ettercap works by putting the network interface into promiscuous mode and by ARP poisoning the target machines. Thereby it can act as a 'man in the middle' and unleash various attacks on the victims. Ettercap has plugin support so that the features can be extended by adding new plugins.

16.2 Features

Ettercap supports active and passive dissection of many protocols (including ciphered ones) and provides many features for network and host analysis. Ettercap offers four modes of operation:

- IP-based: packets are filtered based on IP source and destination.

- MAC-based: packets are filtered based on MAC address, useful for sniffing connections through a gateway.

- ARP-based: uses ARP poisoning to sniff on a switched LAN between two hosts (full-duplex).

- PublicARP-based: uses ARP poisoning to sniff on a switched LAN from a victim host to all other hosts (half-duplex).

In addition, the software also offers the following features:

- Character injection into an established connection: characters can be injected into a server (emulating commands) or to a client (emulating replies) while maintaining a live connection.

- SSH1 support: the sniffing of a username and password, and even the data of an SSH1 connection. Ettercap is the first software capable of sniffing an SSH connection in full duplex.

- HTTPS support: the sniffing of HTTP SSL secured data—even when the connection is made through a proxy.

- Remote traffic through a GRE tunnel: the sniffing of remote traffic through a GRE tunnel from a remote Cisco router, and perform a man-in-the-middle attack on it.

- Plug-in support: creation of custom plugins using Ettercap's API.

- Password collectors for: TELNET, FTP, POP, IMAP, rlogin, SSH1, ICQ, SMB, MySQL, HTTP, NNTP, X11, Napster, IRC, RIP, BGP, SOCKS 5, IMAP 4, VNC, LDAP, NFS, SNMP, *Half-Life*, *Quake 3*, MSN, YMSG

- Packet filtering/dropping: setting up a filter that searches for a particular string (or hexadecimal sequence) in the TCP or UDP payload and replaces it with a custom string/sequence of choice, or drops the entire packet.

- OS fingerprinting: determine the OS of the victim host and its network adapter.

- Kill a connection: killing connections of choice from the connections-list.

- Passive scanning of the LAN: retrieval of information about hosts on the LAN, their open ports, the version numbers of available services, the type of the host (gateway, router or simple PC) and estimated distances in number of hops.

- Hijacking of DNS requests.

Ettercap also has the ability to actively or passively find other poisoners on the LAN.

16.3   See also

- ArpON

- arpwatch

16.4   External links

- Official website

- An article "Реагирование на инциденты информационной безопасности"

- An article "Ettercap: универсальный анализатор трафика"

Chapter 17

Fiddler (software)

Fiddler is an HTTP debugging proxy server application written by Eric Lawrence, formerly a Program Manager on the Internet Explorer development team at Microsoft.[1]

17.1 Features

Fiddler captures HTTP and HTTPS traffic and logs it for the user to review (the latter by implementing man-in-the-middle interception using self-signed certificates).[5]

Fiddler can also be used to modify ("fiddle with") HTTP traffic for troubleshooting purposes as it is being sent or received.[4] By default, traffic from Microsoft's WinINET HTTP(S) stack is automatically directed to the proxy at runtime, but any browser or web application (and most mobile devices) can be configured to route its traffic through Fiddler.

17.2 History

On 6 October 2003, Eric Lawrence released the initial official version of Fiddler.[2]

On 12 September 2012, Eric Lawrence announced that Fiddler was acquired by Telerik and he would join the company to work on Fiddler on a full-time basis.[6]

17.3 See also

- Packet analyzer

- Wireshark

- Burp suite, a Java-based HTTP/HTTPS debugging and security testing tool

17.4 References

[1] Lawrence, Eric (2005-06-06). "HTTP Performance". *IEBlog*. MSDN (Microsoft corporation).

[2] "Fiddler HTTP Debugger - Version Info". Retrieved 2012-08-17.

[3] "Fiddler Web Debugger - Get Fiddler". Retrieved 2012-10-11.

[4] "Fiddler Web Debugger - Fiddler". Retrieved 2010-08-20.

[5] Lawrence, Eric (January 2005). "Fiddler PowerToy - Part 1: HTTP Debugging". MSDN (Microsoft corporation). Retrieved 2007-01-15.

[6] "Fiddler Telerik". Fiddler. September 2012. Retrieved 2012-09-12.

17.5 External links

- Fiddler 2 Homepage

- Fiddler Web Debugger developer blog

- Old Fiddler Blog

- Fiddler PowerToy - Part 1: HTTP Debugging

- Fiddler PowerToy - Part 2: HTTP Performance

- Web Debugging: Fiddler tutorial

17.6 Further reading

- Lawrence, Eric (15 June 2012). *Debugging with Fiddler: The complete reference from the creator of the Fiddler Web Debugger*. ISBN 978-1475024487.

Chapter 18

FlowMon

FlowMon is a name for monitoring probe which is the result of academic research activity on CESNET and also a name for a commercial product which is marketed by university spin-off company INVEA-TECH.

18.1 FlowMon probe - result of research activities

FlowMon probe is an appliance for monitoring and reporting information of IP flows in high-speed computer networks. The probe is being developed by Liberouter team within the scope of CESNET research plan *Optical National Research Network and its New Applications*, research activity *602 - Programmable hardware*.

FlowMon probe is build upon a pair of programmable network cards, called COMBO, and a host computer with Linux operating system. The pair of COMBO cards consists of a main card with PCI, PCI-X or PCI-Express connector for a connection to a motherboard of the host computer and of an add-on card with 2 or 4 network interfaces. Both cards contain programmable chips (FPGAs) which are able to process high amount of data at multi-gigabit speed. The flow monitoring process itself is split between the hardware (acceleration cards) and the application software running on the host computer. Following the principle of hardware/software codesign, all time-critical tasks are implemented in FPGA chips on acceleration cards while more complex operations are carried out by the application software. This concept enables monitoring of modern high-speed (1 Gbps, 10 Gbps) networks with no packet loss and with no necessity of input sampling. At the same time, a flexible and user-friendly interface is provided by software.

FlowMon probe is a passive monitoring device, i.e. it does not alter passing traffic in any way. Therefore, its detection is hardly possible. When connected to a network, FlowMon probe observes all passing traffic/packets, extracts and aggregates information of IP flows into flow records. FlowMon probe is able to export aggregated data to external collectors in NetFlow (version 5 and 9) and IPFIX format. Collectors collect incoming flow records and store them for automated or manual and visual analysis (automated malicious traffic detection, filter rules, graphs and statistical schemas). The whole system allows monitoring of actual state of monitored network as well as long-term traffic analysis.

FlowMon probe is part of GÉANT2 Security Toolset, which consists of the netflow analysis tools NfSen and Nf-Dump and the FlowMon appliance.

18.2 FlowMon solution - commercial product

FlowMon is network traffic monitoring and security solution of INVEA-TECH company. INVEA-TECH was established in 2007 as a university spin-off, made a technology transfer from CESNET (Czech NREN) and continue in R&D, finish prototypes and put them on the market.

FlowMon solution was initially based on FlowMon probes developed by CESNET. Nowadays FlowMon is a complete flow solution which consists of FlowMon Probes, FlowMon Collectors and additional plugins. FlowMon Probes provide NetFlow/IPFIX statistics about network traffic and come in standard version suitable for most of standard networks (10Mbit/s - 10Gbit/s) or hardware-accelerated version based on CESNET's FPGA boards suitable for high-speed networks (10Gbit/s - 100Gbit/s). FlowMon Collectors are appliances for NetFlow/sFlow/IPFIX storage and analysis. FlowMon plugins are modules to FlowMon Probes or FlowMon Collectors which brings additional functionality - e.g. network behavior analysis (NBA), anomaly detection, HTTP logging.

18.3 See also

- Network traffic measurement

- IP Flow Information Export

- NetFlow

18.4 External sources

- Flexible FlowMon technical report

- User and Test Report on NetFlow Probe (DJ2.2.2,2)
  from GÉANT2

- Liberouter project web page

- CESNET web page

- GÉANT2 Security Toolset

- INVEA-TECH's FlowMon

Chapter 19

Glasswire

GlassWire is a commercial Personal Firewall and Network Monitor with a free and limited version, developed by SecureMix. The software includes a network security monitoring feature that alerts the user to online threats including changes in network related files, ARP spoofing, Proxy changes, DNS changes, Host File changes, and suspicious hosts.

GlassWire visualizes all end-point network activity on an easy to use graph[1] that helps the user understand what their computer is doing in the background. Users can block any network connection connection via the "Firewall" tab[2] that shows a list of applications currently accessing the network along with what host they are currently communicating with. The GlassWire "Usage" tab show more detailed information about what hosts and applications are generating the most data over the network. GlassWire can alert the user if their device is getting close to using a certain amount of bandwidth so the user can stay under their ISP data limit.

GlassWire was given a 4.5 out of 5 stars by PCWorld Magazine.[3]

19.1 See also

- Firewall (computing)

19.2 References

[1] http://www.fastcolabs.com/3035401/elasticity/glasswire-makes-web-security-beautiful

[2] http://www.makeuseof.com/tag/meet-glasswire-prettiest-bandwidth-internet-security-monitor-windows-pc/

[3] http://www.pcworld.com/article/2686040/glasswire-review-this-free-network-security-tool-tells-all-about-your-network-traffic.html

19.3 External links

- GlassWire Homepage

Chapter 20

hping

hping is a free packet generator and analyzer for the TCP/IP protocol distributed by Salvatore Sanfilippo (also known as Antirez). It is one of the *de facto* tools for security auditing and testing of firewalls and networks, and was used to exploit the idle scan scanning technique (also invented by the hping author), and now implemented in the Nmap Security Scanner. The new version of hping, hping3, is scriptable using the Tcl language and implements an engine for string based, human readable description of TCP/IP packets, so that the programmer can write scripts related to low level TCP/IP packet manipulation and analysis in very short time.

Like most tools used in computer security, hping is useful to both system administrators and hackers.

20.1   See also

- Nmap Security Scanner: Nmap and hping are often considered complementary to one another.

- Mausezahn: Another fast and versatile packet generator that also supports Ethernet header manipulation.

- Packet Sender: A packet generator with a focus on ease of use.

20.2   External links

- The Hping Website

- The Hping Wiki

- Idle Scanning, paper by Nmap author Fyodor.

- Hping 2 Fixed for Windows XP SP2 (Service Pack 2)

- The Mausezahn Website

Chapter 21

HTTP Debugger

HTTP Debugger is a HTTP protocol analyzing tool written by Khachatur Petrosyan. It captures HTTP and HTTPS traffic and logs it for the user to review. It can also be used to submit modified HTTP requests back to the server for troubleshooting and debugging purposes.

HTTP Debugger uses man-in-the-middle technique for intercepting SSL traffic.

21.1 See also

- Fiddler (software)
- Wireshark

21.2 External links

- Official website

Chapter 22

Ipsectrace

ipsectrace is a software tool designed by Wayne Schroeder to help profile ipsec connections in a packet capture (PCP) file. The program uses a command line interface to point at a PCP capture and informs the user about what is going on. It is somewhat inspired by tcptrace, which uses the same input of PCP files.[1] Ipsectrace is only available for the Linux operating system. It is coded in C++ and is licensed under the GPL, effectively allowing anyone to modify and redistribute it.[2]

Although its main purpose is to monitor ipsec traffic, ipsectrace can be used to crack extra layers of security brought about by VPN implementations of security such as ipsec and SSH,[3] whereas programs such as Anger, Deceit, and Ettercap can be used to infiltrate PPTP security.[4]

22.1 References

[1] "tcptrace". Retrieved 9 May 2011.

[2] "Frequently Asked Questions about the GNU Licenses". GNU. Retrieved 9 May 2011.

[3] Dean, Tamara (2009). *Network+ guide to networks* (5th ed.). Boston, Mass.: Cengage Course Technology. pp. 575–615. ISBN 978-1-4239-0245-4.

[4] Beaver, Kevin; Akin, Peter T. Davis. Foreword by Devin K. (2005). *Hacking wireless networks for dummies : [find and fix network loopholes before invaders exploit them]* (1st ed.). Hoboken, NJ: Wiley. ISBN 0-7645-9730-2.

22.2 External links

- ipsectrace download at OStatic

Chapter 23

Ipswitch, Inc.

Ipswitch develops and markets software products and services for businesses worldwide. Headquartered in Lexington, Massachusetts, Ipswitch also has Research & Development centers in Atlanta and Augusta, Georgia, American Fork, Utah, and Madison, Wisconsin, and a European support office in Amsterdam, The Netherlands. Ipswitch sells its products directly, as well as through distributors, resellers and OEMs in the United States, Canada, Latin America, Europe and the Pacific Rim.

23.1 History

Roger Greene founded Ipswitch in 1991 with the aim of crafting user-friendly software for small businesses. Roger started the company out of his apartment without any Venture capital funding or bank financing. The company became profitable in its second year. The first product from Ipswitch was a gateway that allowed the Novell Inc. IPX networking protocol to connect with the Internet Protocol.[1] In the mid-1990s, it was a value-added reseller of the Spyglass Mosaic browser.[2]

23.2 Acquisitions

In 2010, Ipswitch purchased Dorian Software, which produces system log analysis and compliance software.[3]

23.3 Products

Ipswitch, Inc. sells and markets following products:

- **iMacros**: Client-side scripting, Macro recorder, Web testing developed by iOpus

- WhatsUp Gold for network management

- Log Management Suite for network security management

- MOVEit and WS FTP MessageWay for file transfer

- IMail Server for messaging

Ipswitch was also selling its Telnet VT320 terminal emulation and communications package for PC. The software duplicated virtually all functions of the DEC VT320, VT220, VT102, VT100, and VT52 terminals, allowing to work on UNIX and VMS host systems from PC running Microsoft Windows 16-bit and 32-bit operating systems.[4]

23.4 Awards & recognitions

- Ipswitch was named as one of the best places to work in Boston by Boston Business Journal under Mid-Size Company category in 2010, 2011 and 2012.[5]

23.5 Community Involvement

The company commits 5% of its profits to a variety of community investment programs, designed to support the interests of its employees.[6] Recently, Ipswitch Inc.'s network management division, claimed that the company achieved over 5,000 downloads of its WhatsUp Gold Engineer's Toolkit in the first month of its release. Through a unique partnership with Trees for Life International, they planted over 5,000 trees, one for each download.[7]

23.6 References

[1] Rodney H. Brown (2009-09-23). "Roger Greene bootstrapped Ipswitch, sans bank funding". Mass High Tech. Retrieved 2011-02-19.

[2] Ayre, Rick; Mace, Thomas (12 March 1996). "Just Browsing". *PC Mag* (Ziff Davis).

[3] "WhatsUp Gold buys Windows security management vendor". Networkworld.com. 2010-01-26. Retrieved 2010-08-12.

[4] "VT320 pdf manual." (PDF). Ipswitch.com. Retrieved 2014-05-08.

[5] "The BBJ's 2010 Best Places to Work". 2010-04-30.

[6] http://www.ipswitch.com/company/index.asp

[7] http://it.tmcnet.com/channels/
network-management/articles/
94461-ipswitch-network-managements-whatsup-gold-engineers-toolkit-surpasses.
htm

Coordinates: 42°28′5.4″N 71°15′44.3″W / 42.468167°N 71.262306°W

Chapter 24

Isyvmon

isyVmon was a computer system and network monitoring software application system created by iT-CUBE SYSTEMS. It was designed to monitor and track the status of various applications, network services, servers, and other network hardware.

24.1 Overview

isyVmon was based on the Open Source Software Nagios and Centreon licensed under the GNU GPL V3.

Special features:

- monitoring hosts, networks, applications & business processes

- ready-to-run distribution

- real-time exploitation and management frontends

- Web2.0 GUI, dashboards, alerting, databases, reporting, administration

- prebuilt content inclusive templates and plugins

- extended status-map

- integration of extensions

- scalability through single or distributed deployment

- encrypted communication between core and satellites

- freeware edition is limited up to ten hosts

- virtual and hardware appliance, vmware ready

24.2 History

24.2.1 2013

no further development

24.2.2 2012 (isyVmon v3.0)

isyVmon „Full Discovery (ANH)" (Freeware / Enterprise Edition) Enhancements of isyVmon „Simple Discovery (ADI)" (Freeware / Enterprise Edition) More than 300 Bugs fixed in the isyVmon Monitoring GUI (Freeware / Enterprise Edition) Simplified Setup for ESX(i) Monitoring (Freeware / Enterprise Edition) Improvements of the isyVmon worker (Freeware / Enterprise Edition) Improvements of the Commandline API (Freeware / Enterprise Edition) Simplified getting Support for isyVmon (Freeware / Enterprise Edition) Tactical Overview - Dashboard improvements (Freeware / Enterprise Edition) Scheduled periodic downtimes available (Freeware / Enterprise Edition) Secure LDAP (TLS) support (Freeware / Enterprise Edition)

24.2.3 2011 (isyVmon v2.4)

Auto Discovery (ADI) (also available in Freeware Edition) Advanced Notification (ANO) released (Enterprise Edition only) Extended Status Map (ESM) v3.0 (also available in Freeware Edition) Android/iPhone APP turns from "technical preview" to "beta" state

24.2.4 2011 (isyVmon v2.2)

introduced connection for splunk (www.splunk.com) and isyVmon introduced several new features you asked for (SMS, license GUI, Satellite GUI, and many more) many enhancements in usability and functionality based on customer projects. focus on even more scalability and stability. participated vmware ready process.

24.2.5 2010 (isyVmon v2.0)

isyVmon's first world open public release. complete new product website with community based support (KB, Forum, Downloads, ...) introduced isyVmon Standalone as a freeware edition. major focus on scalability and stability. integration of many enhancements from customer projects. based on complete new development framework.

24.2.6   2009 (isyVmon v1.5 - v1.6)

isyVmon's first official release. increased development and big steps in the integration of features based on customer needs. partnership with merethis - the company behind centreon. opened distributed monitoring for the public version. integrated upgrade function in isyVmon.

24.2.7   2008 (isyVmon v1.0)

the idea of isyVmon was born and introduced based on the 2007 created standardized toolkit. increased development depending on customer needs. started to use a complete development framework based on VMware toolkits. several projects with major focus at distributed monitoring. development of an upgrade function in isyVmon. first virtual appliance version.

24.2.8   2007 (monitoring toolkit v0.1 - v0.8)

evaluated all (relevant) available monitoring tools because nagios interface and handling was very unhandy starting to use centreon at top of nagios. first versions of a standardized toolkit for customers. first implementations of the standardized toolkit in larger environments.

24.3   See also

- Comparison of network monitoring systems

- Nagios

- Opsview: Nagios derivative

24.4   References

24.5   Books

- Schubert, Max et al.; (2008) *Nagios 3 Enterprise Network Monitoring* - Syngress ISBN 978-1-59749-267-6

- Kocjan, Wojciech; (2008) "Learning Nagios 3.0" - Packt Publishing ISBN 1-84719-518-0

24.6   External links

- centreon.com

24.6.1   Support sites

- isyvmon.com

Chapter 25

justniffer

Justniffer is a TCP packet sniffer. It can log network traffic in a 'standard' (web server-like) or in a customized way. It can also log response times, useful for tracking network services performances (e.g. web server, application server, etc.). The output format of the traffic can be easily customized. An example written in Python (delivered with the official package) stores the transferred contents in an output directory separated by domains. This means that the transferred files like html, css, javascript, images, sounds, etc. can be saved to a directory.

25.1 Overview

justniffer was born to help in troubleshooting performance in network TCP-based services: HTTP, RTSP, SIP, SMTP, IMAP, POP, LDAP, Telnet etc.

It can collect low and high level protocol and performance information, reconstructing the TCP flow in a reliable way using portions of the Linux kernel code. It uses a slightly modified version of the libnids libraries that already include a modified version of Linux kernel code in a more reusable way. It can be extended with external scripts (bash, Python, or any executable) and generate logs in a customizable way

The man page for justniffer explains all the options.

25.2 External links

- Official website
- Justniffer - tcp packet sniffer
- Lars Michelsen

25.3 Examples

- Examples

25.4 Grab http traffic and observe

- Grab Http traffic

25.5 See also

- Comparison of packet analyzers
- tcpdump, a packet analyzer
- pcap, an application programming interface (API) for capturing network traffic
- snoop, a command line packet analyzer included with Solaris
- wireshark, a network packet analyzer
- dsniff, a packet sniffer and set of traffic analysis tools
- netsniff-ng, a free Linux networking toolkit
- ngrep, a tool that can match regular expressions within the network packet payloads
- etherape, a network mapping tool that relies on sniffing traffic
- tcptrace, a tool for analyzing the logs produced by tcpdump
- Microsoft Network Monitor, a packet analyzer

Chapter 26

KisMAC

KisMAC is a wireless network discovery tool for Mac OS X. It has a wide range of features, similar to those of Kismet (its Linux/BSD namesake). The program is geared toward network security professionals, and is not as novice-friendly as similar applications. Distributed under the GNU General Public License,[2] KisMAC is free software.

KisMAC will scan for networks passively on supported cards - including Apple's AirPort, and AirPort Extreme, and many third-party cards, and actively on any card supported by Mac OS X itself.

Cracking of WEP and WPA keys, both by brute force, and exploiting flaws such as weak scheduling and badly generated keys is supported when a card capable of monitor mode is used, and packet reinjection can be done with a supported card (Prism2 and some Ralink cards). GPS mapping can be performed when an NMEA compatible GPS receiver is attached.[3]

Data can also be saved in pcap format and loaded into programs such as Wireshark.

26.1 KisMAC Features

- Reveals hidden / cloaked / closed SSIDs
- Shows logged in clients (with MAC Addresses, IP addresses and signal strengths)
- Mapping and GPS support
- Can draw area maps of network coverage
- PCAP import and export
- Support for 802.11b/g
- Different attacks against encrypted networks
- Deauthentication attacks
- AppleScript-able
- Kismet drone support (capture from a Kismet drone)

26.2 KisMAC and Germany

The project was created and led by Michael Rossberg until July 27, 2007, when he removed himself from the project due to changes in German law (specifically, StGB Section 202c) that "prohibits the production and distribution of security software".[4] On this date, project lead was passed on to Geoffrey Kruse, maintainer of KisMAC since 2003, and active developer since 2001. KisMAC is no longer being actively being developed. Primary development, and the relocated KisMAC web site are now based in the United States. The KisMAC project can be found at http://kismac-ng.org/ .

As of August 6, 2007, the former homepage now denounces the new German law.

26.3 See also

- Aircrack-ng
- iStumbler
- Kismet
- Netspot
- WiFi Explorer

26.4 References

[1] KisMAC 0.3.3 Changes

[2] "Under What License is KisMAC Published?". kismac-ng.org. Retrieved 2008-02-22.

[3] GPSd "gpsd — a GPS service daemon" Check |url= scheme (help). berlios.de. Retrieved 2008-02-22.

[4] "Germany says goodbye KisMAC!". kismac.de. Retrieved 2008-02-22.

26.5   External links

- Current homepage

- Binaries of latest versions

- KisMAC Newbie Guide

- Former homepage

- KisMAC Svn

- KisMAC2, a currently maintained fork of the original project

Chapter 27

Kismet (software)

This article is about the network monitoring software. For the gameplay scripting tool, see Kismet (gameplay scripting).

Kismet is a network detector, packet sniffer, and intrusion detection system for 802.11 wireless LANs. Kismet will work with any wireless card which supports raw monitoring mode, and can sniff 802.11a, 802.11b, 802.11g, and 802.11n traffic. The program runs under Linux, FreeBSD, NetBSD, OpenBSD, and Mac OS X. The client can also run on Microsoft Windows, although, aside from external drones (see below), there's only one supported wireless hardware available as packet source.

Distributed under the GNU General Public License,[2] Kismet is free software.

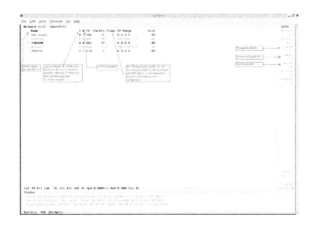

An explanation of the headings displayed in Kismet.

27.1 Features

Kismet differs from other wireless network detectors in working passively. Namely, without sending any loggable packets, it is able to detect the presence of both wireless access points and wireless clients, and to associate them with each other. It is also the most widely used and up to date open source wireless monitoring tool.

Kismet also includes basic wireless IDS features such as detecting active wireless sniffing programs including NetStumbler, as well as a number of wireless network attacks.

Kismet features the ability to log all sniffed packets and save them in a tcpdump/Wireshark or Airsnort compatible file format. Kismet can also capture "Per-Packet Information" headers.

Kismet also features the ability to detect default or "not configured" networks, probe requests, and determine what level of wireless encryption is used on a given access point.

In order to find as many networks as possible, Kismet supports channel hopping. This means that it constantly changes from channel to channel non-sequentially, in a user-defined sequence with a default value that leaves big holes between channels (for example, 1-6-11-2-7-12-3-8-13-4-9-14-5-10). The advantage with this method is that it will capture more packets because adjacent channels overlap.

Kismet also supports logging of the geographical coordinates of the network if the input from a GPS receiver is additionally available.

27.2 Server / Drone / Client infrastructure

Kismet has three separate parts. A *drone* can be used to collect packets, and then pass them on to a *server* for interpretation. A server can either be used in conjunction with a drone, or on its own, interpreting packet data, and extrapolating wireless information, and organizing it. The *client* communicates with the server and displays the information the server collects.

41

27.3   Plugins

With the updating of Kismet to -ng, Kismet now supports a wide variety of scanning plugins including DECT, Bluetooth, and others.

27.4   See also

- KisMAC (for Mac OS X)

27.5   References

[1] http://www.kismetwireless.net/ Kismet web site

[2] "Kismet Readme". kismetwireless.net. Retrieved 2008-02-22.

27.6   External links

- Official Website
- Introduction to Kismet
- Java Kismet TCP/IP Client

Chapter 28

Layer four traceroute

Layer Four Traceroute (LFT) is a fast, multi-protocol traceroute engine, that also implements numerous other features including AS number lookups through Regional Internet Registries and other reliable sources, Loose Source Routing, firewall and load balancer detection, etc. LFT is best known for its use by network security practitioners to trace a route to a destination host through many configurations of packet-filters / firewalls, and to detect network connectivity, performance or latency problems.

28.1 How it Works

LFT sends various TCP SYN and FIN probes (differing from Van Jacobson's UDP-based method) or UDP probes utilizing the IP protocol 'time to live' field and attempts to elicit an ICMP TIME_EXCEEDED response from each gateway along the path to some host. LFT also listens for various TCP, UDP, and ICMP messages along the way to assist network managers in ascertaining per-protocol heuristic routing information, and can optionally retrieve various information about the networks it traverses. The operation of layer four traceroute is described in detail in several prominent security books.[1][2]

28.2 Origins

The lft command first appeared in 1998 as 'fft'. Renamed as a result of confusion with Fast Fourier transforms, lft stands for 'layer four traceroute.' Results are often referred to as a 'layer four trace.'

28.3 External links

- Layer Four Traceroute Project

28.4 Sources

[1] Extreme Exploits: Advanced Defenses Against Hardcore Hacks (2005) McGraw-Hill ISBN 0-07-225955-8

[2] The Tao of Network Security Monitoring (2004) Addison-Wesley ISBN 0-321-24677-2

Chapter 29

lorcon

lorcon (acronym for *Loss Of Radio CONnectivity*) is an open source network tool. It is a library for injecting 802.11 (WLAN) frames, capable of injecting via multiple driver frameworks, without the need to change the application code. Lorcon is built by patching the third-party MadWifi-driver for cards based on the Qualcomm Atheros wireless chipset.[1][2][3]

The project is maintained by Joshua Wright and Michael Kershaw ("dragorn").

29.1 References

[1] Maynor, David. "Beginner's Guide to Wireless Auditing". Symantec. Retrieved 25 February 2013.

[2] McMillan, Robert. "Researchers Use Wi-Fi Driver to Hack Laptop". PCWorld. Retrieved 25 February 2013.

[3] Judge, Peter. "Poor Wi-Fi drivers can expose laptops". ZDNet. Retrieved 25 February 2013.

29.2 External links

- Official Home Page
- pylorcon2 on GitHub

Chapter 30

Microsoft Network Monitor

Microsoft Network Monitor is a packet analyzer. It enables capturing, viewing, and analyzing network data and deciphering network protocols. It can be used to troubleshoot network problems and applications on the network. Microsoft Network Monitor 1.0 (codenamed *Bloodhound*) was originally designed and developed by Raymond Patch, a transport protocol and network adapter device driver engineer on the Microsoft LAN Manager development team.

Network Monitor has been replaced by Microsoft Message Analyzer which is available for download.

30.1 History

The LAN Manager development team had one shared hardware-based analyzer at the time. Netmon was conceived when the hardware analyzer was taken during a test to reproduce a networking bug, and the first Windows prototype was coded over the Christmas holiday. The first 4 bytes of the Netmon capture file format were used to validate the file. The values were 'RTSS' for Ray, Tom, Steve, and Steve - the first four members of the team. The code was originally written for OS/2 and had no user interface; a symbol was placed in the device driver where the packet buffers were kept so received data could be dumped in hex from within the kernel debugger.

Netmon caused a bit of a stir for Microsoft IT since networks and e-mail were not encrypted at the time. Only a few software engineers had access to hardware analyzers due to their cost, but with Netmon many engineers around the company had access to network traffic for free. At the request of Microsoft IT, two simple identification features were added - a non-cryptographic password and an identification protocol named the Bloodhound-Oriented Network Entity (BONE) (created and named by Raymond Patch as a play on the codename *Bloodhound*).

Network Monitor 3 is a complete overhaul of the earlier Network Monitor 2.x version. Originally versions of Network Monitor were only available through other Microsoft products, such as Systems Management Server (SMS). But now the fully featured product with public parsers is available as a free download.

Microsoft Network Monitor has been superseded by Microsoft Message Analyzer [1]

30.2 Features

Some key features of Network Monitor 3.4 include the following:

- Process tracking

- Grouping by network conversation

- Support for over 300 public and Microsoft proprietary protocols

- Simultaneous capture sessions

- Wireless Monitor Mode with supported wireless NICs

- Real-time capture and display of frames

- Reassembly of fragmented data

- Sniffing of promiscuous mode traffic

- Can read libpcap capture files

- API to access capture and parsing engine

30.3 External links

- Download Network Monitor 3.4

- Forum Support for Network Monitor 3

- Download Microsoft Message Analyzer 1.1

- Forum Support for Microsoft Message Analyzer 1.1

- MS Support KB Article

- Blog for Network Monitor

- Message Analyzer (Network Monitor's successor) on Microsoft Connect

- Latest Parser Updates

- Network Monitor Experts on CodePlex

- Message Analyzer has Released – A New Beginning

30.4   References

[1] http://blogs.technet.com/b/messageanalyzer/archive/2012/09/17/meet-the-successor-to-microsoft-network-monitor.aspx

Chapter 31

Monitor mode

Monitor mode, or RFMON (Radio Frequency MONitor) mode, allows a computer with a wireless network interface controller (WNIC) to monitor all traffic received from the wireless network. Unlike promiscuous mode, which is also used for packet sniffing, monitor mode allows packets to be captured without having to associate with an access point or ad hoc network first. Monitor mode only applies to wireless networks, while promiscuous mode can be used on both wired and wireless networks. Monitor mode is one of the seven modes that 802.11 wireless cards can operate in: Master (acting as an access point), Managed (client, also known as station), Ad hoc, Mesh, Repeater, Promiscuous, and Monitor mode.

31.1 Uses

Some uses for monitor mode include: geographical packet analysis, observing of widespread traffic; esp. for unsecure channels (such as through WEP), and acquiring knowledge of Wi-Fi technology through hands-on experience. This mode is also somewhat useful during the design phase of Wi-Fi network construction to discover how many Wi-Fi devices are already using spectrum in a given area and how busy various Wi-Fi channels are in that area. This helps to plan the Wi-Fi network better and reduce interference with other Wi-Fi devices by choosing the least used channels for a new Wi-Fi network.

Software such as KisMAC or Kismet, in combination with packet analyzers that can read pcap files, provide a user interface for passive wireless network monitoring.

31.2 Limitations

Usually the wireless adapter is unable to transmit in monitor mode and is restricted to a single wireless channel, though this is dependent on the wireless adapter's driver, its firmware, and features of its chipset. Also, in monitor mode the adapter does not check to see if the cyclic redun-

dancy check (CRC) values are correct for packets captured, so some captured packets may be corrupted.

31.3 Operating system support

The Microsoft Windows Network Driver Interface Specification (NDIS) API does not support any extensions for wireless monitor mode in older versions of Windows. With NDIS 6, available in Windows Vista and later versions of Windows, it is possible to enable monitor mode.[1] NDIS 6 supports exposing 802.11 frames to the upper protocol levels;[2] with previous versions of NDIS only fake Ethernet frames translated from the 802.11 data frames can be exposed to the upper protocol levels. Monitor mode support in NDIS 6 is an optional feature and may or may not be implemented in the client adapter driver. The implementation details and compliance with the NDIS specifications vary from vendor to vendor. In many cases, monitor mode support is not properly implemented by the vendor. For example, Ralink drivers report incorrect dBm readings and Realtek drivers do not include trailing 4-byte CRC values.

For versions of Windows prior to Windows Vista, some packet analyzer applications such as Wildpackets' OmniPeek and TamoSoft's CommView for WiFi provide their own device drivers to support monitor mode.

Linux's interfaces for 802.11 drivers support monitor mode and many drivers offer that support.[3] FreeBSD, NetBSD, OpenBSD, and DragonFly BSD also provide an interface for 802.11 drivers that supports monitor mode, and many drivers for those operating systems support monitor mode as well. In Mac OS X 10.4 and later releases, the drivers for AirPort Extreme network adapters allow the adapter to be put into monitor mode. Libpcap 1.0.0 and later provides an API to select monitor mode when capturing on those operating systems.

31.4   See also

- Promiscuous mode

- Comparison of open-source wireless drivers

31.5   References

[1] "Network Monitor Operation Mode". *Windows Driver Kit: Network Devices and Protocols*. Microsoft. Retrieved 2007-11-30.

[2] "Indicating Raw 802.11 Packets". *Windows Driver Kit: Network Devices and Protocols*. Microsoft. Retrieved 2007-11-30.

[3] *Aircrack/Aireplay-ng Under Packet Injection Monitor Mode in Windows* retrieved September 11, 2007

31.6   External links

- AirSnort FAQ: What is the difference between monitor and promiscuous mode?

Chapter 32

MTR (software)

My traceroute, originally named **Matt's traceroute** (**MTR**) is a computer program which combines the functions of the traceroute and ping programs in one network diagnostic tool.[1]

MTR probes routers on the route path by limiting the number of hops individual packets may traverse, and listening to responses of their expiry. It will regularly repeat this process, usually once per second, and keep track of the response times of the hops along the path.

32.1 History

The original *Matt's traceroute* program was written by Matt Kimball in 1997. Roger Wolff took over maintaining MTR (renamed *My traceroute*) in October 1998.[2]

32.2 Fundamentals

MTR is licensed under the terms of the GNU General Public License (GPL) and works under modern Unix-like operating systems. It normally works under the text console, but it also has an optional GTK+-based graphical user interface (GUI).

MTR relies on Internet Control Message Protocol (ICMP) Time Exceeded (type 11, code 0) packets coming back from routers, or ICMP Echo Reply packets when the packets have hit their destination host. MTR also has a User Datagram Protocol (UDP) mode (invoked with "-u" on the command line or pressing the "u" key in the curses interface) that sends UDP packets, with the time to live (TTL) field in the IP header increasing by one for each probe sent, toward the destination host. When the UDP mode is used, MTR relies on ICMP port unreachable packets (type 3, code 3) when the destination is reached.

MTR also supports IPv6 and works in a similar manner but instead relies on ICMPv6 messages.

The tool is often used for network troubleshooting. By showing a list of routers traversed, and the average round-trip time as well as packet loss to each router, it allows users to identify links between two given routers responsible for certain fractions of the overall latency or packet loss through the network. This can help identify network overuse problems.[3]

32.3 Examples

This example shows MTR running on Linux tracing a route from the host machine (example.lan) to a web server at Yahoo! (p25.www.re2.yahoo.com) across the Level 3 Communications network.

My traceroute [v0.71] example.lan Sun Mar 25 00:07:50 2007 Packets Pings Hostname %Loss Rcv Snt Last Best Avg Worst 1. example.lan 0% 11 11 1 1 1 2 2. ae-31-51.ebr1.Chicago1.Level3.n 19% 9 11 3 1 7 14 3. ae-1.ebr2.Chicago1.Level3.net 0% 11 11 7 1 7 14 4. ae-2.ebr2.Washington1.Level3.ne 19% 9 11 19 18 23 31 5. ae-1.ebr1.Washington1.Level3.ne 28% 8 11 22 18 24 30 6. ge-3-0-0-53.gar1.Washington1.Le 0% 11 11 18 18 20 36 7. 63.210.29.230 0% 10 10 19 19 19 19 8. t-3-1.bas1.re2.yahoo.com 0% 10 10 19 18 32 106 9. p25.www.re2.yahoo.com 0% 10 10 19 18 19 19

An additional example below shows a recent version of MTR running on FreeBSD. MPLS labels are displayed by default when the "-e" switch is used on the command line (or the "u" key is pressed in the curses interface):

My traceroute [v0.82] dax.prolixium.com (0.0.0.0) Sun Jan 1 12:58:02 2012 Keys: Help Display mode Restart statistics Order of fields quit Packets Pings Host Loss% Snt Last Avg Best Wrst StDev 1. voxel.prolixium.net 0.0% 13 0.4 1.7 0.4 10.4 3.2 2. 0.ae2.tsr1.lga5.us.voxel.net 0.0% 12 10.8 2.9 0.2 10.8 4.3 3. 0.ae59.tsr1.lga3.us.voxel.net 0.0% 12 0.4 1.7 0.4 16.0 4.5 4. rtr.loss.net.internet2.edu 0.0% 12 4.8 7.4 0.3 41.8 15.4 5. 64.57.21.210 0.0% 12 5.4 15.7 5.3 126.7 35.0 6. nox1sumgw1-vl-530-nox-mit.nox.org

0.0% 12 109.5 60.6 23.0 219.5 66.0 [MPLS: Lbl 172832
Exp 0 S 1 TTL 1] 7. nox1sumgw1-peer-—207-210-142-
234.nox.org 0.0% 12 25.0 23.2 23.0 25.0 0.6 8. B24-RTR-
2-BACKBONE-2.MIT.EDU 0.0% 12 23.2 23.4 23.2 24.9
0.5 9. MITNET.TRANTOR.CSAIL.MIT.EDU 0.0% 12
23.4 23.4 23.3 23.5 0.1 10. trantor.helicon.csail.mit.edu
0.0% 12 23.7 25.0 23.5 26.5 1.3 11. zermatt.csail.mit.edu
0.0% 12 23.1 23.1 23.1 23.3 0.1

32.4   WinMTR

WinMTR is a Windows GUI application functionally
MTR-equivalent, developed by Appnor. Although it is very
similar, it shares no common code with MTR. No MTR-
equivalent console application exists for Windows.

32.5   See also

- traceroute

- Ping (networking utility)

- PathPing - a network utility supplied in Windows NT
  and beyond that combines the functions of ping with
  those of traceroute, or tracert

- Bufferbloat

32.6   References

[1] Upstream Provider Woes? Point the Ping of Blame. (linux-
    planet.com)

[2] Cisco router configuration and troubleshooting By Mark Tri-
    pod (Google Books)

[3] Linode: Diagnosing Network Issues with MTR

32.7   External links

- Official website

- MTR man page

- MTR, BitWizard's MTR page with Unix downloads

- WinMTR, the equivalent of MTR for Windows platforms

Chapter 33

Multi Router Traffic Grapher

"MRTG" redirects here. It may also be an abbreviation for mortgage loan.

The **Multi Router Traffic Grapher**, or just simply **MRTG**, is free software for monitoring and measuring the traffic load on network links. It allows the user to see traffic load on a network over time in graphical form.

It was originally developed by Tobias Oetiker and Dave Rand to monitor router traffic, but has developed into a tool that can create graphs and statistics for almost anything.

MRTG is written in Perl and can run on Windows, Linux, Unix, Mac OS and NetWare.

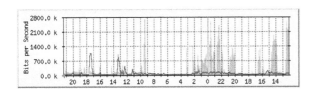

A sample MRTG bandwidth graph.

33.1 How it works

33.1.1 SNMP

MRTG uses the Simple Network Management Protocol (SNMP) to send requests with two object identifiers (OIDs) to a device. The device, which must be SNMP-enabled, will have a management information base (MIB) to look up the OIDs specified. After collecting the information it will send back the raw data encapsulated in an SNMP protocol. MRTG records this data in a log on the client along with previously recorded data for the device. The software then creates an HTML document from the logs, containing a list of graphs detailing traffic for the selected devices in the server..

33.1.2 Script output

Alternatively, MRTG can be configured to run a script or command, and parse its output for counter values. The MRTG website contains a large library of external scripts to enable monitoring of SQL database statistics, firewall rules, CPU fan RPMs, or virtually any integer-value data.

33.2 Features

- Measures two values (I for Input, O for Output) per target.

- Gets its data via an SNMP agent, or through the output of a command line.

- Typically collects data every five minutes (it can be configured to collect data less frequently).

- Creates an HTML page per target that features four graphs (GIF or PNG images).

- Results are plotted vs time into day, week, month and year graphs, with the **I** plotted as a full green area, and the **O** as a blue line.

- Automatically scales the Y axis of the graphs to show the most detail.

- Adds calculated Max, Average and Current values for both **I** and **O** to the target's HTML page.

- Can also send warning emails if targets have values above a certain threshold.

33.3 See also

- RRDtool - Reimplementation of MRTG's graphing and logging features

- Munin - Another monitoring application with web interface, based on RRDtool

- PRTG - Windows GUI implementation of MRTG's functionality (limited freeware version available)

- Cacti - A similar tool using RRDtool

- Observium - A heavily automated platform for network graphing using RRDtool

33.4   References

[1] "Index of /mrtg/pub". Oss.oetiker.ch. Retrieved 2013-01-12.

33.5   External links

- MRTG Home page

- MRTG at Freecode

- Helpful page with example MRTG grabs and explanations.

- Solaris MRTG examples

- Red Hat Enterprise Linux MRTG Configuration HOW-TO

- MRTGEXT module for supporting MRTG and Nagios monitoring systems on Novell Servers project

- Trend View a MRTG Frontend for Windows

- MRTG-XTRA, a Windows distribution of MRTG --DISCONTINUED--

Chapter 34

Naemon

Naemon is an open source computer system monitoring, network monitoring and infrastructure monitoring software application. Naemon offers monitoring and alerting services for servers, switches, applications, and services. It alerts the users when things go wrong and alerts them a second time when the problem has been resolved.

It is available for Red Hat, CentOS, SUSE, Debian and Ubuntu Linux distribution.[1]

34.1 Overview

Naemon is open source software licensed under the GNU GPL V2. It provides:

- Monitoring of network services (SMTP, POP3, HTTP, NNTP, PING, etc.).

- Monitoring of host resources (processor load, disk usage, etc.).

- A simple plugin design that allows users to easily develop their own service checks.

- Parallelized service checks.

- Thruk Monitoring Webinterface.

- The ability to define network host hierarchies using 'parent' hosts, allowing the detection of and distinction between hosts that are down or unreachable.

- Contact notifications when service or host problems occur and get resolved (via e-mail, pager, or any user-defined method through plugin system).

- The ability to define event handlers to be run during service or host events for proactive problem resolution

- Automatic log file rotation

- Support for implementing redundant monitoring hosts

34.2 See also

- Comparison of network monitoring systems

- Nagios

- Icinga – A fork of Nagios

- Shinken – A Nagios compatible replacement

34.3 References

[1] http://www.naemon.org/download/

34.4 External links

- Official Naemon Website

Chapter 35

Nagios

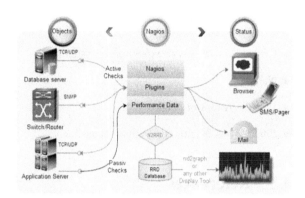

Operating principle of Nagios

35.1 Overview

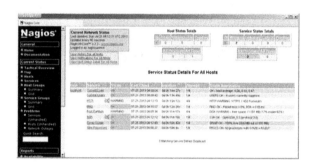

Status reporting in Nagios

Nagios /ˈnɑːɡiːoʊs/, an open-source computer-software application, monitors systems, networks and infrastructure. Nagios offers monitoring and alerting services for servers, switches, applications and services. It alerts users when things go wrong and alerts them a second time when the problem has been resolved.

Ethan Galstad and a group of developers originally wrote Nagios as *NetSaint*. As of 2015 they actively maintain both the official and unofficial plugins. Nagios is a recursive acronym: "Nagios Ain't Gonna Insist On Sainthood"[3] - "sainthood" makes reference to the original name *NetSaint*, which changed in response to a legal challenge by owners of a similar trademark.[4] "Agios" (or "hagios") also transliterates the Greek word άγιος, which means "saint".

Nagios was originally designed to run under Linux, but it also runs well on other Unix variants. It is free software licensed under the terms of the GNU General Public License version 2 as published by the Free Software Foundation.

In 2006 a survey asked members of the nmap-hackers mailing-list to identify their favorite network-security tools. In the survey 3243 people voted; Nagios came in 67th overall and 5th among traffic-monitoring tools. (Nmap itself was excluded from the list.) Another survey, in 2011, placed Nagios at 69th place.[5]

Nagios is open source software licensed under the GNU GPL V2. It provides:

- Monitoring of network services (SMTP, POP3, HTTP, NNTP, ICMP, SNMP, FTP, SSH)

- Monitoring of host resources (processor load, disk usage, system logs) on a majority of network operating systems, including Microsoft Windows with the NSClient++ plugin or Check MK.

- Monitoring of anything else like probes (temperature, alarms,etc.) which have the ability to send collected data via a network to specifically written plugins

- Monitoring via remotely run scripts via Nagios Remote Plugin Executor

- Remote monitoring supported through SSH or SSL encrypted tunnels.

- A simple plugin design that allows users to easily develop their own service checks depending on needs, by using their tools of choice (shell scripts, C++, Perl, Ruby, Python, PHP, C#, etc.)

- Available data graphing plugins

- Parallelized service checks

- The ability to define network host using 'parent' hosts, allowing the detection of and distinction between hosts that are down or unreachable

- Contact notifications when service or host problems occur and get resolved (via e-mail, pager, SMS, or any user-defined method through plugin system)

- The ability to define event handlers to be run during service or host events for proactive problem resolution

- Automatic log file rotation

- Support for implementing redundant monitoring hosts

- An optional web-interface for viewing current network status, notifications, problem history, log files, etc.

- Data storage via text files rather than database

35.2 Nagios Agents

35.2.1 NRPE

Nagios Remote Plugin Executor (NRPE) is a Nagios agent that allows remote system monitoring using scripts that are hosted on the remote systems. It allows for monitoring of resources such as disk usage, system load or the number of users currently logged in. Nagios periodically polls the agent on remote system using the check_nrpe plugin.

NRPE allows you to remotely execute Nagios plugins on other Linux/Unix machines. This allows you to monitor remote machine metrics (disk usage, CPU load, etc.). NRPE can also communicate with some of the Windows agent addons, so you can execute scripts and check metrics on remote Windows machines as well.

35.2.2 NRDP

Nagios Remote Data Processor (NRDP) is a Nagios agent with a flexible data transport mechanism and processor. It is designed with an architecture that allows it to be easily extended and customized. NRDP uses standard ports and protocols (HTTP(S) and XML) and can be implemented as a replacement for NSCA.

35.2.3 NSClient++

This program is mainly used to monitor Windows machines. Being installed on a remote system NSClient++ listens to port TCP 12489. Nagios plugin that is used to collect information from this addon is called check_nt. As NRPE, NSClient++ allows to monitor the so-called 'private

services' (memory usage, CPU load, disk usage, running processes, etc.) Nagios is a host and service monitor which is designed to inform your network problems

35.3 Controversial takeover of nagios-plugins site

On 16 January 2014, Nagios Enterprises redirected the nagios-plugins.org domain to a web server controlled by Nagios Enterprises without notifying the Nagios Plugins community team. In response, the original community plugin team has renamed the project to Monitoring Plugins and created a new project website at monitoring-plugins.org. [6][7]

35.4 See also

- Comparison of network monitoring systems

- Icinga – A fork of Nagios

- Shinken – A Nagios compatible replacement

- op5 Monitor – A network monitoring suite using the Nagios core

- N2rrd – A Nagios add-on to record data in a Round Robin Database

- NConf – A tool for configuring Nagios

- Opsview – An integrated bundle of tools that includes Nagios core

- Check MK – An extension to Nagios that offloads work from the Nagios core, and allows distributed monitoring from several Nagios servers

35.5 Further reading

- Barth, Wolfgang; (2006) *Nagios: System And Network Monitoring* - No Starch Press ISBN 1-59327-070-4

- Barth, Wolfgang; (2008) "Nagios: System And Network Monitoring, 2nd edition - *No Starch Press ISBN 1-59327-179-4*

- Turnbull, James; (2006) *Pro Nagios 2.0* - San Francisco: Apress ISBN 1-59059-609-9

- Josephsen, David; (2007) *Building a Monitoring Infrastructure with Nagios* - Prentice Hall ISBN 0-13-223693-1

- Dondich, Taylor; (2006) *Network Monitoring with Nagios* - O'Reilly ISBN 0-596-52819-1

35.6   References

[1] "NetSaint Change Log". 2002-03-01. Archived from the original on 2006-05-01.

[2] "Nagios Core 4.x Version History". 2014-06-03. Retrieved 2014-06-15.

[3] Galstad, Ethan (2009-08-24). "FAQ Database: Miscellaneous: What does Nagios mean?". *Nagios: Frequently Asked Questions*. Nagios Enterprises, LLC. Retrieved 2014-06-02. The official meaning is that N.A.G.I.O.S. is a recursive acronym which stands for "Nagios Ain't Gonna Insist On Sainthood".

[4] "2005-02-22 - Ethan Galstad". *FOSDEM 2005*. 2005-02-22. Retrieved 2014-06-02. Although we were able to eventually reach an amicable agreement on my future use of the name "NetSaint", I felt it was prudent to change the name in order to prevent any future mishaps.

[5] "SecTools.Org: Top 125 Network Security Tools". Retrieved 2014-06-02.

[6] Holger Weiß (2014-01-16). "HEADS UP New project name: Monitoring Plugins". Retrieved 2014-06-02.

[7] "Bug 1054340: Update upstream URL to https://www. monitoring-plugins.org". Red Hat. 2014-01-16. Retrieved 2014-06-02.

35.7   External links

- Official Nagios Website

Chapter 36

NeDi

NeDi is an open source computer software tool which discovers and maps devices and traffic on a network.[1][2]

36.1 References

[1] Mann, Harper (26 June 2006). "Open Source Network Management Tool You Should Care About: NeDi". InfoWorld.

[2] Venezia, Paul. "Free Open Source Network Monitoring Tools You Must Have". CIO. Retrieved 5 April 2012.

36.2 External links

- Official website

Chapter 37

Nessus (software)

Nessus is a proprietary comprehensive vulnerability scanner which is developed by Tenable Network Security. It is free of charge for personal use in a non-enterprise environment.

According to surveys done 2009 by sectools.org, Nessus is the world's most popular vulnerability scanner, taking first place in the 2000, 2003, and 2006 security tools survey.[2] Tenable Network Security estimated year 2005 that it was used by over 75,000 organizations worldwide.[3]

37.1 Operation

Nessus allows scans for the following types of vulnerabilities:

- Vulnerabilities that allow a remote hacker to control or access sensitive data on a system.

- Misconfiguration (e.g. open mail relay, missing patches, etc.).

- Default passwords, a few common passwords, and blank/absent passwords on some system accounts. Nessus can also call Hydra (an external tool) to launch a dictionary attack.

- Denials of service against the TCP/IP stack by using malformed packets

- Preparation for PCI DSS audits

Initially, Nessus consisted of two main components; nessusd, the Nessus daemon, which does the scanning, and nessus, the client, which controls scans and presents the vulnerability results to the user. Later versions of Nessus (4 and greater) utilize a web server which provides the same functionality as the client.

In typical operation, Nessus begins by doing a port scan with one of its four internal portscanners (or it can optionally use AmapM[4] or Nmap[5]) to determine which ports

are open on the target and then tries various exploits on the open ports. The vulnerability tests, available as subscriptions, are written in NASL(Nessus Attack Scripting Language), a scripting language optimized for custom network interaction.

Tenable Network Security produces several dozen new vulnerability checks (called plugins) each week, usually on a daily basis. These checks are available for free to the general public; commercial customers are not allowed to use this Home Feed any more. The Professional Feed (which is not free) also give access to support and additional capabilities (e.g. audit files, compliance tests, additional vulnerability detection plugins).

Optionally, the results of the scan can be reported in various formats, such as plain text, XML, HTML and LaTeX. The results can also be saved in a knowledge base for debugging. On UNIX, scanning can be automated through the use of a command-line client. There exist many different commercial, free and open source tools for both UNIX and Windows to manage individual or distributed Nessus scanners.

If the user chooses to do so (by disabling the option 'safe checks'), some of Nessus' vulnerability tests may try to cause vulnerable services or operating systems to crash. This lets a user test the resistance of a device before putting it in production.

Nessus provides additional functionality beyond testing for known network vulnerabilities. For instance, it can use Windows credentials to examine patch levels on computers running the Windows operating system, and can perform password auditing using dictionary and brute force methods. Nessus 3 and later can also audit systems to make sure they have been configured per a specific policy, such as the NSA's guide for hardening Windows servers. This functionality utilizes Tenable's proprietary audit files or Security Content Automation Protocol (SCAP) content.

37.2 History

The "Nessus" Project was started by Renaud Deraison in 1998 to provide to the Internet community a free remote security scanner.[6] On October 5, 2005, Tenable Network Security, the company Renaud Deraison co-founded, changed Nessus 3 to a proprietary (closed source) license.[3] The earlier versions appear to have been removed from the official website since then. The Nessus 3 engine is still free of charge, though Tenable charges $100/month per scanner for the ability to perform configuration audits for PCI, CIS, FDCC and other configuration standards, technical support, SCADA vulnerability audits, the latest network checks and patch audits, the ability to audit anti-virus configurations and the ability for Nessus to perform sensitive data searches to look for credit card, social security number and many other types of corporate data.

In July 2008, Tenable sent out a revision of the feed license which will allow home users full access to plugin feeds.[7] A professional license is available for commercial use.

The Nessus 2 engine and a minority of the plugins are still GPL, leading to forked open source projects based on Nessus like OpenVAS and Porz-Wahn.[6][8] Tenable Network Security has still maintained the Nessus 2 engine and has updated it several times since the release of Nessus 3.[6]

Nessus 3 is available for many different Unix-like and Windows systems, offers patch auditing of UNIX and Windows hosts without the need for an agent and is 2-5 times faster than Nessus 2.[9]

On April 9, 2009, Tenable released Nessus 4.0.0.[10] On February 15, 2012, Tenable released Nessus 5.0.[11] On October 14, 2014, Tenable released Nessus 6.0. [12]

37.3 See also

- Penetration test
- Metasploit Project
- Security Administrator Tool for Analyzing Networks (SATAN)
- SAINT (software)
- Snort (software)
- Wireshark

37.4 References

[1] "Nessus 6.3.3 Now Available FAQ". Retrieved 2014-10-14.

[2] "sectools.org". Retrieved 2009-10-21.

[3] LeMay, Renai (2005-10-06). "Nessus security tool closes its source". CNet.

[4] http://freeworld.thc.org/thc-amap/

[5] http://www.nessus.org/documentation/index.php?doc=nmap-usage

[6] Carey, Mark; Russ Rogers; Paul Criscuolo; Mike Petruzzi. *Nessus Network Auditing*. O'reilly. ISBN 978-1-59749-208-9.

[7] "Nessus feed letter" (PDF).

[8] "OpenVAS". Retrieved 2009-10-21.

[9] "Nessus 3 documentation".

[10] http://static.tenable.com/prod_docs/upgrade_nessus.html. Retrieved 2015-09-08. Missing or empty |title= (help)

[11] http://static.tenable.com/prod_docs/upgrade_nessus.html. Retrieved 2015-09-08. Missing or empty |title= (help)

[12] http://static.tenable.com/prod_docs/upgrade_nessus.html. Retrieved 2015-09-08. Missing or empty |title= (help)

37.5 External links

- Official website
- Nessus 2.2.11 files and source code
- Nessus source code up to 2.2.9

Chapter 38

Netcat

Netcat (often abbreviated to **nc**) is a computer networking service for reading from and writing to network connections using TCP or UDP. Netcat is designed to be a dependable back-end that can be used directly or easily driven by other programs and scripts. At the same time, it is a feature-rich network debugging and investigation tool, since it can produce almost any kind of connection its user could need and has a number of built-in capabilities.

Its list of features includes port scanning, transferring files, and port listening, and it can be used as a backdoor.

38.1 Features

netcat's features include:[1]

- Outbound or inbound connections, TCP or UDP, to or from any ports

- Full DNS forward/reverse checking, with appropriate warnings

- Ability to use any local source port

- Ability to use any locally configured network source address

- Built-in port-scanning capabilities, with randomization

- Built-in loose source-routing capability

- Can read command line arguments from standard input

- Slow-send mode, one line every N seconds

- Hex dump of transmitted and received data

- Optional ability to let another program service establish connections

- Optional telnet-options responder

- Featured tunneling mode which permits user-defined tunneling, e.g., UDP or TCP, with the possibility of specifying all network parameters (source port/interface, listening port/interface, and the remote host allowed to connect to the tunnel).

38.2 Examples

38.2.1 Opening a raw connection to port 25 (like SMTP)

nc mail.server.net 25

38.2.2 Setting up a one-shot webserver on port 8080 to present the content of a file

{ echo -ne "HTTP/1.0 200 OK\r\nContent-Length: $(wc -c <some.file)\r\n\r\n"; cat some.file; } | nc -l 8080

The file can then be accessed via a web browser under http://servername:8080/. Netcat only serves the file once to the first client that connects and then exits, it also provides the content length for browsers that expect it. (This should work fine in a LAN, but probably may fail with any kind of firewall between.).

38.2.3 Checking if UDP ports (-u) 80-90 are open on 192.168.0.1 using zero mode I/O (-z)

nc -vzu 192.168.0.1 80-90

Note that UDP tests will always show as "open". The -uz argument is useless.

60

38.2.4 Test if UDP port is open: simple UDP server and client

This test is useful, if you have shell access to the server that should be tested, but you do not know whether there is a firewall blocking a specific UDP port on the server.

On the listening host, i.e. on the server whose port needs to be checked, do the following:

nc -ul 7000

On the sending host, do the following – note that servname is the hostname of the listening host:

nc -u servname 7000

If text typed on the sending host (type something and hit enter) is displayed also on the listening host, then the UDP port 7000 is open. If it is not open, you will get an error such as "Connection refused".

There is a caveat. On some machines, IPv6 may be the default IP version to use by netcat. Thus, the host specified by the hostname is contacted using IPv6, and the user might not know about this. Ports may appear closed in the test, even though they would be open when using IPv4. This can be difficult to notice and may cause the false impression that the port is blocked, while it is actually open. You can force the use of IPv4 by using adding −4 to the options of the nc commands.

38.2.5 Pipe via UDP (-u) with a wait time (-w) of 1 second to 'loggerhost' on port 514

echo '<0>message' | nc -w 1 -u loggerhost 514

38.2.6 Port scanning

An uncommon use of netcat is port scanning. Netcat is not considered the best tool for this job, but it can be sufficient (a more advanced tool is nmap)

nc -v -n -z -w 1 192.168.1.2 1-1000

The "-n" parameter here prevents DNS lookup, "-z" makes nc not receive any data from the server, and "-w 1" makes the connection timeout after 1 second of inactivity.

38.2.7 Proxying

Another useful behaviour is using netcat as a proxy. Both ports and hosts can be redirected. Look at this example:

nc -l 12345 | nc www.google.com 80

Port 12345 represents the request

This starts a nc server on port 12345 and all the connections get redirected to google.com:80. If a web browser makes a request to nc, the request will be sent to google but the response will not be sent to the web browser. That is because pipes are unidirectional. This can be worked around with a named pipe to redirect the input and output.

mkfifo backpipe nc -l 12345 0<backpipe | nc www.google. com 80 1>backpipe

The "-c" option may also be used with the 'ncat' implementation:[2]

ncat -l 12345 -c 'nc www.google.com 80'

Using a named pipe is a more reliable method because using "-c" option provides only a one-shot proxy.

Another useful feature is to proxy SSL connections. This way, the traffic can not be viewed in wire sniffing applications such as wireshark. This can be accomplished on UNIXes by utilizing mkfifo, netcat, and openssl.

mkfifo tmp mkfifo tmp2 nc -l 8080 -k > tmp < tmp2 & while [1] do openssl s_client -connect www.google.com:443 -quiet < tmp > tmp2 done

38.2.8 Making any process a server

netcat can be used to make any process a network server. It can listen on a port and pipe the input it receives to that process.

The -e option spawns the executable with its input and output redirected via network socket.

For example, it is possible to expose a bourne shell process to remote computers.

To do so, on a computer A with IP 192.168.1.2, run this command:

nc -l -p 1234 -e /bin/sh

Then, from any other computer on the same network, one could run this nc command:

nc 192.168.1.2 1234 ls -las

And the output one would see might be like this:

total 4288 4 drwxr-xr-x 15 imsovain users 4096 2009-02-17 07:47 . 4 drwxr-xr-x 4 imsovain users 4096 2009-01-18 21:22 .. 8 -rw------- 1 imsovain users 8192 2009-02-16 19:30 .bash_history 4 -rw-r--r-- 1 imsovain users 220 2009-01-18 21:04 .bash_logout ...

In this way, the -e option can be used to create a rudimentary backdoor. Some administrators perceive this as a risk, and thus do not allow netcat on a computer.

38.2.9 Port Forwarding or Port Mapping

On Linux, NetCat can be used for port forwarding. Below are nine different ways to do port forwarding in NetCat (-c switch not supported though - these work with the 'ncat' incarnation of netcat):

nc -l -p port1 -c 'nc -l -p port2' nc -l -p port1 -c 'nc host2 port2' nc -l -p port1 -c 'nc -u -l -p port2' nc -l -p port1 -c 'nc -u host2 port2' nc host1 port1 -c 'nc host2 port2' nc host1 port1 -c 'nc -u -l -p port2' nc host1 port1 -c 'nc -u host2 port2' nc -u -l -p port1 -c 'nc -u -l -p port2' nc -u -l -p port1 -c 'nc -u host2 port2'

Example, see #Proxying

38.3 Ports and reimplementations

The original version of netcat was a Unix program. The last version (1.10) was released in March 1996.[1]

There are several implementations on POSIX systems, including rewrites from scratch like GNU netcat[3] or OpenBSD netcat,[4] the latter of which supports IPv6. The OpenBSD version has been ported to the FreeBSD base[5] and Windows/Cygwin[6] as well. Mac OS X users can use MacPorts to install a *netcat* variant.[7] There is also a Microsoft Windows version of *netcat* available.[8]

Known ports for embedded systems includes versions for Windows CE (named "Netcat 4 wince"[9]) or for the iPhone.[10]

BusyBox includes by default a lightweight version of netcat.

Solaris 11 includes netcat implementation based on OpenBSD netcat.

Socat[11] is a more complex variant of *netcat*. It is larger and more flexible and has more options that must be configured for a given task.

Cryptcat[12] is a version of *netcat* with integrated transport encryption capabilities.

In the middle of 2005, Nmap announced another netcat incarnation called Ncat.[13] It features new possibilities such as "Connection Brokering", TCP/UDP Redirection, SOCKS4 client and server support, ability to "Chain" Ncat processes, HTTP CONNECT proxying (and proxy chaining), SSL connect/listen support and IP address/connection filtering. Like Nmap, Ncat is cross-platform.

On some systems, modified versions or similar netcat utilities go by the command name(s) nc, ncat, pnetcat, socat, sock, socket, sbd.

38.4 See also

- List of Unix programs
- Nmap
- OpenSSL
- Telnet
- Plink
- Packet Sender

38.5 References

[1] "Netcat 1.10". 2008-02-14. Retrieved 2013-08-11.

[2] "Ncat Command Execution". Retrieved 2013-12-01.

[3] Giovanni Giacobbi (2006-11-01). "The GNU Netcat project". Retrieved 2013-08-11.

[4] "OpenBSD CVSWeb: src/usr.bin/nc/". Retrieved 2013-08-11.

[5] delphij (2005-02-06). "Contents of /release/5.4.0/usr.bin/nc/Makefile". Retrieved 2013-08-11.

[6] Thomas Linden (2011-03-02). "Netcat OpenBSD Cygwin Port 1.10.2.3". Retrieved 2013-08-11.

[7] "MacPorts Portfiles". MacPorts. Retrieved 2013-08-11.

[8] Chris Wysopal. "netcat(Windows)". Securityfocus. Retrieved 2013-08-11.

[9] Andreas Bischoff (2010-06-07). "Netcat 4 wince". Retrieved 2013-08-11.

[10] "Revision 772: /trunk/data/netcat". telesphoreo.org. 2008-08-18. Retrieved 2013-08-11.

[11] "socat - Multipurpose relay". 2013-05-26. Retrieved 2013-08-11.

[12] "CryptCat Project". 2005-10-18. Retrieved 2013-08-11.

[13] "Ncat - Netcat for the 21st Century". 2009-07-08. Retrieved 2013-08-11.

38.6 External links

- Official website
- nc(1) – Linux User Commands Manual

Chapter 39

NetCrunch

AdRem **NetCrunch** is a commercial software product for agentless, cross-platform network monitoring developed by AdRem Software, Inc. The program monitors 65 network services, Windows applications; Windows, Linux, NetWare, BSD, Mac OS X systems and SNMP (v1-3) devices without agents; centralizes fault management by collecting and alerting on events from sources including Windows Event Log, syslogs, and SNMP traps; presents physical and logical network topology as automatically updated dynamic graphical views.

39.1 Features

AdRem NetCrunch key features: [1]

- Auto-discovery- initial and scheduled discovery and classification of network resources

- Network views - physical and logical network topology including predefined views like: IP networks, Routing Map, Physical segments, Servers, Maps with Issues, and others.

- Automatic monitoring dependencies (incl. ESX hosts) - view dependent nodes, and prevent cascading alerts from dependent nodes.

- Network Self-Healing - set corrective actions to be taken in response to an alert

- Event management - events from Windows, Syslog and SNMP traps

- Monitoring policies - sets of rules defining events to be monitored and data to be collected for later reporting, including predefined policies for:

    - Operating system - Windows (Active Directory, Network Services Health, Security Audit, Terminal Services, Windows Server, Basic Windows Monitoring), Linux, Mac OS, BSD, Netware, Other (AIX, AS/400, MIB-II host resources).

    - Hardware – Network devices (Nortel, Alcatel OmniSwitch, Cisco), IBM Director, Dell OpenManage, HP Systems Insight Manager, APC PowerChute.

    - Applications – Microsoft (Exchange 2003, IIS 5.0/6.0, ISA Server 2000, ISA Server 2004, MS SQL Server 7.0/2000, MS SQL Server 2005), APC Windows Events, ARCServe, CA eTrust Alert Manager, Lotus Notes 6, McAfee AlertManager, Norton AntiVirus Corporate Edition, Oracle 9i, Sophos Enterprise Manager, Trend Micro ServerProtect, Veritas Backup Exec.

- Availability monitoring - network devices and services (HTTP, POP3, SMTP, etc.)

- Performance monitoring - real-time statistics, multi-server charts, and performance trends (devices, systems, and applications)

- Long-term trend analysis – reports generated on demand or delivered on schedule via email.

- Remote access – remote administration console and access via web browser.

- User experience monitors – advanced monitoring of crucial network services. The program simulates user's action e.g. sends an email for POP3 service monitoring, etc.

- Smart monitoring - limiting monitoring traffic for specific sub networks.

- Inventory - ability to gather the basic inventory information of Windows machines (i.e. mainboard, processor type and memory), with options to schedule inventory audits to be performed, automatically discover and view installed software

- Localization - language versions of AdRem NetCrunch include: English, Japanese, Polish, German, French, Spanish and Italian.

- TLS encryption - support for sending emails to external SMTP servers

- SNMPv3 encryption - DES, 3DES, AES 128, AES 192 and AES 256 keys

- Automatically sets monitoring dependencies - prevents alert floods when one node goes down

39.2 Platform

Recommended platforms for NetCrunch Server are Windows 2008 x32/x64 or Windows 2003 SP2 x32/x64. AdRem NetCrunch Remote Administration Console runs on Windows 7/Vista SP2/XP SP3 or Windows Server 2003/2008 (x32/x64).

39.3 Editions

There are two editions: Premium and Premium XE. The Premium XE edition is designed for large networks and intended to run on a dedicated Windows 2008 server.

Common Premium XE usage scenarios include:

- Network with more than a 1000 nodes for availability monitoring

- Network with more than a 1000 network services for availability monitoring

- Network with more than a 100 servers and routers for performance monitoring

- Network with sub networks

- Network with external servers connected over WAN Links

- Network with CISCO or Nortel switches

- MS SQL, Exchange application performance monitoring and trending

39.4 Technology overview

- Client-server architecture—User manages NetCrunch server using Remote Administration Consoles.

- Multithreading—NetCrunch Premium XE uses multithreading to take advantage of multi-core x64 machine.

- Prioritized monitoring—The program automatically sets up node monitoring order and time upon monitoring dependencies hierarchy.

- Event suppression—In case of failure of an intermediate node, the program suppresses alerts from nodes located beyond that node.

- SQL event database (up to 128GB)

- Web access—By implementing AJAX technology the server/browser interactions run asynchronously without reloading the Web page.

39.5 References

[1] "AdRem NetCrunch Technical Specifications". Adrem Software. 9 September 2014. Retrieved 26 September 2014.

39.6 External links

- AdRem Software's Website

39.6.1 Reviews

- "Gartner Monitoring Technology Pick, 12 May 2014"

- "WindowsNetworking.com Gold Award, 8 Jan. 2014"

- IT Professional, December 2013, "Product of the Year 2013"

- Network World Magazine, November 2013, "Product of the Week 11/11/2013"

- Network World Magazine, September 2013, "Product of the Week 9/23/2013"

- Network World Magazine, May 2013, "Hottest products from Interop 2013"

- LANline Magazin Germany, Dr. Werner Degenhardt, July 2013, "Netzwerk-Monitoring in Seide gekleidet"

- Bjoerns Windows Blog, December 2010, "Netzwerküberwachung mit NetCrunch 6"

- LanLine Magazine, November 2010, Werner Degenhardt, "Netzwerküberwachung für viele Plattformen"

- Networld Magazine, Michał Witkowski, February 2010. "Spokojnie, to tylko awaria"

- Processor Magazine, Robin Weisman, January 2010. "Straightforward Network Server Management"

- LANline Magazin Germany, Dr. Werner Degenhardt, June 2008. "Der neue Netzwerkatlas"

- Processor Magazine, May 2008. "Easy Network Monitoring"

- PC Magazine Russia February 2008. "AdRem Software выпускает систему мониторинга и управления сетью NetCrunch 5"

- Datamation, Cynthia Harvey, February 2007. "Datamation Readers Name NetCrunch Number One"

39.6.2 News

- "AdRem Software Launches NetCrunch 8 Monitoring Platform"

- "Agentless Monitoring: AdRem's NetCrunch 8 Released"

Chapter 40

netsniff-ng

netsniff-ng is a free Linux network analyzer and networking toolkit originally written by Daniel Borkmann. Its gain of performance is reached by zero-copy mechanisms for network packets (RX_RING, TX_RING),[2] so that the Linux kernel does not need to copy packets from kernel space to user space via system calls such as recvmsg().[3] libpcap, starting with release 1.0.0, also supports the zero-copy mechanism on Linux for capturing (RX_RING), so programs using libpcap also use that mechanism on Linux.

40.1 Overview

netsniff-ng was initially created as a network sniffer with support of the Linux kernel packet-mmap interface for network packets, but later on, more tools have been added to make it a useful toolkit such as the iproute2 suite, for instance. Through the kernel's zero-copy interface, efficient packet processing can be reached even on commodity hardware. For instance, Gigabit Ethernet wire-speed has been reached with netsniff-ng's **trafgen**.[4][5] The netsniff-ng toolkit does not depend on the libpcap library. Moreover, no special operating system patches are needed to run the toolkit. netsniff-ng is free software and has been released under the terms of the GNU General Public License version 2.

The toolkit currently consists of a network analyzer, packet capturer and replayer, a wire-rate traffic generator, an encrypted multiuser IP tunnel, a Berkeley Packet Filter compiler, networking statistic tools, an autonomous system trace route and more:[6]

- **netsniff-ng**, a zero-copy analyzer, packet capturer and replayer, itself supporting the pcap file format

- **trafgen**, a zero-copy wire-rate traffic generator

- **mausezahn**, a packet generator and analyzer for HW/SW appliances with a Cisco-CLI

- **bpfc**, a Berkeley Packet Filter compiler

- **ifpps**, a top-like kernel networking statistics tool

- **flowtop**, a top-like netfilter connection tracking tool with Geo-IP information

- **curvetun**, a lightweight multiuser IP tunnel based on elliptic curve cryptography

- **astraceroute**, an autonomous system trace route utility with Geo-IP information

Distribution specific packages are available for all major operating system distributions such as Debian[7] or Fedora Linux. It has also been added to Xplico's Network Forensic Toolkit,[8] GRML Linux, SecurityOnion,[9] and to the Network Security Toolkit.[10] The netsniff-ng toolkit is also used in academia.[11][12]

40.2 Basic commands working in netsniff-ng

In these examples, it is assumed that *eth0* is the used network interface. Programs in the netsniff-ng suite accept long options, e.g., --in (-i), --out (-o), --dev (-d).

- For geographical AS TCP SYN probe trace route to a website:

astraceroute -d eth0 -N -S -H <host e.g., netsniff-ng.org>

- For kernel networking statistics within promiscuous mode:

ifpps -d eth0 -p

- For high-speed network packet traffic generation, *trafgen.txf* is the packet configuration:

trafgen -d eth0 -c trafgen.txf

- For compiling a Berkeley Packet Filter *fubar.bpf*:

bpfc fubar.bpf

- For live-tracking of current TCP connections (including protocol, application name, city and country of source and destination):

flowtop

- For efficiently dumping network traffic in a pcap file:

netsniff-ng -i eth0 -o dump.pcap -s -b 0

40.3   Platforms

The **netsniff-ng** toolkit currently runs only on Linux systems. Its developers decline a port to Microsoft Windows.[13]

40.4   See also

- Comparison of packet analyzers
- Packet generator
- Traffic generation model
- OpenVPN
- Traceroute
- Wireshark
- Tcpdump
- Xplico

40.5   References

[1] "netsniff-ng license".

[2] "Description of the Linux packet-mmap mechanism". Retrieved 6 November 2011.

[3] "netsniff-ng Homepage, Abstract, Zero-copy". Retrieved 6 November 2011.

[4] "Network Security Toolkit Article about trafgen's performance capabilities". Retrieved 6 November 2011.

[5] "Developer's Blog about trafgen's Performance". Retrieved 6 November 2011.

[6] "Tools that are part of netsniff-ng". Retrieved 6 November 2011.

[7] "netsnif-ng in Debian".

[8] "Xplico support of netsniff-ng". Retrieved 6 November 2011.

[9] "Security Onion 12.04 RC1 Available Now!". Retrieved 16 December 2012.

[10] "Network Security Toolkit adds netsniff-ng". Retrieved 6 November 2011.

[11] "netsniff-ng's trafgen at University of Napoli Federico II". Retrieved 7 November 2011.

[12] "netsniff-ng's trafgen at Columbia University". Retrieved 7 November 2011.

[13] "netsniff-ng FAQ declining a port to Microsoft Windows". Retrieved 21 June 2015.

40.6   External links

- Official netsniff-ng website
- netsniff-ng FAQ
- netsniff-ng at GitHub
- netsniff-ng mailing list archive
- Linux' packet mmap(), BPF, and the netsniff-ng toolkit, talk at DevConf (long)
- Packet Sockets, BPF, netsniff-ng, talk at OpenSourceDays (short)
- netsniff-ng(8) – Linux Administration and Privileged Commands Manual

Chapter 41

Network intelligence

Network Intelligence (NI) is a technology that builds on the concepts and capabilities of Deep Packet Inspection (DPI), Packet Capture and Business Intelligence (BI). It examines, in real time, IP data packets that cross communications networks by identifying the protocols used and extracting packet content and metadata for rapid analysis of data relationships and communications patterns. Also, sometimes referred to as Network Acceleration or piracy.

NI is used as a middleware to capture and feed information to network operator applications for bandwidth management, traffic shaping, policy management, charging and billing (including usage-based and content billing), service assurance, revenue assurance, market research mega panel analytics, lawful interception and cyber security. It is currently being incorporated into a wide range of applications by vendors who provide technology solutions to Communications Service Providers (CSPs), governments and large enterprises. NI extends network controls, business capabilities, security functions and data mining for new products and services needed since the emergence of Web 2.0 and wireless 3G and 4G technologies.[1][2][3][4]

41.1 Background

The evolution and growth of Internet and wireless technologies offer possibilities for new types of products and services,[4][5] as well as opportunities for hackers and criminal organizations to exploit weaknesses and perpetrate cyber crime.[6][7][8] Network optimization and security solutions therefore need to address the exponential increases in IP traffic, methods of access, types of activity and volume of content generated.[9][10] Traditional DPI tools from established vendors have historically addressed specific network infrastructure applications such as bandwidth management, performance optimization and Quality of Service (QoS).

DPI focuses on recognizing different types of IP traffic as part of a CSP's infrastructure. NI provides more granular analysis. It enables vendors to create an information layer with metadata from IP traffic to feed multiple applications for more detailed and expansive visibility into network-based activity.

NI technology goes beyond traditional DPI, since it not only recognizes protocols but also extracts a wide range of valuable metadata. NI's value-add to solutions traditionally based on DPI has attracted the attention of industry analysts who specialize in DPI market research. For example, Heavy Reading now includes NI companies on its Deep Packet Inspection Semi-Annual Market Tracker.[4]

41.2 Business Intelligence for data networks

In much the same way that BI technology synthesizes business application data from a variety of sources for business visibility and better decision-making, NI technology correlates network traffic data from a variety of data communication vehicles for network visibility, enabling better cyber security and IP services. With ongoing changes in communications networks and how information can be exchanged, people are no longer linked exclusively to physical subscriber lines. The same person can communicate in multiple ways – FTP, Webmail, VoIP, instant messaging, online chat, blogs, social networks – and from different access points via desktops, laptops and mobile devices.

NI provides the means to quickly identify, examine and correlate interactions involving Internet users, applications, and protocols whether or not the protocols are tunneled or follow the OSI model. The technology enables a global understanding of network traffic for applications that need to correlate information such as who contacts whom, when, where and how, or who accesses what database, when, and the information viewed. When combined with traditional BI tools that examine service quality and customer care, NI creates a powerful nexus of subscriber and network data.

41.3 Use in telecommunications

Telcos, Internet Service Providers (ISPs) and Mobile Network Operators (MNOs) are under increasing competitive pressures to move to smart pipe business models. The cost savings and revenue opportunities driving smart pipe strategies also apply to Network Equipment Providers, Software Vendors and Systems Integrators that serve the industry.

Because NI captures detailed information from the hundreds of IP applications that cross mobile networks, it provides the required visibility and analysis of user demand to create and deliver differentiating services, as well as manage usage once deployed.

NI as enabling technology for smart pipe applications

Customer metrics are especially important for telecom companies to understand consumer behaviors and create personalized IP services. NI enables faster and more sophisticated Audience Measurement, User Behavior Analysis, Customer Segmentation, and Personalized Services.

Real-time network metrics are equally important for companies to deliver and manage services. NI classifies protocols and applications from layers 2 through 7, generates metadata for communication sessions, and correlates activity between all layers, applicable for Bandwidth & Resource Optimization, Quality of Service (QoS), Content-Based Billing, Quality of Experience (QoE), VoIP Fraud Monitoring and Regulatory Compliance.

41.4 Use in cloud computing

The economics and deployment speed of cloud computing is fueling rapid adoption by companies and government agencies.[11][12][13] Among concerns, however, are risks of information security, e-discovery, regulatory compliance and auditing.[14][15][16] NI mitigates the risks by providing Infrastructure as a Service (IaaS), Platform as a Service (PaaS) and Software as a Service (SaaS) vendors with real-time situational awareness of network activity, and critical transparency to allay fears of potential customers. A vendor can demonstrate hardened network security to prevent Data Leakage or Data Theft and an irrefutable audit trail of all network transaction – communication and content – related to a customer's account, assuming compliance to regulation and standards.

41.5 Use in government

NI extracts and correlates information such as who contacts whom, when where and how, providing situational awareness for Lawful Interception and Cyber Security. Real-time data capture, extraction and analysis allow security specialists to take preventive measures and protect network assets in real time as a complement post-mortem analysis after an attack.

41.6 Use in business

Because NI combines real-time network monitoring with IP metadata extraction, it enhances the effectiveness of applications for Database Security, Database Auditing and Network Protection. The network visibility afforded by NI can also be used to build enhancements and next-generation solutions for Network Performance Management, WAN Optimization, Customer Experience Management, Content Filtering, and internal billing of networked applications.

41.7 References

[1] Jessica Schieve (2011-02-23). "Light Reading report: Network Acceleration - Managing Data Growth". Light Reading. Retrieved 2011-03-15.

[2] Brian Partridge (2010-05-17). "Network Intelligence is Key to Profiting from Anywhere Demand". Yankee Group Anchor Report. Retrieved 2010-06-15.

[3] Thibaut Bechetoille (2009-03-25). "The Everyday Relationship Between You and 'Your' Information: What's Out There on the Internet". TMCnet. Retrieved 2010-06-15.

[4] Simon Sherrington (2010-06). "Deep Packet Inspection Semi-Annual Market Tracker". Heavy Reading. Retrieved 2010-06-15. Check date values in: |date= (help)

[5] Aditya Kishore (2008-07-21). "Market Research: New Opportunity for Service Providers?". Light Reading. Retrieved 2009-07-27.

[6] Shireen Dee (2009-02-03). "Qosmos Network Intelligence Helps Development of Smart Pipe Solutions". TMCnet. Retrieved 2009-07-27.

[7] "MessageLabs Intelligence: 2008 Annual Security Report" (PDF). MessageLabs. 2009. Retrieved 2009-07-27.

[8] "Big Data and Bigger Breaches With Alex Pentland of Monument Capital Group". 2015. Retrieved 2015-01-14.

[9] "2008 Internet Security Trends". IronPort. 2008. Retrieved 2009-07-27.

[10] Jordan Golson (2009-07-21). "A Brave New World: 700M New Net Users Seen By 2013". GigaOM. Retrieved 2009-07-27.

[11] Stacey Higginbotham (2009-07-21). "Will P2P Soon Be the Scourge of Mobile Networks?". GigaOM. Retrieved 2009-07-27.

[12] "IDC Finds Cloud Computing Entering Period of Accelerating Adoption and Poised to Capture IT Spending Growth Over the Next Five Years". IDC. 2008-10-20. Retrieved 2009-07-28.

[13] Tom Sullivan (2008-03-29). "More Cash for Cloud Computing in 2009". PC World. Retrieved 2009-07-28.

[14] Henry Sienkiewicz (2008-04-30). "DISA's Cloud Computing Initiatives". Government Information Security Podcasts. Retrieved 2009-07-28.

[15] Ephraim Schwartz (2008-07-07). "The dangers of cloud computing". Info World. Retrieved 2009-07-28.

[16] Jon Brodkin (2008-07-02). "Gartner: Seven cloud-computing security risks". Info World. Retrieved 2009-07-28.

Chapter 42

Network Security Toolkit

The **Network Security Toolkit** (NST) is a Linux-based Live CD that provides a set of open source computer security and networking tools to perform routine security and networking diagnostic and monitoring tasks. The distribution can be used as a network security analysis, validation and monitoring tool on servers hosting virtual machines. The majority of tools published in the article "Top 125 security tools" by Insecure.org are available in the toolkit. NST has package management capabilities similar to Fedora and maintains its own repository of additional packages.

42.1 Features

Many tasks that can be performed within NST are available through a web interface called NST WUI. Among the tools that can be used through this interface are nmap with the vizualization tool ZenMap, ntop, a Network Interface Bandwidth Monitor, a Network Segment ARP Scanner, a session manager for VNC, a minicom-based terminal server, serial port monitoring, and WPA PSK management.

Other features include visualization of ntopng, ntop, wireshark, traceroute, netflow and kismet data by geolocating the host addresses, IPv4 Address conversation, traceroute data and wireless access points and displaying them via Google Earth or a Mercator World Map bit image, a browser-based packet capture and protocol analysis system capable of monitoring up to four network interfaces using Wireshark, as well as a Snort-based intrusion detection system with a "collector" backend that stores incidents in a MySQL database. For web developers, there is also a JavaScript console with a built-in object library with functions that aid the development of dynamic web pages.

42.1.1 Host Geolocations

The following example ntop host geolocation images were generated by NST.

ntop World Map Hosts

42.1.2 Network Monitors

The following image depicts the *interactive* dynamic SVG/AJAX enabled Network Interface Bandwidth Monitor which is integrated into the NST WUI. Also shown is a **Ruler Measurement** tool overlay to perform time and bandwidth rate analysis.

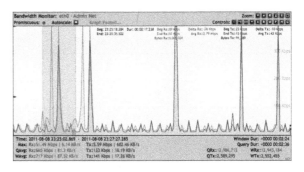

Network Interface Bandwidth Monitor - Interface: eth0

42.2   See also

- BackTrack

- Kali Linux

- Computer Security

- List of Live CDs

42.3   Notes

42.4   References

- Network Security Toolkit distribution aids network security administrators

- Screencast: Opening Up the Network Security Toolkit

- Security Matters: NST Goes Virtual Too}

42.5   External links

- Official website

- NST at SourceForge

- Network Security Geolocation Matrix

Chapter 43

Network weathermap

Network Weathermap, also called PHP Weathermap, is an open source (GNU GPL 2.0) network traffic tool that displays, in a graphical way, how network links are utilized within a given network.[1][2]

43.1 References

[1] Duling, Mark. "Visualize Traffic with Network Weathermap". Retrieved 5 April 2012.

[2] Mann, Harper (May 1, 2006). "Network Weathermap -- A Free Monitoring Tool You Should be Using". Retrieved 5 April 2012.

43.2 External links

- Official website

Chapter 44

ngrep

ngrep (network grep) is a network packet analyzer written by Jordan Ritter.[2] It runs under the command line, and relies upon the pcap library and the GNU regex library.

ngrep supports Berkeley Packet Filter (BPF) logic to select network sources or destinations or protocols, and also allows to match patterns or regular expressions in the data payload of packets using GNU grep syntax, showing packet data in a human-friendly way.

ngrep is an open source application, and the source code is available to download from the ngrep site at SourceForge. It can be compiled and ported to multiple platforms, it works in many UNIX-like operating systems: Linux, Solaris, BSD, AIX, and also works on Microsoft Windows.[3]

44.1 Functionality

ngrep is similar to tcpdump, but it has the ability to look for a regular expression in the payload of the packet, and show the matching packets on a screen or console. It allows users to see all unencrypted traffic being passed over the network, by putting the network interface into promiscuous mode.

ngrep with an appropriate BPF filter syntax, can be used to debug plain text protocols interactions like HTTP, SMTP, FTP, DNS, among others, or to search for a specific string or pattern, using a grep regular expression syntax.[4][5]

ngrep also can be used to capture traffic on the wire and store pcap dump files, or to read files generated by other sniffer applications, like tcpdump, or wireshark.

ngrep has various options or command line arguments. The ngrep man page in UNIX-like operating systems show a list of available options.

44.2 Using ngrep

In these examples, it is assumed that *eth0* is the used network interface.

- Capture network traffic incoming/outgoing to/from eth0 interface and show parameters following HTTP (TCP/80) GET or POST methods

ngrep -l -q -d eth0 -i "^GET |^POST " tcp and port 80

- Capture network traffic incoming/outgoing to/from eth0 interface and show the HTTP (TCP/80) User-Agent string

ngrep -l -q -d eth0 -i "User-Agent: " tcp and port 80

- Capture network traffic incoming/outgoing to/from eth0 interface and show the DNS (UDP/53) querys and responses

ngrep -l -q -d eth0 -i "" udp and port 53

44.3 Security

Capturing raw network traffic from an interface requires special privileges or superuser privileges on some platforms, especially on Unix-like systems. ngrep default behavior is to drop privileges in those platforms, running under a specific unprivileged user.

Like tcpdump, it is also possible to use ngrep for the specific purpose of intercepting and displaying the communications of another user or computer, or an entire network.

A privileged user running ngrep in a server or workstation connected to a device configured with port mirroring on a switch, router, or gateway, or connected to any other device used for network traffic capture on a LAN, MAN, or WAN, can watch all unencrypted information related to login ID's, passwords, or URLs and content of websites being viewed in that network.[6]

44.4 Supported Platforms

- Linux: Unix operating system running the Linux kernel

- Solaris: Unix operating system developed by Sun Microsystems

- BSD: Unix operating system family (FreeBSD, NetBSD, OpenBSD)

- OS X: Unix operating system developed by Apple Inc.

- AIX, Unix operating system developed by IBM

- Windows, operating system developed by Microsoft

44.5 Supported Protocols

- IPv4 and IPv6, Internet Protocol version 4 and version 6

- TCP, Transmission Control Protocol

- UDP, User Datagram Protocol

- ICMPv4 and ICMPv6, Internet Control Message Protocol version 4 and version 6

- IGMP, Internet Group Management Protocol

- Ethernet, IEEE 802.3

- PPP, Point to Point Protocol

- SLIP, Serial Line Internet Protocol

- FDDI, Fiber Data Distribution Protocol

- Token Ring, IEEE 802.5

44.6 See also

- Comparison of packet analyzers

- tcpdump, a packet analyzer

- pcap, an application programming interface (API) for capturing network traffic

- snoop, a command line packet analyzer included with Solaris

- wireshark, a network packet analyzer

- dsniff, a packet sniffer and set of traffic analysis tools

- netsniff-ng, a free Linux networking toolkit

- etherape, a network mapping tool that relies on sniffing traffic

- tcptrace, a tool for analyzing the logs produced by tcpdump

- Microsoft Network Monitor, a packet analyzer

- xplico, a network forensics analysis tool

- flowgrep, a tool for filtering packet streams

44.7 References

[1] LICENSE.txt file in the tarball

[2] Jordan Ritter at CrunchBase

[3] ngrep supported platforms

[4] ngrep and regular expressions

[5] ngrep usage

[6] Network monitoring with ngrep

44.8 External links

- Official site for ngrep

- Ngrep - Linux man page

- Flowgrep TCP/UDP/IP stream grep tool

- Official site for tcpdump (and libpcap)

- Official site for WinDump

- Other Packet Sniffers at sectools.org

Chapter 45

Nimsoft

Nimsoft was an independent company software vendor that offered information technology (IT) monitoring and service desk products and services. It was acquired by CA Inc. in 2010, and since October 2012 its products were integrated into that business. The Nimsoft brand is still used by CA.

Nimsoft products monitor and manage business services and specific systems within the IT infrastructure, including network components, servers, databases, applications, and virtualized environments.

With Nimsoft products, customers can monitor systems hosted in internal data centers, as well as in externally hosted environments, including software as a service (SaaS) and cloud computing environments.[1]

45.1 History

Nimbus Software was founded in Oslo, Norway in 1998 (not to be confused with Nimbus Data). Converse Software, the exclusive US distributor of Nimbus Software was founded in Silicon Valley in 2002. Nimbus Software and Converse Software merged in 2004 to form Nimsoft. Gary Read, the founder of the US distributor, was appointed CEO and the new company's headquarters were established in Silicon Valley.[2] In 2007 a 10.3 million Series A round of funding from JMI Equity and Northzone Ventures closed.[3] Nimsoft acquired Indicative Software in April 2008 to offer business service management and established a new research and development base in Fort Collins, Colorado.[4] Nimsoft received the *San Francisco Business Times* 2008 "Best Place to Work Award".[5] Nimsoft closed a $12 million funding round led by Goldman Sachs in October 2008.[3]

In May 2009 Nimsoft acquired the intellectual property assets of Cittio. Its product capabilities included network discovery, topology mapping, and root cause analysis (RCA) utilizing graph theory.[6] That October Nimsoft announced its unified monitoring architecture to monitor externally hosted systems and services, including SaaS and cloud computing based IT infrastructures.[7]

In March 2010 CA Inc. announced it would acquired Nimsoft for $350 million.[8] Nimsoft was one of the "Hottest Silicon Valley Companies" by Lead411.[9] In September 2010, Nimsoft extended its software to support Vblock products from the VCE Company.[10]

In April 2011, Nimsoft announced its Unified Manager, software combining IT monitoring and service management.[11] Enhanced management support for NetApp storage was announced in June.[12] CA acquired Netherlands-based WatchMouse in July, and its software was integrated into Nimsoft .[13]

Nimsoft ceased to exist as an independent operating unit within CA in 2012, although the same products are still offered under that brand name.

45.2 References

[1] Denise Dubie , Network World. "Managing IT assets where they live: Nimsoft extends monitoring capabilities beyond data center to cloud computing environments, SaaS provided apps." October 21, 2009.

[2] Tony C. Yang, San Francisco Business Times. "Keeping an eye on IT." May 30, 2008.

[3] Denise Dubie, Network World. "Goldman Sachs leads $12 million investment in Nimsoft." October 7, 2008.

[4] Denise Dubie, Network World. "Nimsoft, Indicative join forces to take on the Big Four". April 9, 2008.

[5] "Nimsoft Wins "Best Place to Work Award", Sponsored by San Francisco Business Times". *Press release* (Nimsoft). May 1, 2008. Archived from the original on May 17, 2008. Retrieved August 13, 2013.

[6] Ellen Messmer, Network World. "Nimsoft acquires the assets of Cittio". May 19, 2009.

[7] Denise Dubie, Network World. "Managing IT assets where they live: Nimsoft extends monitoring capabilities beyond

data center to cloud computing environments, SaaS provided apps." October 21, 2009.

[8] Charles Babcock, InformationWeek, "CA to buy Nimsoft for USD 350 million", March 11, 2010.

[9] Lead411 launches "Hottest Silicon Valley Companies" awards

[10] Beth Schultz, Network World, "Nimsoft delivers integrated monitoring for Vblock units", September 28, 2010.

[11] John Rath, Darlington College, "Nimsoft Broadens Offerings With Unified Manager", April 6, 2011.

[12] "Nimsoft enhances management support for NetApp storage". *Press release* (Computer Technology Review). June 17, 2011. Retrieved August 13, 2013.

[13] Charles Babcock (July 29, 2011). "CA Buys Watchmouse, For Remote App Testing Power". *Information Week*. Retrieved August 13, 2013.

45.3   External links

- Nimsoft Unified Monitoring Site

- Nimsoft Network Monitoring Site

- Nimsoft Server Monitoring Site

Chapter 46

Nmap

Nmap (*Network Mapper*) is a security scanner originally written by Gordon Lyon (also known by his pseudonym *Fyodor Vaskovich*)[1] used to discover hosts and services on a computer network, thus creating a "map" of the network. To accomplish its goal, Nmap sends specially crafted packets to the target host and then analyzes the responses.

The software provides a number of features for probing computer networks, including host discovery and service and operating system detection. These features are extensible by scripts that provide more advanced service detection,[2] vulnerability detection,[2] and other features. Nmap is also capable of adapting to network conditions including latency and congestion during a scan. Nmap is under development and refinement by its user community.

Nmap was originally a Linux-only utility,[3] but it was ported to Windows, Solaris, HP-UX, BSD variants (including OS X), AmigaOS, and IRIX.[4] Linux is the most popular platform, followed closely by Windows.[5]

46.1 Features

Nmap features include:

- Host discovery – Identifying hosts on a network. For example, listing the hosts that respond to TCP and/or ICMP requests or have a particular port open.

- Port scanning – Enumerating the open ports on target hosts.

- Version detection – Interrogating network services on remote devices to determine application name and version number.[6]

- OS detection – Determining the operating system and hardware characteristics of network devices.

- Scriptable interaction with the target – using Nmap Scripting Engine (NSE) and Lua programming language.

Nmap can provide further information on targets, including reverse DNS names, device types, and MAC addresses.[7]

Typical uses of Nmap:

- Auditing the security of a device or firewall by identifying the network connections which can be made to, or through it.[8]

- Identifying open ports on a target host in preparation for auditing.[9]

- Network inventory, network mapping, maintenance and asset management.

- Auditing the security of a network by identifying new servers.[10]

- Generating traffic to hosts on a network.[11]

- Find and exploit vulnerabilities in a network.[12]

46.2 Graphical interfaces

NmapFE, originally written by *Zach Smith*, was Nmap's official GUI for Nmap versions 2.2 to 4.22.[13] For Nmap 4.50 (originally in the 4.22SOC development series) NmapFE was replaced with Zenmap, a new official graphical user interface based on UMIT, developed by *Adriano Monteiro Marques*.

Various web-based interfaces allow controlling Nmap or analysing Nmap results from a web browser. These include LOCALSCAN,[14] nmap-web,[15] and Nmap-CGI.[16]

Microsoft Windows specific GUIs exist, including NMapWin,[17] which has not been updated since June 2003 (v1.4.0), and NMapW[18] by Syhunt.

- *Zenmap*, showing results for a port scan against Wikipedia

- *NmapFE*, showing results for a port scan against Wikipedia

- *XNmap*, a Mac OS X GUI

46.3 Reporting results

Nmap provides four possible input formats. All but the interactive output is saved to a file. Nmap output can be manipulated by text processing software, enabling the user to create customized reports.[19]

Interactive presented and updated real time when a user runs Nmap from the command line. Various options can be entered during the scan to facilitate monitoring.

XML a format that can be further processed by XML tools. It can be converted into a HTML report using XSLT.

Grepable output that is tailored to line-oriented processing tools such as grep, sed or awk.

Normal the output as seen while running Nmap from the command line, but saved to a file.

Script kiddie meant to be an amusing way to format the interactive output replacing letters with their visually alike number representations. For example, *Interesting ports* becomes *Int3rest1ng p0rtz*.

46.4 History

Nmap was first published in September 1997, as an article in Phrack Magazine with source-code included.[20] With help and contributions of the computer security community, development continued. Enhancements included operating system fingerprinting, service fingerprinting,[6] code rewrites (C to C++), additional scan types, protocol support (e.g. IPv6, SCTP[21]) and new programs that complement Nmap's core features. Changes include:

- 12 December 1998—Nmap 2.00 is released, including Operating System fingerprinting[22]

- 11 April 1999—NmapFE, a GTK+ front end, is bundled with Nmap[22]

- 7 December 2000—Windows port[13]

- 28 August 2002—Rewrite from C to C++[13]

- 16 September 2003—The first public release to include service version detection[13]

- 31 August 2004—Core scan engine rewritten for version 3.70. New engine is called *ultra_scan*[23]

- Summer 2005—Nmap selected for participation in Google Summer of Code.[24] Added features included Zenmap, NSE, Ncat, and 2nd-generation OS detection.

- 13 December 2007—Nmap 4.50, the 10th Anniversary Edition, was released. Included Zenmap, 2nd-generation OS detection, and the Nmap Scripting Engine[25]

- 30 March 2009—Emergency release of Nmap 4.85BETA5, leveraging NSE to detect Conficker infections[26]

- 16 July 2009—5.00 included netcat-replacement Ncat and Ndiff scan comparison tool[27]

- 28 January 2011—5.50 included Nping packet generation[28]

- 21 May 2012—6.00 released with full IPv6 support.

The Nmap Changelog records all changes.[13]

46.5 Ethical issues and legality

Nmap is a tool that can be used to discover services running on Internet connected systems. Like any tool it could potentially be used for *black hat* hacking,[29] as a precursor to attempts to gain unauthorized access to computer systems. Nmap is more often used by security and systems administration to assess networks for vulnerabilities.

System administrators can use Nmap to search for unauthorized servers, or for computers that do not conform to security standards.[30]

Nmap is related to vulnerability assessment tools such as Nessus, which test for common vulnerabilities in open ports. The included NSE[31] scripts that are packaged with modern versions of Nmap are able to perform vulnerability checks against discovered services.

In some jurisdictions, unauthorized port scanning is illegal.[32]

46.6 In popular culture

In *The Matrix Reloaded*, Trinity is seen using Nmap to access a power plant's computer system,[33] allowing Neo to "physically" break in to a building. The appearance of

Nmap in the film was widely discussed on Internet forums and hailed as an unusually realistic example of hacking.[34]

Nmap and NmapFE were used in *The Listening*, a 2006 movie about a former NSA officer who defects and mounts a clandestine counter-listening station high in the Italian alps.

Nmap source code can be seen in the movie *Battle Royale*, as well as brief views of the command line version of Nmap executing in *Live Free or Die Hard* and *Bourne Ultimatum*.[33] In 2013, Nmap continued to make appearances in movies including popular sci-fi movie *Elysium*.

The film *Dredd*, a film adaptation of the famous Judge Dredd comics, was released in 2012 and also contains multiple Nmap scenes.[33] Nmap is used for network reconnaissance and exploitation of the slum tower network. It is even seen briefly in the movie's trailer.

46.7   In academia

Nmap is an integral part of academic activities. It has been used for research involving the TCP/IP protocol suite and networking in general.[35] As well as being a research tool, Nmap has become a research topic as well.[36]

46.8   Sample output

Command:- nmap -A scanme.nmap.org Starting Nmap 6.47 (http://nmap.org) at 2014-12-29 20:02 CET Nmap scan report for scanme.nmap.org (74.207.244.221) Host is up (0.16s latency). Not shown: 997 filtered ports PORT STATE SERVICE VERSION 22/tcp open ssh OpenSSH 5.3p1 Debian 3ubuntu7.1 (Ubuntu Linux; protocol 2.0) | ssh-hostkey: | 1024 8d:60:f1:7c:ca:b7:3d:0a:d6:67:54:9d:69:d9:b9:dd (DSA) |_ 2048 79:f8:09:ac:d4:e2:32:42:10:49:d3:bd:20:82:85:ec (RSA) 80/tcp open http Apache httpd 2.2.14 ((Ubuntu)) |_http-title: Go ahead and ScanMe! 9929/tcp open nping-echo Nping echo Warning: OSScan results may be unreliable because we could not find at least 1 open and 1 closed port Device type: general purpose|phone|storage-misc|WAP Running (JUST GUESSING): Linux 2.6.X|3.X|2.4.X (94%), Netgear RAIDiator 4.X (86%) OS CPE: cpe:/o:linux:linux_kernel:2.6.38 cpe:/o:linux:linux_kernel:3 cpe:/o:netgear:raidiator:4 cpe:/o:linux:linux_kernel:2.4 Aggressive OS guesses: Linux 2.6.38 (94%), Linux 3.0 (92%), Linux 2.6.32 - 3.0 (91%), Linux 2.6.18 (91%), Linux 2.6.39 (90%), Linux 2.6.32 - 2.6.39 (90%), Linux 2.6.38 - 3.0 (90%), Linux 2.6.38 - 2.6.39 (89%), Linux 2.6.35 (88%), Linux 2.6.37 (88%) No exact OS matches for host (test

conditions non-ideal). Network Distance: 13 hops Service Info: OS: Linux; CPE: cpe:/o:linux:linux_kernel TRACEROUTE (using port 80/tcp) HOP RTT ADDRESS 1 14.21 ms 151.217.192.1 2 5.27 ms ae10-0.mx240-iphh.shitty.network (94.45.224.129) 3 13.16 ms hmb-s2-rou-1102.DE.eurorings.net (134.222.120.121) 4 6.83 ms blnb-s1-rou-1041.DE.eurorings.net (134.222.229.78) 5 8.30 ms blnb-s3-rou-1041.DE.eurorings.net (134.222.229.82) 6 9.42 ms as6939.bcix.de (193.178.185.34) 7 24.56 ms 10ge10-6.core1.ams1.he.net (184.105.213.229) 8 30.60 ms 100ge9-1.core1.lon2.he.net (72.52.92.213) 9 93.54 ms 100ge1-1.core1.nyc4.he.net (72.52.92.166) 10 181.14 ms 10ge9-6.core1.sjc2.he.net (184.105.213.173) 11 169.54 ms 10ge3-2.core3.fmt2.he.net (184.105.222.13) 12 164.58 ms router4-fmt.linode.com (64.71.132.138) 13 164.32 ms scanme.nmap.org (74.207.244.221) OS and Service detection performed. Please report any incorrect results at http://nmap.org/submit/ . Nmap done: 1 IP address (1 host up) scanned in 28.98 seconds

46.9   See also

- Metasploit Framework
- Netcat
- Wireshark
- Nessus_(software)
- SAINT_(software)

46.10   References

[1] "Matrix mixes life and hacking". *BBC News*. 2003-05-19. Retrieved 2009-01-14.

[2] Nmap Scripting Engine. Nmap.org. Retrieved on 2013-02-01.

[3] The History and Future of Nmap. Nmap.org. Retrieved on 2013-02-01.

[4] Other Platforms. Nmap.org. Retrieved on 2013-02-01.

[5] "Nmap Installation for Windows". nmap.org. Retrieved 2008-05-14.

[6] Service and Application Version Detection

[7] "Chapter 15. Nmap Reference Guide". Nmap.org. 2011-03-25. Retrieved 2011-04-23.

[8] Nmap Overview and Demonstration.

[9] When Good Scanners Go Bad, From , ComputerWorld 22 March 1999

[10] nmap-audit – Network auditing with Nmap. heavyk.org

[11] Nping - Network packet generation tool / ping utiliy.

[12] Leyden, John. "Revealed ... GCHQ's incredible hacking tool to sweep net for vulnerabilities: Nmap". *theregister.co.uk*. The Register. Retrieved 14 December 2014.

[13] "Nmap Change Log". Nmap.org. Retrieved 2011-09-17.

[14] archive copy on Archive.org

[15] nmap-web: quick-n-dirty web interface to Nmap. Komar.org. Retrieved on 2011-09-17.

[16] nmap-cgi homepage. Nmap-cgi.tuxfamily.org. Retrieved on 2011-09-17.

[17] NMapWin v1.2.3. Nmapwin.sourceforge.net. Retrieved on 2011-09-17.

[18] Syhunt Technology: Web Application Security and Testing Tools. Syhunt.com (2010-10-23). Retrieved on 2011-09-17.

[19] Output. Nmap.org. Retrieved on 2011-12-10.

[20] Nmap Introduction – Phrack 51, Article 11. Phrack.org. Retrieved on 2011-09-17.

[21] SCTP Support for Nmap. Roe.ch (2007-01-26). Retrieved on 2011-09-17.

[22] "The History and Future of Nmap". Nmap.org.

[23] "Nmap Hackers—Nmap 3.70 Released—Core Scan Engine Rewrite!". Seclists.org. Retrieved 2011-09-17.

[24] "Google sponsors Nmap summer student developers". Seclists.org. Retrieved 2011-09-17.

[25] "Nmap 4.50 Press Release". Insecure.org. Retrieved 2011-09-17.

[26] "Nmap Development—Nmap 4.85BETA5—Now with Conficker detection!". Seclists.org. Retrieved 2011-09-17.

[27] "Nmap 5.00 Release Notes". Nmap.org. Retrieved 2011-09-17.

[28] "Nmap 5.50—Now with Gopher protocol support!". Seclists.org. Retrieved 2011-09-17.

[29] "Hacking tool reportedly draws FBI subpoenas". Securityfocus.com. 2004-11-24. Retrieved 2011-09-17.

[30] "120 – How to conduct a security audit" (PDF). Tech Support Alert. Retrieved 2011-09-17.

[31] "NSE scripts with brief summaries". nmap.org. Retrieved 2014-01-12.

[32] "First ruling by the Supreme Court of Finland on attempted break-in". Osborne Clarke. 2003. Retrieved 2010-02-21.

[33] "nmap in the movies".

[34] Kevin Poulsen (2003-05-16). "Matrix Sequel Has Hacker Cred". The Register.

[35] "Validation of Sensor Alert Correlators" (PDF).

[36] "A Data Mining Based Analysis of Nmap Operating System Fingerprint Database".

46.11 Bibliography

- Fyodor Lyon, Gordon (1 January 2009). *Nmap Network Scanning: The Official Nmap Project Guide to Network Discovery and Security Scanning*. Insecure.com LLC. p. 468. ISBN 0-979-95871-7.

46.12 External links

- Official website

- nmap-online.com – Online tool to check your computer

- HackerTarget.com – Online version of the Nmap Port Scanner

Chapter 47

ntop

ntop is a network probe that shows network usage in a way similar to what top does for processes. In interactive mode, it displays the network status on the user's terminal. In Web mode, it acts as a web server, creating a HTML dump of the network status. It supports a NetFlow/sFlow emitter/collector, a HTTP-based client interface for creating ntop-centric monitoring applications, and RRD for persistently storing traffic statistics.[1]

ntop is available for both Unix and Win32-based platforms. It has been developed by Luca Deri, an Italian research scientist and network manager at University of Pisa.

Common usage on a GNU/Linux system is to start the ntop daemon (/etc/init.d/ntopd start), then one can use the web interface to ntop via visiting http://127.0.0.1:3000 provided the loopback device has been started (/etc/init.d/net.lo start) and the listening port for ntop is 3000 (look out for the -w option in ps aux | grep ntop).

47.1   See also

- Zero-copy
- Netsniff-ng
- Iftop
- ntopng

47.2   References

[1] Ntop Feature Overview

47.3   External links

- ntop

Chapter 48

ntopng

"ntopng" is an open-source network traffic monitor. It is designed to be a high-performance, low-resource replacement for ntop. The name is derived from "ntop next generation." ntopng is released under the GPLv3 software license, and is available for Unix, Linux, BSD, Mac OS X, and Windows. Binaries are available for CentOS, Ubuntu, and Mac OS X. A Windows demo binary is available that limits analysis to 2,000 packets. The engine is written in C++, and the optional web interface is written in Lua.

ntopng relies on the Redis key-value server rather than a traditional database, takes advantage of nDPI for protocol detection, supports geolocation of hosts, and is able to display real-time flow analysis for connected hosts.

48.1 Sample usage

ntopng --dns-mode 1 --interface 5 --daemon --redis localhost:6379 --verbose

Explanation: run ntopng executable, set DNS mode to decode DNS responses and resolve all numeric IPs, use fifth network interface, operate in daemon mode, use Redis server running on local host, and operate in verbose mode.

48.2 External links

- ntop

48.3 See also

- ntop

48.4 References

Chapter 49

OmniPeek

OmniPeek is a packet analyzer software tool from Wild-Packets Inc., for network troubleshooting and protocol analysis. It supports an application programming interface (API) for plugins.

49.1 History

WildPackets was founded in 1990 by Mahboud Zabetian and Tim McCreery. The first product by WildPackets was written for the Mac, and called EtherPeek. It was a protocol analyzer for Ethernet networks. It was later ported to Microsoft Windows, which was released in 1997. In 2001, AiroPeek was released, which added support for wireless IEEE 802.11 (marketed with the Wi-Fi brand) networks. In 2003, the OmniEngine Distributed Capture Engine was released as software, and as a hardware network recorder appliance.

On the morning of July 15, 2002, the WildPackets' building in Walnut Creek, California burnt to the ground. However, the company survived the fire.[1]

49.2 Acquisitions

WildPackets acquired Net3 Group in November 2000. Their product, NetSense, an expert system for network troubleshooting, was converted into a plug-in and integrated into a new version of the product called EtherPeekNX.[2]

WildPackets acquired Optimized Engineering Corporation in 2001. Optimized network analysis training courses and instructors were added to WildPackets' services.[3]

49.3 Extensibility

OmniPeek has APIs on the front-end for automation, APIs on the back-end for analysis, as well as other mechanisms to extend and enhance the program.[4]

There are 40 **plug-ins** available for the OmniPeek Platform. These plug-ins range from logging extensions to full-blown applications that are hosted by OmniPeek.

Remote Adapters: provide a means to capture packets and stats. There are remote adapters to capture from RMON, NetFlow, SFlow, Cisco AP's, Aruba AP's, and Linux boxes. Adapters are available to aggregate packets from multiple network segments and wireless channels at the same time.

The most notable **decoders** are the protospecs and decoder files, which are interpreted text files that can be extended by the user to enhance the display and analysis of existing protocols, and add knowledge of completely new protocols, without releasing new versions of the application.[5]

The **plugin Wizards** for the OmniPeek Console and the OmniEngine are Microsoft Visual Studio Project Templates that generate working plug-ins. When the wizard is run, a dialog appears providing options for types of functionality that sample code will be generated for. When the wizard is complete, the user is left with a working plugin with entry points for adding application logic. These plug-in wizards enable the development of extensions to OmniPeek.

The **MyPeek Community Portal** is a website dedicated to the extension of OmniPeek. It provides plug-ins, scripts, adapters, tools, and various levels of support for the plug-ins posted there, and expertise for those interested in extending OmniPeek themselves.[6]

PlaceMap: is a freely available standalone Google Maps Packet sniffer application for Windows that captures network traffic and maps nodes to the Google Map. PlaceMap is a notable example of extensibility in that it uses exactly the same Google Map plugin that is also available for the OmniPeek, and is uses the peek driver API to capture packets.[7]

49.4 Example Plugins

- Google Map Plugin - map nodes to a Google Map[8]

- SQLFilter Plugin - save and query packets from a database

- PeekPlayer Plugin - send packet an adapter or a capture window

- PowerBar Plugin - write scripts that process packets

- Decoder Plugin - decode packets

- WatchMe Plugin - display web sites in real-time from URLs

- Browser Plugin - construct and display web pages from packets

- IM Plugin - display instant message screen names and chat

- WebStats Plugin - collect and report web statistics

- Remote TCPDump Adapter Plugin - stream packets from any machine with SSH and tcpdump

- Cisco Remote Adapter Plugin - stream packets from Cisco Access Points

- Aruba Remote Adapter Plugin - stream packets from Aruba Networks Air Monitors

49.5 References

[1] "WildPackets Survives Fire". Retrieved 2009-07-23.

[2] "WildPackets to buy Net3". 2000-11-20. Retrieved 2009-07-23.

[3] "WildPackets to Acquire Optimized Engineering Corporation; Expands Protocol Analysis Training and Services.". *Business Wire*. 2001-01-31. Retrieved 2009-07-23.

[4] "An Open API Sets WildPackets Apart". Retrieved 2009-07-23.

[5] "Throwin' Down The Decoder Gauntlet!". Retrieved 2009-07-23.

[6] "WildPackets Launches MyPeek Community Portal". Retrieved 2009-07-23.

[7] "PlaceMap 1.0.0.4". Retrieved 2009-07-23.

[8] "WildPackets Offers Free Google Map Plug-In". Retrieved 2009-07-23.

49.6 External links

- Official website

- Official forum

- Network World, Sept. 18, 2006: Review of Wild-Packets' OmniPeek. By Anthony Mosco, Robert Smithers, Robert Tarpley

- Network World , April 23, 2007: WLAN analyzers: WildPackets' OmniPeek For Windows 4.1. By Tom Henderson, Rand Dvorak

- IT Week. Network IT Week, 19 Aug 2006, by Dave Bailey. WildPackets' latest OmniPeek tool makes it easier to inspect traffic and troubleshoot networks. Tested: WildPackets OmniPeek Enterprise 4.0

- Network World, March 10, 2008: Clear Choice Test VoIP analysis tools. By Rob Smithers of Miercom

- Cisco Website, Mar. 22, 2006: LWAPP Decodes Enablement on WildPackets OmniPeek and EtherPeek 3.0 Software

Chapter 50

Openkore

OpenKore is a community-maintained descendant of Solos Kore,[6] a custom client and an advanced automated assistant for the MMORPG Ragnarok Online. It's free and open-source software, application licensed under GNU General Public License. OpenKore is mainly written in Perl, but some code is also in C++ XS modules. The Perl interpreter allows for a cross-platform usability and an ability to work with the source code without recompiling or even interrupting the program.[7] OpenKore is not associated with Gravity (developers of Ragnarok Online). Developers work on the project pseudonymously, mostly due to privacy issues and internet gaming community traditions.[1]

50.1 History

The OpenKore project was started by VCL in late November 2003. At the moment, there was original Kore, probably the only well-known free software Ragnarok Online bot, but due to lack of organization, many forks and modifications existed. OpenKore is based on Skore-revamped, which is a modified version of Skore (Solos Kore), which is a fork of the original Kore developed by Kura.[8][9] It was started as an attempt to unite contributors to Kore forks, and that was quite successful. Gradually, other Ragnarok Online bot projects have phased out, mostly due to server-side updates and lack of development. Many developers have come from other inactive Ragnarok Online bot program projects (e.g. ApezBot, Kore, Modkore, Revemu, Skore, etc.) to develop on OpenKore.[1]

Nearing the end of 2008, the Openkore project is the only Ragnarok Online bot that currently provides support to many Ragnarok Online servers and continual development on an international level. On May 4, there was a vote to choose the logo to OpenKore, having gained what logo made by battlemode, used even today.[10] As of November 8, 2010, Openkore releases has been downloaded from SourceForge.net approximately more than 6,071,820 times since its availability in 2003.[11]

After version 2.0.7's release in mid-2009, there were no releases for a long time, with recommendation[10] to use trunk instead due to server updates, bug fixes and new features.

50.2 Features

OpenKore acts as a Ragnarok Online game client and can perform anything a player's character can do manually in the game client. It's highly configurable and tweakable; reasonable default configuration provided as well.[12][13]

The software can be configured to automatically and repeatedly perform assigned tasks without human involvement. The automated actions are state-based and with the macro plug-in be also script-based. These automations cover almost every action available in the game client. When a bot program is running, it continuously reports the latest information and the current status of the game, e.g., a character's location, the current action, the "hit" point, and information about nearby monsters. Openkore allows users to give commands anytime, regardless of the prearranged actions by scripts, i.e., the bot is script-based and interactive. Basically, Openkore is meant to automate and simplify actions by the user of the software within the Ragnarok Online environment through the use of extensive scripting.[14]

50.2.1 Controls

There are several interfaces which all have console log with the latest information and console input for commands which cover current status inspection, manual actions and AI management. The most basic interface is just a console application. There is also slightly more tuned Curses-based console interface and wxWidgets-based GUI with graphical map display etc.

50.2.2 Automation Features

These features are generally triggered by state-based triggers and can be tuned in many aspects.

- Walk seamlessly between maps, automatically finding the shortest, cheapest or safest path

- Automatically find (randomly wandering or teleporting) and attack monsters

- Automatically use items and skills

- Automatically manage (loot, gather, buy, sell, drop) items in inventory, cart and storage

- Automatically find (party members only) and follow another character, mimicking his movements, attacks and other actions

- Automatically manage various requests (party, guild, deal)

- Avoiding monsters, players, GMs, tough damage, death

- Automatically chat with players with self-training chat plugin

- Control semi-independent entities such as Homunculus and Mercenary using semi-independent AI

50.2.3 Logging Features

- Log the number of monsters killed

- Log private, public and guild chats

- Log console

- Log raw network packets

- Automatically visit vendors, collect data on offers and store it in database with a web interface (plugin)

- Automatically collect data on other players (levels, equipment, parties, guilds)

50.2.4 Miscellaneous Features

- Hook on game client's connection to the game server, using the client as the ultimate view and control tool and acting as a packet editor ("XKore 1")

- Integrated game server game client can connect to without interrupting ("XKore 2")

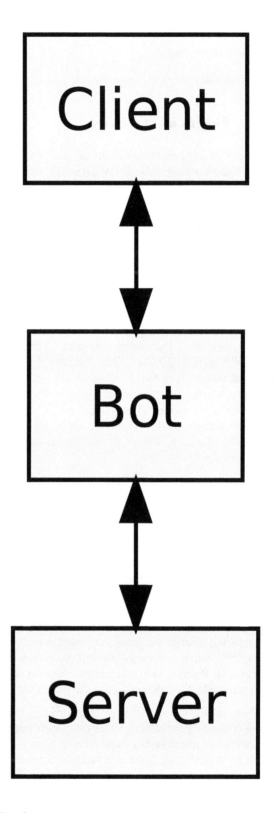

XKore 2

- Remote controlling via socket (included) or IRC (plugin)

- Anti spam (plugin)

- Sound alerts (plugin)

- Growl and Snarl alerts (plugin)

50.2.5 Plugins and Scripting

Third-party plugins, written in Perl, can add and modify available functions using provided API (hooks) or reflective features of Perl.

Macro plugin provides a simple way to create a script-based triggers and action sequences.

50.3 Community

OpenKore's community is diverse with contributions to the project coming from communities that are English,[15] French, German, Indonesian, Korean, Portuguese, Russian,[16] Spanish, Filipino, Thai, Traditional Chinese, and Vietnamese. This diverse range of cultures enables OpenKore to provide international support for various Ragnarok Online servers all over the world. Currently, OpenKore supports bRO, iRO, idRO, inRO, mRO, pRO, rRO and most private servers.;[17] euRO was supported when it shut down.

50.4 Impact and Reception

Bots, unlike normal players, can play and do repetitive actions endlessly long, including gaining experience points, ingame items and currency, which can affect so-called balance of the game. They can affect real economy, as well as human players, due to these things being sold for real money. High amount of obvious bots (not well-configured) may negatively change the gaming experience for human players,[12][13] but due to being obvious they can be banned easily as well. If server staff is concerned about botting issue, negative effects can be reduced to the minimum.

OpenKore itself is just an alternative client and tries to conform to common game rules and ethics: it doesn't kill steal and doesn't loot, there isn't any options or plugins for that and it's forbidden to ask about it at OpenKore forums.[18] However, there isn't any strict countermeasures against implementing it, as it's pointless to do in free software.

With free software game clients, everyone can enrich the overall gaming experience.[19] Many harmless features added, like efficient and configurable spam blocking, automatic reconnection after disconnect and play statistics. Various types of bot-based services exist, for example market search[19] (found in other games and finally implemented in Ragnarok Online too, but poorly), global events/quests availability viewer, database of players,[20] buff and teleport service. Bots can act as a flexible NPCs for client-side controlled quests and minigames.[21][22]

Some anti-bot measures expose complete incompetence and/or indifference of game management on official servers. HackShield was installed on rRO[23] despite being already circumvented by OpenKore for years.[24] CAPTCHA was added on kRO[25] and become supported for manual and automated passing shortly.[26] Such measurements usually only introduce additional problems for all players.

50.5 Related Projects

- ModKore, another fork of Kore; went closed source and is not supported anymore

- VisualKore, OpenKore variant with simplified configuration and interface, is not supported anymore; some of its features were implemented in OpenKore

- Ragnarok Online Plugin System,[27] game client plugin framework; similar functionality is now included in iRO's client together with antispam plugin[28][29][30]

- RCX (RoCha),[31] proprietary software which extends game client without automation features

50.6 See also

- Internet bot

- Ragnarok Online

50.7 References

[1] "About OpenKore". Retrieved 2008-11-29.

[2] "OpenKore | Download OpenKore software for free at SourceForge.net". 2003-11-07.

[3] "The OpenKore Open Source Project on Ohloh : Commits Summary Page".

[4] "OpenKore - Ohloh".

[5] "OpenKore Runtime - Package Details - repo.openpandora.org Repository of Software for the Open Pandora open source console".

[6] "Home Page of Solos Kore".

[7] "Openkore Online Manual - Console Commands".

[8] "Disclaimer - Solos Kore Page".

[9] "Kore Ragnarok bot project".

[10] "Topic of the vote on the logo".

[11] "SourceForge.net: Openkore - Download History Statistics". 2003-11-07. Retrieved 2010-11-08.

[12] Adam Cornelissen; Franc Grootjen (October 2008). "A Modern Turing Test: Bot Detection in MMORPGs" (PDF). *Proceedings 20th Belgian-Netherlands Conference on Artificial Intelligence* (Enschede: University of Twente): 49–55. ISSN 1568-7805.

[13] Marlieke van Kesteren; Jurriaan Langevoort; Franc Grootjen (October 2009). "A step in the right direction: Botdetection in MMORPGs using movement analysis" (PDF). *Proceedings of the 21st Belgian-Dutch Conference on Artificial Intelligence* (Eindhoven).

[14] Chen, K.T.; Jiang, J.W.; Huang, P.; Chu, H.H.; Lei, C.L.; Chen, W.C. (2006-06-01). "Identifying MMORPG Bots: A Traffic Analysis Approach". ACM. |= ignored (help)

[15] "OpenKore community forums".

[16] "Клуб любителей пляски с бубном вокруг Openkore" [Club dancing with a tambourine around Openkore] (in Russian).

[17] "Openkore - List of (un)supported servers". 2003-11-07. Archived from the original on 2008-06-19. Retrieved 2008-11-29.

[18] Bibian. "Global Forum Rules". Retrieved 2008-04-07. DON'T <...> Request or divulge howto modify OpenKore to KS.

[19] "About » RagnaStats.com » Ragnarok Online, iRO market information and more".

[20] "Ragnarok Online Player Database".

[21] richjkl (2008-11-21). "Pong? In Ragnarok?". A plugin I made for Ragnarok to turn a character into a pong ball. It asks who wants to play and when two people say they're up for it, the game begins!

[22] KeplerBR (2013-02-22). "Scattergories? In Ragnarok?". The BOT will manage the Scattergories game with this plug-in.

[23] "Новая система защиты HackShield для игрового клиента" [The new protection system for the game client HackShield] (in Russian). Gravity CIS, Inc. 2009-06-22. В эту среду, 24 июня, будет установлено обновление, с помощью которого будет увеличена защита от различных методов нечестной игры (ботов, модификации клиента и т.д.).

[24] "Copy CVS's Base::Server to the 1.6 branch; add Poseidon to CVS". 2006-01-31.

[25] "Re: 09/23/2009 - Maintenance (Genetic Update)". 2009-09-23.

[26] "support: kRO (src)". 2009-10-25.

[27] "Ragnarok Online Plugin System".

[28] "Anti-Spam Bot". Retrieved 2011-11-01.

[29] "Spambots Malfunction". Retrieved 2011-10-26.

[30] "Re: XKore 1 with 18.10.2011 iRO update". 2012-05-04.

[31] "RCX temporary".

50.8 Further reading

- eAthena

50.9 External links

- OpenKore User Documentation

Chapter 51

OpenVAS

OpenVAS (*Open Vulnerability Assessment System*,[1] the name of the fork originally known as *GNessUs*) is a framework of several services and tools offering a vulnerability scanning and vulnerability management solution.

All OpenVAS products are Free Software. Most components are licensed under the GPL.

The latest version is 8.0, released April 2015.[2]

51.1 History

OpenVas began, under the name of GNessUs, as a fork of the previously open source Nessus scanning tool after Tenable Network Security changed it to a proprietary (closed source) license in October 2005.[3] OpenVAS was originally proposed by pentesters at Portcullis Computer Security[4] and then announced[5] by Tim Brown on Slashdot.

OpenVAS is a member project of Software in the Public Interest.[6]

51.2 Structure

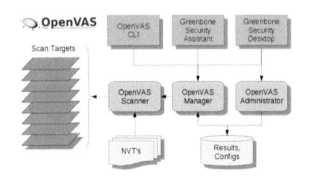

The OpenVAS 4 Structure

There is a daily updated feed of Network Vulnerability

Tests (NVTs) - over 35,000 in total (as of April 2014).

51.3 Documentation

The OpenVAS protocol structure is known to be well documented to assist developers. The OpenVAS Compendium is a publication of the OpenVAS Project that delivers a large amount of documentation on OpenVAS. OpenVAS Protocol Documentation OpenVAS Compendium - A Publication of The OpenVAS Project

51.4 References

[1] http://www.openvas.org/

[2] OpenVAS release announcement

[3] LeMay, Renai (2005-10-06). "Nessus security tool closes its source". CNet.

[4] Portcullis Computer Security

[5] Slashdot

[6] Log from SPI board meeting

51.5 External links

- OpenVAS web site

- OpenVAS, Nessus and NexPose Tested

Chapter 52

PA Server Monitor

PA Server Monitor is a server monitoring and network monitoring software application, developed by Power Admin LLC.[1]

The main function of the software is to monitor performance of servers and network devices in Windows and Linux environments. Data is kept on customers servers, not stored in the cloud. An agentless monitoring software to watch ping, CPU, memory, disk, SNMP + traps, events, with available historical reports. Apps are available for iOS and Android.

52.1 History

Power Admin LLC is a privately held company founded by IT professionals, located in Olathe, Kansas, just outside the downtown Kansas City area. Power Admin has been providing professional grade system monitoring products since 1992 for all types of business from SMBs to Fortune 500 companies.

Power Admin also developed two other popular utilities that are used all over the world.

PAExec[2] allows a user to launch Windows programs[3] on remote Windows computers without needing to install software on the remote computer first.[4] This was written as an alternative to Microsoft's PsExec[5] tool (originally by SysInternals's Mark Russinovich), because it could not be redistributed, and sensitive command-line options like username and passwords were sent as clear text. Source code is readily available on GitHub.[6]

Power Admin also developed SpeedFanHttpAgent.[7] The SpeedFan HTTP Agent exports and allows you to access SpeedFan's (utility by Alfredo Milani Comparetti) temperature data from across the network via a simple HTTP request.

52.2 What it Does

PA Server Monitor monitors event logs, disk space, running services, web page content, SNMP object values, log files, processes, ping response time, directory quotas, changed files and directories. Equipped to monitor thousands of servers/devices from a single installation, and more via satellite monitoring services.

It has extensive reporting to get status reports for servers/devices, group summaries, uptime and historic stats, providing actions and alerts by customizable email, SMS and other types of notifications, and suppression and escalation of certain notifications. It can also automatically restart services and run custom scripts.

Other capabilities include satellite monitoring of remote offices/locations across firewalls and/or across the internet without a VPN, agentless server monitoring and a bulk config feature to speed changes across many servers/devices.

52.3 Version History[8]

- v.5.6.0.163 (2014)
- v.5.2.112 (2013)
- v.5.2.49 (2012)
- v.4.0.8.120 (2011)
- v.4.0.1.71 (2010)
- v.3.7.5.40 (2009)
- v.3.6.0.48 (2008)
- v.3.4.10.14 (2007)
- v.3.3.1.5 (2006)
- v.2.2.15 (2005)
- v.2.0.0.12 (2004)
- v.1.0.6 (First Beta Release (2004))

52.4   See also

- Comparison of network monitoring systems

- Computer performance

- Remote administration

- Application performance management

- Website monitoring

- Network management

- System monitor

52.5   References

[1] "CrunchBase". *CrunchBase*.

[2] "PAExec". *PowerAdmin.com*. Power Admin.

[3] Chen, Kent. "PAExec to Launch Applications on Remote Computers". Next of Windows.com. Retrieved 2012-03-14.

[4] Williams, Mike. "Take Control of Remote PCs with PAExec". BetaNews. Retrieved 2012-05-05.

[5] "PsExec". Microsoft.

[6] "PAExec". GitHub.

[7] "SpeedFanHTTPAgent". Power Admin LLC.

[8] "PA Server Monitor Version History".

52.6   External links

- Official website

- PA Server Monitor

- PA File Sight

- Blog - Network Wrangler

Chapter 53

Packet analyzer

A **packet analyzer** (also known as a **network analyzer**, **protocol analyzer** or **packet sniffer**—or, for particular types of networks, an **Ethernet sniffer** or **wireless sniffer**) is a computer program or piece of computer hardware that can intercept and log traffic that passes over a digital network or part of a network.[1] As data streams flow across the network, the sniffer captures each packet and, if needed, decodes the packet's raw data, showing the values of various fields in the packet, and analyzes its content according to the appropriate RFC or other specifications.

Packet capture is the process of intercepting and logging traffic.

53.1 Capabilities

On wired broadcast LANs, depending on the network structure (hub or switch), one can capture traffic on all or parts of the network from a single machine on the network. However, some methods avoid traffic narrowing by switches to gain access to traffic from other systems on the network (e.g., ARP spoofing). For network monitoring purposes, it may also be desirable to monitor all data packets in a LAN by using a network switch with a so-called *monitoring port* that mirrors all packets that pass through all ports of the switch when systems (computers) are connected to a switch port. To use a network tap is an even more reliable solution than to use a monitoring port, since taps are less likely to drop packets during high traffic load.

On wireless LANs, one can capture traffic on a particular channel, or on several channels using multiple adapters.

On wired broadcast and wireless LANs, to capture traffic other than unicast traffic to the machine running the sniffer, multicast traffic to a multicast group that machine is monitoring, or broadcast traffic—the network adapter capturing the traffic must be in promiscuous mode. Some sniffers support this, but not all. On wireless LANs, even if the adapter is in promiscuous mode, packets not for the service set the adapter is configured for are usually ignored. To see those packets, the adapter must be in monitor mode.

When traffic is captured, either the entire contents of packets are recorded, or the headers are recorded without recording the total content of the packet. This can reduce storage requirements, and avoid legal problems, yet provide sufficient information to diagnose problems.

Captured information is decoded from raw digital form into a human-readable format that lets users easily review exchanged information. Protocol analyzers vary in their abilities to display data in multiple views, automatically detect errors, determine root causes of errors, generate timing diagrams, reconstruct TCP and UDP data streams, etc.

Some protocol analyzers can also generate traffic and thus act as the reference device. These can act as protocol testers. Such testers generate protocol-correct traffic for functional testing, and may also have the ability to deliberately introduce errors to test the DUT's ability to handle errors.

Protocol analyzers can also be hardware-based, either in probe format or, as is increasingly common, combined with a disk array. These devices record packets (or a slice of the packet) to a disk array. This allows historical forensic analysis of packets without users having to recreate any fault.

53.2 Uses

Packet sniffers can:

- Analyze network problems

- Detect network intrusion attempts

- Detect network misuse by internal and external users

- Documenting regulatory compliance through logging all perimeter and endpoint traffic

- Gain information for effecting a network intrusion

93

- Isolate exploited systems

- Monitor WAN bandwidth utilization

- Monitor network usage (including internal and external users and systems)

- Monitor data-in-motion

- Monitor WAN and endpoint security status

- Gather and report network statistics

- Filter suspect content from network traffic

- Serve as primary data source for day-to-day network monitoring and management

- Spy on other network users and collect sensitive information such as login details or users cookies (depending on any content encryption methods that may be in use)

- Reverse engineer proprietary protocols used over the network

- Debug client/server communications

- Debug network protocol implementations

- Verify adds, moves and changes

- Verify internal control system effectiveness (firewalls, access control, Web filter, spam filter, proxy)

Packet capture can be used to fulfill a warrant from a law enforcement agency (LEA) to produce all network traffic generated by an individual. Internet service providers and VoIP providers in the United States must comply with CALEA (Communications Assistance for Law Enforcement Act) regulations. Using packet capture and storage, telecommunications carriers can provide the legally required secure and separate access to targeted network traffic and are able to use the same device for internal security purposes. Collecting data from a carrier system without a warrant is illegal due to laws about interception.

53.3   Notable packet analyzers

For a more comprehensive list, see Comparison of packet analyzers.

- Cain and Abel

- Capsa Network Analyzer

- Carnivore (FBI)

- CommView

- dSniff

- ettercap

- Fiddler

- Kismet

- Lanmeter

- Microsoft Network Monitor

- NarusInsight

- NetScout Systems nGenius Infinistream

- ngrep, Network Grep

- OmniPeek

- SkyGrabber

- snoop

- tcpdump

- Wireshark (formerly known as Ethereal)

- Xplico Open source Network Forensic Analysis Tool

53.4   See also

- Bus analyzer

- Logic analyzer

- Network detector

- Network intrusion detection system

- Network tap

- Packet generation model

- pcap

- Signals intelligence

53.5   References

[1] Kevin J. Connolly (2003). *Law of Internet Security and Privacy*. Aspen Publishers. p. 131. ISBN 978-0-7355-4273-0.

53.6   External links

- Protocol Analyzers at DMOZ

- Multi-Tap Network Packet Capture

Chapter 54

Packet crafting

Packet crafting is a technique that allows network administrators to probe firewall rule-sets and find entry points into a targeted system or network. This is done by manually generating packets to test network devices and behaviour, instead of using existing network traffic.[1] Testing may target the firewall, IDS, TCP/IP stack, router or any other component of the network.[1][2] Packets are usually created by using a packet generator or packet analyzer which allows for specific options and flags to be set on the created packets. The act of packet crafting can be broken into four stages: Packet Assembly, Packet Editing, Packet Play and Packet Decoding.[1][2] Tools exist for each of the stages - some tools are focussed only on one stage while others such as Ostinato try to encompass all stages.

54.1 Packet Assembly

Packet Assembly is the creation of the packets to be sent. Some popular programs used for packet assembly are Hping, Nemesis, Ostinato, Cat Karat packet builder, Libcrafter, libtins, Scapy, Wirefloss and Yersinia.[1][2][3] Packets may be of any protocol and are designed to test specific rules or situations. For example, a TCP packet may be created with a set of erroneous flags to ensure that the target machine sends a RESET command or that the firewall blocks any response.[1][2]

54.2 Packet Editing

Packet Editing is the modification of created or captured packets. This involves modifying packets in manners which are difficult or impossible to do in the Packet Assembly stage, such as modifying the payload of a packet.[2] Programs such as Ostinato, Netdude allow a user to modify recorded packets' fields, checksums and payloads quite easily.[1] These modified packets can be saved in packet streams which may be stored in pcap files to be replayed later.

54.3 Packet Play

Packet Play or Packet Replay is the act of sending a pre-generated or captured series of packets. Packets may come from Packet Assembly and Editing or from captured network attacks. This allows for testing of a given usage or attack scenario for the targeted network. Tcpreplay is the most common program for this task since it is capable of taking a stored packet stream in the pcap format and sending those packets at the original rate or a user-defined rate. Ostinato added support for pcap files in version 0.4.[4] Some packet analyzers are also capable of packet replay.

54.4 Packet Decoding

Packet Decoding is the capture and analysis of the network traffic generated during Packet Play. In order to determine the targeted network's response to the scenario created by Packet Play, the response must be captured by a packet analyzer and decoded according to the appropriate specifications. Depending on the packets sent, a desired response may be no packets were returned or that a connection was successfully established, among others.

54.5 See also

- Comparison of packet analyzers
- Packetsquare
- Replay attack

54.6 References

[1] Zereneh, William. "Packet Crafting" (PDF). Retrieved 2010-08-01.

[2] Poor, Mike. "Packet Craft for Defense-in-Depth" (PDF). InGuardians. Retrieved 2010-08-01.

[3] "Top 4 Packet Crafting Tools". SecTools.org. Retrieved 2010-08-01.

[4] "Ostinato ChangeLog". Retrieved 2011-04-30.

54.7 External links

- Packet Crafting for Firewall & IDS Audits (Part 1 of 2) by Don Parker

- Wikiformat article detailing Packet crafting

- Bit-Twist - Libpcap-based Ethernet packet generator

Chapter 55

Packet generator

A **packet generator or packet builder** is a type of software that generates random packets or allows the user to construct detailed custom packets. Depending on the network medium and operating system, packet generators utilize raw sockets, NDIS function calls, or direct access to the network adapter kernel-mode driver.

This is useful for testing implementations of IP stacks for bugs and security vulnerabilities.

55.1   Comparison

55.1.1   General Information

[1] Custom: free for personal use

55.2   See also

- Packet crafting

- Packet analyzer

- Packetsquare

Chapter 56

Packet Sender

Packet Sender is an open source utility to allow sending and receiving TCP and UDP packets. It is available for Windows, Mac, and Linux. It is licensed GNU General Public License v2 and is free software.[1] Packet Sender's web site says "*It's designed to be very easy to use while still providing enough features for power users to do what they need.*".[2]

56.1 Uses

Typical applications of Packet Sender include:

- Troubleshooting network devices that use network servers (send a packet and then analyze the response)

- Troubleshooting network devices that use network clients (devices that "phone home" via UDP or TCP—Packet Sender can capture these requests)

- Testing and development of new network protocols (send a packet, see if device behaves appropriately)

- Reverse-engineering network protocols for security analysis (such as malware)

- Automation (via Packet Sender's command line interface or resend feature)

Packet Sender comes with a built-in TCP and UDP server on a port number a user specifies. This remains running listening for packets while sending other packets.

56.2 Features

As of version 2015-8-22 Packet Sender supports the following features:[3]

- Live traffic log (Time / From IP / From Port / To IP / Method / Error / ASCII / HEX)

- Persistent TCP Connections

- Portable Mode

- IPv4 Subnet Calculator

- Saved packets (with sending directly from saved list)

- Mixed ASCII packet notation (ASCII with embedded syntax to allow hex)

- TCP server

- UDP server

- Packet resending at n intervals (where n is seconds)

- Multi-threaded TCP connections

- Command-line interface

- Packet responses

- Packet search (for saved packets)

- Packet export/import

- Quick-send from traffic log

- Save traffic log

56.3 Platforms

- Windows (XP through Windows 10)

- OS X (Intel-based x86-64)

- Linux (ARM, x86, and x86-64 with Qt 5.5)

Packet Sender once had mobile versions for iOS and Android, but these efforts have been abandoned.[4][5]

56.4 See also

- Hping

- Wireshark

- Netcat

56.5 References

[1] "http://packetsender.com/LICENSE.txt".   Retrieved 15
    February 2015.

[2] "http://packetsender.com/". Retrieved 22 February 2014.

[3] "http://packetsender.com/documentation".   Retrieved 23
    August 2015.

[4] "https://github.com/dannagle/PacketSender-iOS/".   Re-
    trieved 19 April 2015.

[5] "https://github.com/dannagle/PacketSender-Android/".
    Retrieved 19 April 2015.

56.6 External links

- Original website

- Packet Sender source code on GitHub

Chapter 57

Packetsquare

PacketSquare (CapEdit) is a free and open-source pcap-based network protocol testing tool.[1] It is used for testing network devices (IDS/IPS, firewall, routers switches etc.,), network troubleshooting, analysis, software and communications protocol development, and education.

Currently PacketSquare-CapEdit runs on Linux, using the GTK+ widget toolkit to implement its user interface, and written in C. Released under the terms of the GNU General Public License v3, PacketSquare-CapEdit is free software.

57.1 Functionality

PacketSquare-CapEdit works by editing protocol fields of the saved packet capture file and replaying. In addition to editing and replaying it supports many features for extrapolation of captured traffic.

57.2 History

PacketSquare is an open source community started in April 2010 by Vijay Mohan, Sushant Gupta and Anant Dixit for developing computer network testing tools.[2] The Community is currently working on CapEdit, used for testing wide range of network security and monitoring products.

57.3 Features

- Currently supports pcap standard packet capture format, as used by tcpdump, Wireshark, and other programs.

- Protocols supported: Ethernet II, VLAN, MPLS, ARP, IPv4, IPv6, ICMPv4, IGMPv3, GRE, IP-in-IP, UDP and TCP.[3]

- Protocol field value modification.

- Packet deletion.

- Packet duplication.

- Packet reordering.

- Fragmentation of packets.

- VLAN, MPLS tags can be added to the packets.

- TCP and UDP stream-based field value modification.

- IP and MAC address find and replace.

- Auto checksum for IP, ICMP, IGMP, TCP and UDP protocols.

- Interface selection for sending packets.

- Option for sending a single selected packet or all packets.

- Pcap edit and replay.

57.4 See also

- tcpdump, a packet analyzer

- pcap, an application programming interface (API) for capturing network traffic

- snoop, a command line packet analyzer included with Solaris

- wireshark, a network packet analyzer

- dsniff, a packet sniffer and set of traffic analysis tools

- netsniff-ng, a free Linux networking toolkit

- etherape, a network mapping tool that relies on sniffing traffic

57.5 References

[1] Good tools which work with pcap files

[2] Packetsquare community info

[3] Supported Protocols

57.6 External links

- Official website
- Mailing List
- Blog
- Google Code

Chapter 58

PacketTrap

PacketTrap is a provider of network management and traffic analysis software for midsize companies. The company is headquartered in San Francisco, California. Its corporate parent, Dell is located in Round Rock, Texas.

58.1 Features

PacketTrap features include Desktop Management, Server Management, Monitor Cloud Assets etc [1][2]

58.2 See also

- Comparison of network monitoring systems

58.3 References

[1] PacketTrap gives enterprise "Perspective"

[2] How Can PacketTrap Perspective Help you Manage your Cisco Network?

58.4 External links

- PacketTrap's Products and Services

- Startup City - InformationWeek

- Network World, Denise Dubie, Nov, 2008. "10 IT Management Companies to Watch"

- Information Week, John Foley, Aug, 2008. "Packet-Trap Challenges CA and IBM"

- Microsoft TechNet, Greg Steen, July, 2008. "New Products for IP Pros"

- PC Magazine, Jamie Bernstein, May, 2008. "Review: PacketTrap pt360"

- Network World, Denise Dubie, March, 2008 "Kicking the Tires of Management Software"

- What PC, Tony Luke, Feb, 2008. "A Tough Nut to Crack"

- Information Week, John Foley, Feb, 2008. "The Demise Of Commercial Open Source"

Chapter 59

Paessler Router Traffic Grapher

Paessler Router Traffic Grapher is a server up-time and utilisation, network monitoring and bandwidth usage software for server infrastructure by Paessler AG. It can monitor and classify bandwidth usage in a network using SNMP, Packet Sniffing and Netflow. It services Microsoft Windows as well as Linux. The successor product is PRTG Network Monitor.

59.1 See also

- Paessler AG: Vendor of the software

- Network traffic measurement: Available software tools to measure network traffic

59.2 References

- Posey, Brien M. (July 29, 2003). PRTG makes it easy to monitor bandwidth, *TechRepublic*, accessed on March 7, 2008

- David Davis (May 1, 2007). The ultimate list of Cisco administration tools, Networkworld, accessed on March 7, 2008

- Douglas Toombs (Sep 1,2007). 8 More Absolutely Cool, Totally Free Utilities, WindowsITPro Magazine Sep 2007, accessed on March 7, 2008

- Christian Twardawa (Feb 1, 2008). Plumbing The Depth-the need of professional network monitoring from a business view, Network Computing, accessed on March 7, 2008

- Karen D. Schwartz (Feb 27, 2008). Paessler Upgrades Low-Cost, Easy-to-Use Network Monitoring Tool, www.eweek.com, accessed on March 7, 2008

59.3 External links

- PRTG Project Homepage

Chapter 60

Panorama9

Panorama9 is a cloud-based service within enterprise Network management. The company sells a hosted Dashboard monitoring everything on the network ensuring that servers, pc, peripherals and external Internet related services are all running. Furthermore Panorama9 offers a set of reports on inventory on both hardware, software and users.

Founded in 2010[1][2] by serial entrepreneurs Allan Thorvaldsen and Diego d'Ambra who also founded MSP SoftCom Solutions ApS in 1996 and SoftScan in 2003. By the end of 2009 they had achieved more than 12.000 customers and were later that year sold to Symantec (NASDAQ: SYMC).[3][4]

Panorama9 provides a hosted monitoring service made possible by downloading a simple agent on the PCs and servers that needs to be monitored throughout the network.

In November 2011 an interactive network map was introduced making it possible for IT administrators to have an real-time chart of the network at a very granular level.[5]

During May 2012 Zendesk and Panorama9 announced a partnership strengthening the offering for both Zendesk and Panorama9.[6]

The company was founded in Copenhagen but is now incorporated in the US with headquarter in San Francisco, California.[7][8] [9] [10] [11] [12]

[13]

[14]

60.1 See also

- Software Asset Management

- IT Asset Management

- SNMP

- List of mergers and acquisitions by Symantec

60.2 References

[1] "Iværksættere med rødder i kanalen". crn.dk. Retrieved 2011-10-18.

[2] "Sådan vil Softscan-stifterne banke nyt firma op til global succes". comon.dk. Retrieved 2011-10-19.

[3] "SEC Form 10-K, Symantec Corp, period: April 02, 2010, p. 10" (PDF). Symantec. 2010-05-24. Retrieved 2010-09-06.

[4] "Symantec Corporation Mergers and Acquisitions". Thomson Financial. Retrieved 2008-10-31.

[5] "Danskere i kamp med VMware®Go og Windows Intune". http://www.cloudchecker.dk. Retrieved 2011-11-15.

[6] "Zendesk partners with Panorama9 on cloud help desk". http://www.cloudpro.co.uk/. Retrieved 2012-06-06.

[7] "Singaporeaccent duer ikke i USA". http://www.crn.dk. Retrieved 2011-12-20.

[8] "Panorama9 sets up shop (sort of) in Bay Area". http://www.gigaom.com. Retrieved 2012-03-16.

[9] "Dansk startup dypper tæerne i Silicon Valley". http://www.comon.dk. Retrieved 2012-03-02.

[10] "Startups på pengejagt i USA: Hvor er de danske investorer?". http://www.comon.dk. Retrieved 2012-03-16.

[11] "Panorama9 attacks big IT headaches of small companies". http://gigaom.com/. Retrieved 2012-05-01.

[12] "Panorama9 Simplifies IT Manager's Lives with Cloud-based Dashboard: US Launch Opens New Market". http://www.prlog.org/. Retrieved 2012-05-02.

[13] "Panorama9 attacks big IT headaches of small companies". http://technews.am/. Retrieved 2012-05-02.

[14] "Let Panorama9 monitor your Windows machines and network". http://www.techrepublic.com/. Retrieved 2012-05-04.

60.3 External links

- Official website

Chapter 61

Paping

Paping (pronounced pah ping) is a computer network administration utility used to test the reachability of a host on an Internet Protocol (TCP/IP) network and to measure the time it takes to connect to a specified port. The name is a play on the word ping, another computer network administration utility.

Because ICMP can be used to identify the operating system of a remote machine,[1][2] it is sometimes blocked.[3][4] If ICMP is blocked, ping cannot be used to identify if the service is responding. Publicly available services must keep their relevant TCP or UDP ports open, paping can attempt to make connections to these ports to determine if a service is responding. Similar utilities such as nmap allow a range of ports to be scanned, however they do not allow you to repetitively scan the same ports.

Paping operates by attempting to connect to an Internet Protocol TCP/IP port on the target. In the process it measures the time taken for a connection to be established and records any connection failures. The results of the test are printed in form of a statistical summary of the connections made including the minimum, maximum, and the mean connection times.

Paping is cross-platform software, currently supporting Windows and Linux.[5]

As of April 2013, the project appears to be abandoned with no new fixes or versions being produced.

61.1 Sample paping test

The following is a sample output of paping against en.wikipedia.org on TCP/IP port 80 (http) from a Linux host:

./paping -p 80 en.wikipedia.org -c 10 paping v1.5.1 - Copyright (c) 2010 Mike Lovell Connecting to text.pmtpa.wikimedia.org [208.80.152.2] on TCP 80: Connected to 208.80.152.2: time=64.11ms protocol=TCP port=80 Connected to 208.80.152.2: time=64.03ms protocol=TCP port=80 Connected to 208.80.152.2: time=65.81ms protocol=TCP port=80 Connected to 208.80.152.2: time=63.56ms protocol=TCP port=80 Connected to 208.80.152.2: time=63.95ms protocol=TCP port=80 Connected to 208.80.152.2: time=64.29ms protocol=TCP port=80 Connected to 208.80.152.2: time=64.35ms protocol=TCP port=80 Connected to 208.80.152.2: time=64.99ms protocol=TCP port=80 Connected to 208.80.152.2: time=63.10ms protocol=TCP port=80 Connected to 208.80.152.2: time=64.02ms protocol=TCP port=80 Connection statistics: Attempted = 10, Connected = 10, Failed = 0 (0.00%) Approximate connection times: Minimum = 63.10ms, Maximum = 65.81ms, Average = 64.22ms

61.2 References

[1] "OS Detection over ICMP". Retrieved 29 August 2010.

[2] "OS Detection over ICMP". Retrieved 29 August 2010.

[3] "Blocking ICMP in Linux". Retrieved 29 August 2010.

[4] "Blocking ICMP in Windows". Retrieved 29 August 2010.

[5] "Versions of paping available". Retrieved 10 August 2010.

61.3 External links

- code.google.com/p/paping/

Chapter 62

PathPing

PathPing is a network utility supplied in Windows NT and beyond that combines the functionality of ping with that of tracert.

It provides details of the path between two hosts *and* Ping-like statistics for each node in the path based on samples taken over a time period, depending on how many nodes are between the start and end host.

The advantages of *PathPing* over ping and traceroute are that each node is pinged as the result of a single command, and that the behavior of nodes is studied over an extended time period, rather than the default *ping* sample of four messages or default *traceroute* single route trace. The disadvantage is that it takes a total of 25 seconds per hop to show the ping statistics.[1]

62.1 Usage

C:\Documents and Settings\User>*pathping* Usage: path-ping [-g host-list] [-h maximum_hops] [-i address] [-n] [-p period] [-q num_queries] [-w timeout] [-P] [-R] [-T] [−4] [−6] target_name Options: -g host-list Loose source route along host-list. -h maximum_hops Maximum number of hops to search for target. -i address Use the specified source address. -n Do not resolve addresses to hostnames. -p period Wait period milliseconds between pings. -q num_queries Number of queries per hop. -w timeout Wait timeout milliseconds for each reply. -P Test for RSVP PATH connectivity. -R Test if each hop is RSVP aware. -T Test connectivity to each hop with Layer-2 priority tags. −4 Force using IPv4. −6 Force using IPv6.[2]

62.2 Sample

>*pathping wikipedia.org* Tracing route to wikipedia.com [207.142.131.235] over a maximum of 30 hops: 0 simonslaptop [192.168.0.11] 1 192.168.0.1 2 thus1-hg2.ilford.broadband.bt.net [217.32.64.73] 3 217.32.64.34 4 217.32.64.110 5 anchor-border-1-4-0-2-191.router.demon.net [212.240.162.126] 6 anchor-core-2-g0-0-1.router.demon.net [194.70.98.29] 7 ny1-border-1-a1-0-s2.router.demon.net [194.70.97.66] 8 ge-8-0-153.ipcolo1.NewYork1.Level3.net [209.246.123.177] 9 ae-0-51.bbr1.NewYork1.Level3.net [64.159.17.1] 10 so-2-0-0.mp1.Tampa1.Level3.net [209.247.11.201] 11 ge-6-0.hsa2.Tampa1.Level3.net [64.159.1.10] 12 unknown.Level3.net [63.208.24.2] 13 Computing statistics for 325 seconds... Source to Here This Node/Link Hop RTT Lost/Sent = Pct Lost/Sent = Pct Address 0 simonslaptop [192.168.0.11] 0/ 100 = 0% | 1 0ms 0/ 100 = 0% 0/ 100 = 0% 192.168.0.1 0/ 100 = 0% | 2 18ms 1/ 100 = 1% 1/ 100 = 1% thus1-hg2.ilford.broadband.bt.net [217.32.64.73] 0/ 100 = 0% | 3 18ms 0/ 100 = 0% 0/ 100 = 0% 217.32.64.34 0/ 100 = 0% | 4 21ms 0/ 100 = 0% 0/ 100 = 0% 217.32.64.110 0/ 100 = 0% | 5 21ms 1/ 100 = 1% 1/ 100 = 1% anchor-border-1-4-0-2-191.router.demon.net [212.240.162.126] 0/ 100 = 0% | 6 --- 100/ 100 =100% 100/ 100 =100% anchor-core-2-g0-0-1.router.demon.net [194.70.98.29] 0/ 100 = 0% | 7 --- 100/ 100 =100% 100/ 100 =100% ny1-border-1-a1-0-s2.router.demon.net [194.70.97.66] 0/ 100 = 0% | 8 100ms 0/ 100 = 0% 0/ 100 = 0% ge-8-0-153.ipcolo1.NewYork1.Level3.net [209.246.123.177] 0/ 100 = 0% | 9 94ms 0/ 100 = 0% 0/ 100 = 0% ae-0-51.bbr1.NewYork1.Level3.net [64.159.17.1] 0/ 100 = 0% | 10 134ms 1/ 100 = 1% 1/ 100 = 1% so-2-0-0.mp1.Tampa1.Level3.net [209.247.11.201] 0/ 100 = 0% | 11 137ms 0/ 100 = 0% 0/ 100 = 0% ge-6-0.hsa2.Tampa1.Level3.net [64.159.1.10] 0/ 100 = 0% | 12 131ms 0/ 100 = 0% 0/ 100 = 0% unknown.Level3.net [63.208.24.2] 100/ 100 =100% | 13 --- 100/ 100 =100% 0/ 100 = 0% win2000 [0.0.0.0] Trace complete. >*pathping wikipedia.org -q 10*[3] Tracing route to wikipedia.org [66.230.200.100] over a maximum of 30 hops: 0 Aaron.hsd1.mn.comcast.net. [192.168.11.3] 1 air.setup [192.168.11.1] 2 73.127.68.1 3 ge-1-38-ur01.minnetonka.mn.minn.comcast.net [68.86.234.41] 4 68.86.232.37 5 68.86.232.33 6 * 68.86.232.5 7 68.86.232.1 8 12.116.99.41 9 tbr2.cgcil.ip.att.net [12.122.99.70] 10 * ggr2.cgcil.ip.att.net [12.123.6.69]

11   ar1-a3120s2.wswdc.ip.att.net   [192.205.34.6]   12
66.192.247.163 13 ge8-13.csw5-pmtpa.wikimedia.org
[66.193.50.242]   14   *   rr.pmtpa.wikimedia.org
[66.230.200.100] Computing statistics for 35 seconds...
Source to Here This Node/Link Hop RTT Lost/Sent = Pct
Lost/Sent = Pct Address 0 Aaron.hsd1.mn.comcast.net.
[192.168.11.3] 0/ 10 = 0% | 1 0ms 0/ 10 = 0% 0/ 10 = 0%
air.setup [192.168.11.1] 0/ 10 = 0% | 2 8ms 0/ 10 = 0% 0/
10 = 0% 73.127.68.1 0/ 10 = 0% | 3 8ms 0/ 10 = 0% 0/
10 = 0% ge-1-38-ur01.minnetonka.mn.minn.comcast.net
[68.86.234.41] 0/ 10 = 0% | 4 9ms 0/ 10 = 0% 0/ 10 =
0% 68.86.232.37 0/ 10 = 0% | 5 8ms 0/ 10 = 0% 0/ 10
= 0% 68.86.232.33 0/ 10 = 0% | 6 12ms 0/ 10 = 0% 0/
10 = 0% 68.86.232.5 0/ 10 = 0% | 7 8ms 0/ 10 = 0%
0/ 10 = 0% 68.86.232.1 0/ 10 = 0% | 8 20ms 0/ 10 =
0% 0/ 10 = 0% 12.116.99.41 0/ 10 = 0% | 9 --- 10/ 10
=100% 10/ 10 =100% tbr2.cgcil.ip.att.net [12.122.99.70]
0/ 10 = 0% | 10 --- 10/ 10 =100% 10/ 10 =100%
ggr2.cgcil.ip.att.net [12.123.6.69] 0/ 10 = 0% | 11 --- 10/
10 =100% 10/ 10 =100% ar1-a3120s2.wswdc.ip.att.net
[192.205.34.6] 0/ 10 = 0% | 12 --- 10/ 10 =100% 10/
10 =100% 66.192.247.163 0/ 10 = 0% | 13 63ms 0/
10 = 0% 0/ 10 = 0% ge8-13.csw5-pmtpa.wikimedia.org
[66.193.50.242] 0/ 10 = 0% | 14 63ms 0/ 10 = 0% 0/
10 = 0% rr.pmtpa.wikimedia.org [66.230.200.100] Trace
complete. >*pathping wikipedia.org -n* Tracing route to
wikipedia-lb.eqiad.wikimedia.org   [208.80.154.225]over
a maximum of 30 hops: 0 192.168.1.102 1 192.168.1.1
2 10.202.181.110 3 10.202.182.109 4 10.202.181.153
5 10.202.181.49 6 212.72.4.97 7 82.178.32.102 8
63.218.109.117 9 63.218.44.38 10 206.111.0.249 11
216.156.8.189 12 * * * Computing statistics for 275
seconds...

62.3   See also

- ping (networking utility)

- traceroute

- MTR — computer software which combines the functionality of the traceroute and ping programs in a single network diagnostic tool.

- layer four traceroute, a more modern traceroute (IP
  network tracing) implementation that supports a mul-
  titude of layer-4 protocols

62.4   External links

- Microsoft PathPing - Information about the PathPing
  tool (Microsoft.com)

- WinMTR

62.5   Notes and references

[1] PathPing - TechNet, Microsoft

[2] C:\Documents and Settings\User>ver Microsoft Windows
    XP [Version 5.1.2600]

[3] note the shorter wait with only 10 queries per hop instead of
    the default 100

Chapter 63

pcap

This article is about the packet sniffing API. For the projected capacitance technology for touchscreens, see projected capacitance.

In the field of computer network administration, **pcap** (**p**acket **cap**ture) consists of an application programming interface (API) for capturing network traffic. Unix-like systems implement pcap in the **libpcap** library; Windows uses a port of libpcap known as **WinPcap**.

Monitoring software may use libpcap and/or WinPcap to capture packets travelling over a network and, in newer versions, to transmit packets on a network at the link layer, as well as to get a list of network interfaces for possible use with libpcap or WinPcap.

The pcap API is written in C, so other languages such as Java, .NET languages, and scripting languages generally use a wrapper; no such wrappers are provided by libpcap or WinPcap itself. C++ programs may link directly to the C API or use an object-oriented wrapper.

63.1 Features

libpcap and WinPcap provide the packet-capture and filtering engines of many open source and commercial network tools, including protocol analyzers (packet sniffers), network monitors, network intrusion detection systems, traffic-generators and network-testers.

libpcap and WinPcap also support saving captured packets to a file, and reading files containing saved packets; applications can be written, using libpcap or WinPcap, to be able to capture network traffic and analyze it, or to read a saved capture and analyze it, using the same analysis code. A capture file saved in the format that libpcap and WinPcap use can be read by applications that understand that format, such as tcpdump, Wireshark, CA NetMaster, or Microsoft Network Monitor 3.x.

The MIME type for the file format created and read by libp-cap and WinPcap is application/vnd.tcpdump.pcap. The typical file extension is .pcap, although .cap and .dmp are also in common use.[4]

63.2 libpcap

libpcap was originally developed by the tcpdump developers in the Network Research Group at Lawrence Berkeley Laboratory. The low-level packet capture, capture file reading, and capture file writing code of tcpdump was extracted and made into a library, with which tcpdump was linked.[5] It is now developed by the same tcpdump.org group that develops tcpdump.[6]

63.3 WinPcap

WinPcap consists of:[7]

- x86 and x86-64 drivers for the Windows NT family (Windows NT 4.0, Windows 2000, Windows XP, Windows Server 2003, Windows Vista, Windows 7, etc.), which use NDIS to read packets directly from a network adapter;

- implementations of a lower-level library for the listed operating systems, to communicate with those drivers;

- a port of libpcap that uses the API offered by the low-level library implementations.

Programmers at the Politecnico di Torino wrote the original code; as of 2008 CACE Technologies, a company set up by some of the WinPcap developers, develops and maintains the product. CACE Technologies was acquired by Riverbed Technology on October 21, 2010.[8]

63.4 Programs that use libpcap/WinPcap

- tcpdump, a tool for capturing and dumping packets for further analysis, and WinDump, the Windows port of tcpdump.

- ngrep, aka "network grep", isolate strings in packets, show packet data in human-friendly output.

- Wireshark (formerly Ethereal), a graphical packet-capture and protocol-analysis tool.

- Snort, a network-intrusion-detection system.

- Nmap, a port-scanning and fingerprinting network utility

- the Bro IDS and network-monitoring platform.

- URL Snooper, locate the URLs of audio and video files in order to allow recording them.

- Kismet, for 802.11 wireless LANs

- L0phtCrack, a password auditing and recovery application.

- iftop, a tool for displaying bandwidth usage (like top for network traffic)

- EtherApe, a graphical tool for monitoring network traffic and bandwidth usage in real time.

- Bit-Twist, a libpcap-based Ethernet packet generator and editor for BSD, Linux, and Windows.

- Pirni, a network security tool for jailbroken iOS devices.

- McAfee ePolicy Orchestrator, Rogue System Detection feature

- NetSim a network simulation software for network R & D

- XLink Kai Software that allows various LAN console games to be played online

- Firesheep, an extension for the Firefox web browser, that intercepts unencrypted cookies from certain websites (such as Facebook and Twitter) as the cookies are transmitted over networks, exploiting session hijacking vulnerabilities.

- Suricata, a network intrusion prevention and analysis platform.

- WhatPulse, a statistical (input, network, uptime) measuring application.

- Xplico, a network forensics analysis tool (NFAT).

- Scapy, a packet manipulation tool for computer networks, written in Python by Philippe Biondi.

63.5 Wrapper libraries for libpcap/WinPcap

- Perl: Net::Pcap

- Python: python-libpcap, Pcapy

- Ruby: PacketFu

- Rust: pcap

- Tcl: tclpcap, tcap, pktsrc

- Java: jpcap, jNetPcap, Jpcap, Pcap4j

- .NET: WinPcapNET, SharpPcap, Pcap.Net

- Haskell: pcap

- OCaml: mlpcap

- Chicken Scheme: pcap

- Common Lisp: PLOKAMI

- Racket: SPeaCAP

- Go: pcap by Andreas Krennmair, pcap fork of the previous by Miek Gieben, pcap developed as part of the gopacket package

63.6 Non-pcap code that reads pcap files

- Python: pycapfile

63.7 References

[1] "tcpdump and libpcap latest release". tcpdump & libpcap. Retrieved 2015-05-31.

[2] "tcpdump and libpcap license". tcpdump & libpcap. Retrieved 2012-04-13.

[3] "WinPcap Changelog".

[4] "IANA record of application for MIME type application/vnd.tcpdump.pcap".

[5] Steve McCanne. "libpcap: An Architecture and Optimization Methodology for Packet Capture" (PDF). Retrieved December 27, 2013.

[6] "TCPDUMP/LIBPCAP public repository". Retrieved December 27, 2013.

[7] "WinPcap internals". Retrieved December 27, 2013.

[8] "Riverbed Expands Further Into The Application-Aware Network Performance Management Market with the Acquisition of CACE Technologies". Riverbed Technology. 2010-10-21. Retrieved 2010-10-21.

63.8 External links

- Official site for libpcap (and tcpdump)

- Official site for WinPcap (and WinDump)

- List of publicly available PCAP files

Chapter 64

Ping (networking utility)

An example run of the command-line ping utility on Microsoft Windows

Ping is a computer network administration software utility used to test the reachability of a host on an Internet Protocol (IP) network and to measure the round-trip time for messages sent from the originating host to a destination computer and back. The name comes from active sonar terminology that sends a pulse of sound and listens for the echo to detect objects underwater;[1] however, the acronym "PING" meaning "Packet InterNet Groper" has been in use since early days[2] in computing for testing and measuring networks and the Internet.

Ping operates by sending Internet Control Message Protocol (ICMP) **echo request** packets to the target host and waiting for an ICMP **echo reply**. It measures the round-trip time from transmission to reception, reporting errors and packet loss. The results of the test usually include a statistical summary of the response packets received, including the minimum, maximum, the mean round-trip times, and usually standard deviation of the mean.

The command-line options for the ping utility and its output vary depending on implementation. Options may include the size of the payload, count of tests, and limits for the number of hops (TTL) that probes traverse. Many systems provide a companion utility ping6, for similar testing on Internet Protocol version 6 (IPv6) networks.

64.1 History

The ping utility was written by Mike Muuss in December 1983 as a tool to troubleshoot problems in an IP network. He was inspired by a remark by David Mills on using ICMP echo packets for IP network diagnosis and measurements.[3] The author named it after the sound that sonar makes, since its methodology is similar to sonar's echo location.[1][4]

RFC 1122 prescribes that any host must process an echo-request and issue an echo-reply in return.[5]

64.2 Sample ping test

The following is the output of running ping under Linux for sending five probes to the target host www.example.com:

$ ping -c 5 www.example.com PING www.example.com (93.184.216.119): 56 data bytes 64 bytes from 93.184.216.119: icmp_seq=0 ttl=56 time=11.632 ms 64 bytes from 93.184.216.119: icmp_seq=1 ttl=56 time=11.726 ms 64 bytes from 93.184.216.119: icmp_seq=2 ttl=56 time=10.683 ms 64 bytes from 93.184.216.119: icmp_seq=3 ttl=56 time=9.674 ms 64 bytes from 93.184.216.119: icmp_seq=4 ttl=56 time=11.127 ms --- www.example.com ping statistics --- 5 packets transmitted, 5 packets received, 0.0% packet loss round-trip min/avg/max/stddev = 9.674/10.968/11.726/0.748 ms

The utility summarizes its results after completing the ping probes. The shortest round trip time was 9.674 ms, the average was 10.968 ms, and the maximum value was 11.726 ms. The measurement had a standard deviation of 0.748 ms.

64.3 Error indications

In cases of no response from the target host, most implementations of ping display nothing, or periodically print notifications about timing out. Possible ping outputs indicating a problem include the following:

- H, !N or !P – host, network or protocol unreachable

- S – source route failed

- F – fragmentation needed

- U or !W – destination network/host unknown

- I – source host is isolated

- A – communication with destination network administratively prohibited

- Z – communication with destination host administratively prohibited

- Q – for this ToS the destination network is unreachable

- T – for this ToS the destination host is unreachable

- X – communication administratively prohibited

- V – host precedence violation

- C – precedence cutoff in effect

In case of error, the target host or an intermediate router sends back an ICMP error message, for example "host unreachable" or "TTL exceeded in transit". In addition, these messages include the first eight bytes of the original message (in this case header of the ICMP echo request, including the quench value), so the ping utility can match responses to originating queries.[6]

64.4 Message format

64.4.1 ICMP packet

Generic composition of an ICMP 32-byte packet:[7]

- IP Header (in blue): *protocol* set to 1 (ICMP) and *Type of Service* set to 0.

- ICMP Header (in red):

  - Type of ICMP message (8 bits)

  - Code (8 bits)

- Checksum (16 bits), calculated with the ICMP part of the packet (the IP header is not used). It is the 16-bit one's complement of the one's complement sum of the ICMP message starting with the Type field[8]

- Header Data (32 bits) field, which in this case (ICMP echo request and replies), will be composed of identifier (16 bits) and sequence number (16 bits).

- ICMP Payload: *payload* for the different kind of answers; can be an arbitrary length, left to implementation detail. However, the packet including IP and ICMP headers must be less than the maximum transmission unit of the network or risk being fragmented.

64.4.2 Echo request

The *echo request* ("ping") is an ICMP message.

The Identifier and Sequence Number can be used by the client to match the reply with the request that caused the reply. In practice, most Linux systems use a unique identifier for every ping process, and sequence number is an increasing number within that process. Windows uses a fixed identifier, which varies between Windows versions, and a sequence number that is only reset at boot time.

64.4.3 Echo reply

The *echo reply* is an ICMP message generated in response to an echo request; it is mandatory for all hosts and routers, and must include the exact payload received in the request.

- *Type* and *code* must be set to 0.

- The *identifier* and *sequence number* can be used by the client to determine which echo requests are associated with the echo replies.

64.4.4 Payload

The payload of the packet is generally filled with ASCII characters, as the output of the tcpdump utility shows:

16:24:47.966461 IP (tos 0x0, ttl 128, id 15103, offset 0, flags [none], proto: ICMP (1), length: 60) 192.168.146.22 > 192.168.144.5: ICMP echo request, id 1, seq 38, length 40 0x0000: 4500 003c 3aff 0000 8001 5c55 c0a8 9216 E..<:.....\U.... 0x0010: c0a8 9005 0800 4d35 0001 0026 6162 6364 ......M5...&abcd 0x0020: 6566 6768 696a 6b6c 6d6e 6f70 7172 7374 efghijklmnopqrst 0x0030: 7576 7761 6263 6465 6667 6869 uvwabcdefghi

The payload includes a timestamp of when the message was sent and a sequence number. This allows ping to compute the round trip time in a stateless manner without needing to record when packets were sent.

64.5   Security considerations

The *flood* ping option exists of many implementations, sending requests as fast as possible in an attempt to determine the response of the network under high-load conditions. That option is restricted to users having administrative privileges, but may be used in denial-of-service attacks to induce a ping flood, in which the attacker attempts to overwhelm the victim with ICMP echo requests.

Ping has been considered as a security risk as merely acknowledging a host's presence turns it into a potential target.[9] For these reasons, many systems provide means to disable the reply,[10][11] despite the fact that RFC 1122 mandates hosts to always send a reply.

Host discovery, scanning or ping sweep is a feature of network scanning tools such as nmap, working by utilizing ICMP echo packets.

64.6   See also

- Keepalive
- List of DOS commands
- List of Unix utilities
- Traceroute
- Ping of death
- Ping-pong scheme
- Security through obscurity
- Smurf attack

64.7   References

[1] Mike Muuss. "The Story of the PING Program". U.S. Army Research Laboratory. Archived from the original on 8 September 2010. Retrieved 8 September 2010. I named it after the sound that a sonar makes, inspired by the whole principle of echo-location.

[2] Mills, D.L. (December 1983). *Internet Delay Experiments*. IETF. p. 1. STD 8. RFC 889. https://tools.ietf.org/html/rfc889#page-1. Retrieved June 26, 2015.

[3] "The Story of the PING Program", Mike Muuss

[4] Salus, Peter (1994). *A Quarter Century of UNIX*. Addison-Wesley. ISBN 0-201-54777-5.

[5] "RFC 1122 - Requirements for Internet Hosts -- Communication Layers". p. 42. Retrieved 2012-03-19. Every host MUST implement an ICMP Echo server function that receives Echo Requests and sends corresponding Echo Replies.

[6] "ICMP: Internet   Control   Message   Protocol". *repo.hackerzvoice.net.*   January 13, 2000.   Retrieved December 4, 2014.

[7] "RFC 792 - Internet Control Message Protocol". Tools.ietf.org. Retrieved 2014-02-02.

[8] "RFC Sourcebook's page on ICMP". Retrieved 20 December 2010.

[9] "Shields Up, Firewall Test". Retrieved 4 June 2010. [text shown if your computer replies to ping requests] "Ping" is among the oldest and most common methods used to locate systems prior to further exploitation.

[10] "Windows firewall: how block ICMP echo response".

[11] "redhat linux /proc/sys/net/ipv4 parameters".

64.8   External links

- ping(1M) – Solaris 10 System Administration Commands Reference Manual
- ping(8) – FreeBSD System Manager's Manual

Chapter 65

Pirni

Pirni Pro is a network security tool designed for iOS, and specifically for iPhone and iPod Touch devices. It is capable of intercepting traffic on a wireless network segment, capturing passwords, and regular expressions entered by the user.

The core system of Pirni, written in C, is open-source software,[1] and licensed under the GNU General Public License. Pirni Pro is the succeeding version of Pirni, and is commercial software, available in the Cydia Store, for jailbroken Apple devices.

65.1 Features

Pirni Pro supports active dissection of all non-ciphered protocols (given that the user has supplied a regular expression for dissection). The application description contains the following:

- ARP spoof the entire network or any target

- Watch a live feed over interesting packets collected

- Manage regular expressions to filter out data, such as site credentials

In addition, the software also offers the following features:

- Password collectors for: HTTP

65.2 External links

- Root at Everything official website

- Cydia Link

- Extensive Tutorial

65.3 References

[1] https://code.google.com/p/n1mda-dev/

Chapter 66

Plink

For the genetics software, see PLINK (genetic tool-set). For informal target shooting, see Plinking.

Plink (PuTTY Link) is a free and open-source (MIT license) command-line network connection tool similar to UNIX ssh written by Simon Tatham, author of another popular terminal emulator, serial console and network file transfer application name PuTTY. It is mostly used for automated operations, such as making CVS access a repository on a remote server.[1][2]

66.1 Features

- Interactive logins to a remote SSH server

- Automated SSH connections from Batch File

66.2 See also

- Comparison of SSH clients

- SecureCRT

- mintty

- WinSCP

- Netcat

66.3 References

[1] http://the.earth.li/~{}sgtatham/putty/0.58/htmldoc/Chapter7.html

[2] http://linux.die.net/man/1/plink

66.4 External links

- Author's website

Chapter 67

Plixer International

Plixer International, Inc. is a provider of NetFlow and sFlow network analysis and network security monitoring tools among other network management software.[1]

Plixer sells and supports products that aid Network Administrators in monitoring, troubleshooting, securing and analyzing the behavior of IT networks. Plixer's most recent focus has been on boosting its network security capabilities including methods such as IP Host reputation identifying Advanced Persistent Threats.[2] It also hosts an expansive online community. In late 2008, Plixer introduced the addition of a multi-author daily blog that discusses various challenges faced by administrators of IT networks, and practical methods of approaching them.

67.1 History

Plixer International was founded in 1999 by Michael Patterson (currently the company's CEO) and Marc Bilodeau (currently the company's CTO). The company was built to create full-featured, easy-to-use network monitoring applications that would cost significantly less than traditional network performance and security monitoring software suites.[3]

In 2006, Plixer International merged with Somix Technologies, Inc. and continued to develop and support its network performance and security monitoring software packages. It also partnered with several resellers around the world to establish a global presence in the network monitoring community.[4][5][6]

Plixer International is headquartered in Kennebunk, Maine.

67.2 Products and services

Plixer International's flagship product, Scrutinizer, is made available for download at the company's site. The product is offered as a robust free version that can be used both privately and commercially, with several licensing models

available for full-featured versions.

- **Scrutinizer NetFlow & sFlow Analyzer**, a data warehousing utility that leverages NetFlow, sFlow, j-Flow, IPFIX, and other flow-based technologies to receive and store network traffic data from switches, routers, and other network devices, and to present trends, reports, and network maps based on this data to the user

- **Replicator**, The NetFlow Replicator appliance allows a single stream of log data to be transparently replicated to multiple destinations

- **Flowalyzer NetFlow & sFlow Tester**, Flowalyzer is a NetFlow and sFlow Tool Kit for testing and configuring hardware or software for sending and receiving NetFlow and sFlow data

- **Denika Performance Trender**, a utility that utilizes SNMP to monitor all aspects of nodes and devices on a network

- **IPFIXify**, IPFIXify processes massive volumes of system health data generated by complex IT infrastructures and then leverages Plixer solutions to troubleshoot problems

67.3 Media

Plixer International has written and produced a series of "NetFlow Rap" videos directed at Cisco and NetFlow customers, as well as the IT field in general. They feature a local artist and previous employee of Plixer, Mix Master Mitch. According to Mitch, the goal of the music videos are to entertain and educate at the same time, while promoting awareness of the NetFlow capabilities of Cisco devices.[7] The videos have received thousands of hits on YouTube and have a quickly-growing fan base in the Cisco engineer community.[8] The first video was produced completely independently by Mix Master Mitch, with no budget. Subsequent videos received small production budgets from Plixer as the series grew in popularity.

67.4   Notable customers

- CNN

- The Coca-Cola Company

- Abercrombie & Fitch

- Lockheed Martin

- IBM

- Regal Cinemas

- Raytheon

- NASA

- Eddie Bauer

67.5   References

[1] Michael Patterson, ThomasNet News"Plixer International Supports the Latest Update in Network Management, Flexible NetFlow." June 4, 2007. Retrieved on December 11, 2009.

[2] Michael Patterson, Advanced Persistent Threats"Plixer International Supports the Latest Update in Network Management, Flexible NetFlow." March 4, 2013. Retrieved on March 18, 2013.

[3] Marc Bilodeau, Manta.com"Plixer International profiled by Manta.com." July 12, 2005. Retrieved on December 11, 2009.

[4] Dale Locke, PWeb.com"Plixer Joins the Riverbed Technology Alliance Program." July 2, 2008. Retrieved on December 11, 2009.

[5] Thomas Pore, PWeb.com"Force10 Networks and Plixer Announce Technology Compatible Partnership." June 6, 2008. Retrieved on December 11, 2009.

[6] Matthew St Jean, Plixer.com"Plixer Teams with Enterasys For Mobile IAM Analytics." May 1, 2012. Retrieved on August 23, 2012.

[7] Earthtimes.org "Cisco NetFlow Goes Hip Hop With Mix Master Mitch And Plixer International." December 11, 2009. Retrieved on December 11, 2009.

[8] Brad Reese, Network World. "Lookout Death Row Records, here comes a new hit, the Cisco NetFlow Rap song." March 26, 2009. Retrieved on December 11, 2009.

67.6   External links

- Plixer International official web site

Chapter 68

Prefix WhoIs

```
> whois -h whois.pwhois.org 4.2.2.1
IP: 4.2.2.1
Origin-AS: 3356
Prefix: 4.0.0.0/9
AS-Path: 3257 3356
AS-Org-Name: Level 3 Communications, LLC
Org-Name: Level 3 Communications, Inc.
Net-Name: LVLT-ORG-4-8
Cache-Date: 1240446962
Latitude: 39.913500
Longitude: -105.093000
City: BROOMFIELD
Region: COLORADO
Country: UNITED STATES
```

This example Prefix WhoIs query shows various information about an IP address including its network origin and registrar details

Prefix WhoIs is an open source project that develops and operates a free whois-compatible framework for stockpiling and querying various routing and registry information. Prefix WhoIs uses global BGP routing data learned from many ISP backbone routers. Other information sources are also supported, such as imported data from every Regional Internet Registry (AFRINIC, APNIC, ARIN, LACNIC and RIPE) and geocoding information.

The project has been mentioned in a number of popular network security and network engineering books[1] and articles.[2]

68.1 Public Prefix WhoIs Service

Many public servers around the world operate mirrors of Prefix WhoIs, making the information generally available worldwide. The service may be used with any client using the standard whois protocol. The DNS address *whois.pwhois.org* resolves to the Prefix WhoIs server nearest to the client based on anycast DNS.

68.2 Client Software

Several client software packages are available from both Prefix WhoIs itself and from commercial vendors. These include free, open source utilities such as **WhoB** and Layer Four Traceroute.

68.3 Server Software

- The pWhoIsd server software responds to standard whois queries and supports a variety of output formats (including Prefix WhoIs native, Cymru, and RPSL).

- The pWhoIs-updatedb agent parses routing information bases (RIBs) from Internet routers or digests from route-views servers in text or MRT format and populates a relational database

68.4 Software Development Libraries

The Prefix WhoIs project distributes C and PHP libraries for direct access to Prefix WhoIs servers. A HTTP simple-Query interface is also available.

68.5 Software licensing

The software is made available under a custom license.[3]

68.6 Sources

[1] Extreme Exploits: Advanced Defenses Against Hardcore Hacks (2005) by McGraw-Hill ISBN 0-07-225955-8

[2] SecurityFocus article

[3] http://pwhois.org/license.who

68.7   External links

- The Prefix WhoIs Project Official Web SIte

- RIPE NCC RIS WhoIs is an alternative source of similar information

Chapter 69

Promiscuous mode

In computer networking, **promiscuous mode** (often shortened to "promisc mode" or "promisc. mode") is a mode for a wired network interface controller (NIC) or wireless network interface controller (WNIC) that causes the controller to pass all traffic it receives to the central processing unit (CPU) rather than passing only the frames that the controller is intended to receive. This mode is normally used for packet sniffing that takes place on a router or on a computer connected to a hub (instead of a switch) or one being part of a WLAN. Interfaces are placed into promiscuous mode by software bridges often used with hardware virtualization.

In IEEE 802 networks such as Ethernet, token ring, and IEEE 802.11, and in FDDI, each frame includes a destination Media Access Control address (MAC address). In non-promiscuous mode, when a NIC receives a frame, it normally drops it unless the frame is addressed to that NIC's MAC address or is a broadcast or multicast frame. In promiscuous mode, however, the card allows all frames through, thus allowing the computer to read frames intended for other machines or network devices.

Many operating systems require superuser privileges to enable promiscuous mode. A non-routing node in promiscuous mode can generally only monitor traffic to and from other nodes within the same broadcast domain (for Ethernet and IEEE 802.11) or ring (for token ring or FDDI). Computers attached to the same network hub satisfy this requirement, which is why network switches are used to combat malicious use of promiscuous mode. A router may monitor all traffic that it routes.

Promiscuous mode is often used to diagnose network connectivity issues. There are programs that make use of this feature to show the user all the data being transferred over the network. Some protocols like FTP and Telnet transfer data and passwords in clear text, without encryption, and network scanners can see this data. Therefore, computer users are encouraged to stay away from insecure protocols like telnet and use more secure ones such as SSH.

69.1 Detection

As promiscuous mode can be used in a malicious way to *sniff* on a network, one might be interested in detecting network devices that are in promiscuous mode. In promiscuous mode, some software might send responses to frames even though they were addressed to another machine. However, experienced sniffers can prevent this (e.g., using carefully designed firewall settings).

An example is sending a ping (ICMP echo request) with the wrong MAC address but the right IP address. If an adapter is operating in normal mode, it will drop this frame, and the IP stack never sees or responds to it. If the adapter is in promiscuous mode, the frame will be passed on, and the IP stack on the machine (to which a MAC address has no meaning) will respond as it would to any other ping. The sniffer can prevent this by configuring his or her firewall to block ICMP traffic.

69.2 Some applications that use promiscuous mode

- NetScout Sniffer
- OmniPeek
- Capsa
- Aircrack-ng
- KisMAC (used for WLAN)
- AirSnort (used for WLAN)
- Wireshark (formerly *Ethereal*)
- tcpdump
- IPTraf
- pktstat

- PRTG

- Kismet

- VMware's **VMnet** Bridging (networking)

- Cain and Abel

- Driftnet Software

- Microsoft Windows Network Bridge

- XLink Kai

- WC3Banlist

- Snort

- ntop

- Firesheep

- VirtualBox (bridge networking mode)

- CommView

- AccessData SilentRunner

69.3   See also

- Packet analyzer

- Monitor mode

- MAC spoofing

69.4   References

69.5   External links

SearchSecurity.com definition of promiscuous mode

Chapter 70

PRTG Network Monitor

PRTG Network Monitor (**PRTG**, successor of Paessler Router Traffic Grapher) is network monitoring software from Paessler AG.

PRTG runs on Windows and monitors network availability and network usage using SNMP, Packet Sniffing, WMI, IP SLAs and Netflow and various other protocols. It comes in both freeware and commercial editions. Since the release of PRTG 9, the software supports the monitoring of IPv6 devices.

A web-based interface is available, as well as dedicated apps for iOS and Android

As part of proof of concept a dedicated probe for PRTG runs on Linux, written in Python.[1]

70.1 Version History [2]

- v.7.0 (June 30, 2008)

- v.7.1 (March 30, 2009)

- v.7.2 (September 28, 2009)

- v.7.3 (February 15, 2010)

- v.8.1 (September 21, 2010)

- v.9.1 (September 19, 2011)

- v.9.2 (April 18, 2011)

- v.12.2 (May 9, 2012)

- v.12.3 (July 19, 2012)

- v.12.4 (October 16, 2012)

- v.13.1 (January 15, 2013)

- v.13.2 (April 22, 2013)

- v.13.3 (July 8, 2013)

- v.13.4 (October 8, 2013)

- v.14.1 (February 3, 2014)

- v.15.1 (January 13, 2015)

- v.15.2 (June 6, 2015)

- v.15.3 (July 1, 2015)

70.2 See also

- Paessler AG: Vendor of the software

- Comparison of network monitoring systems

- PRTG Freeware Download

- Skyframe S.R.L.: Paessler Partner

70.3 References

[1] "PRTG Mini Probe on Linux".

[2] "PRTG Network Monitor Version History".

- Wally Bahny (March 22, 2010).   Product Spotlight: PRTG Network Monitor, TechRepublic.com, accessed on March 25, 2010

- Bernd Reder (Nov 17th 2009).   Test: Vier Networkmonitoring-Produkte auf dem Prüfstand (Monitoring Tools Comparison) (German) Network Computing, accessed on March 25, 2010

- Howard Solomon (Sep 3rd 2009). Paessler brings back Windows for Network Monitor

- David Davis (May 1, 2007).   The ultimate list of Cisco administration tools, Networkworld, accessed on March 25, 2010

- David Harris (October 20, 2010).   , accessed on November 1, 2010

- Carolyn Duffy Marsan (October 17, 2011). Net monitoring tool now ships with IPv6, Networkworld, accessed on October 20, 2011

- PRTG news blog (April 26, 2012 updated May 9, 2012)

Chapter 71

SAINT (software)

SAINT (Security Administrator's Integrated Network Tool) is computer software used for scanning computer networks for security vulnerabilities, and exploiting found vulnerabilities.

71.1 SAINT Network Vulnerability Scanner

The SAINT scanner screens every live system on a network for TCP and UDP services. For each service it finds running, it launches a set of probes designed to detect anything that could allow an attacker to gain unauthorized access, create a denial-of-service, or gain sensitive information about the network.[1]

SAINT provides support to the Security Content Automation Protocol (SCAP) specification as an Unauthenticated Vulnerability Scanner and Authenticated Vulnerability and Patch Scanner.[2] SAINT is also an approved scanning vendor with the Payment Card Industry (PCI).[3]

The Four Steps of a SAINT Scan:

- Step 1 – SAINT screens every live system on a network for TCP and UDP services.

- Step 2 – For each service it finds running, it launches a set of probes designed to detect anything that could allow an attacker to gain unauthorized access, create a denial-of-service, or gain sensitive information about the network.

- Step 3 – The scanner checks for vulnerabilities.

- Step 4 – When vulnerabilities are detected, the results are categorized in several ways, allowing customers to target the data they find most useful.

SAINT can group vulnerabilities according to severity, type, or count. It can also provide information about a particular host or group of hosts. SAINT describes each of the vulnerabilities it locates; references Common Vulnerabilities and Exposures (CVE), CERT advisories, and IAVA (Information Assurance Vulnerability Alerts); and describes ways to correct the vulnerabilities. In many cases, the SAINT scanner provides links to patches or new software versions that will eliminate the detected vulnerabilities.[4]

A vulnerability is a flaw in a system, device, or application that, if leveraged by an attacker, could impact the security of the system. Exploits take advantage of a vulnerability by compromising or destructing the vulnerable system, device, or application. Remediation is the process of repairing or providing a remedy for a vulnerability, thereby eliminating the risk of being exploited. Vulnerability scanning is used to identify and evaluate the security posture of a network. Historically, scanners were developed for specific purposes such as scanning only Windows desktops, applications, or network devices. SAINT offers heterogeneous scanning that identifies vulnerabilities across operating systems, desktop applications, network devices, Web applications, databases, and more.

71.2 SAINTexploit Penetration Testing Tool

The integrated penetration testing tool, SAINTexploit, demonstrates the path an attacker could use to breach a network and quantifies the risk to the network. SAINTexploit includes a Web site emulator and e-mail forgery tool.[5]

Penetration testing tools from SAINT are designed to simulate both internal and external real-world attacks. This type of testing identifies the methods of gaining access to a target and understanding the techniques used by attackers. There are many levels and types of penetration testing and the scope of the project should be well defined. Targets included in the scope could include popular protocols, network devices, databases, Web applications, desktop applications, and various flavors of operating systems.

SAINT focuses on the development of exploits where a shell can be established. A shell, or shellcode, is where all exploits included offer a command shell/direct connection to the target from the computer performing the testing. Exploits target operating systems, desktop applications, databases, Web applications, protocols, and network devices. The most common exploit types included in SAINTexploit include the following:

• Remote Exploit – These attacks are launched across the Internet or network against a vulnerable target without the user having previous access to the system.

• Client Exploit – The victim must access the attacker's resource for a successful attack to take place. Common client exploits include e-mail forgery attacks, enticing the user to visit a Web site, or to open a file.

• Local Exploit – In order to launch a local attack, the attacker must have previous access to the victim. (Also known as privilege elevation and tunneling). In this case, the victim's machine is used as the launch pad for connecting to other vulnerable targets.

71.3 SAINTmanager Remote Management Console

SAINT's remote management console, SAINTmanager, enables enterprise-wide vulnerability scanning. The browser-based console provides the ability to centrally manage an entire network of SAINT vulnerability scanners from a single interface.

71.4 SAINTCloud

SAINTCloud enables cloud based vulnerability scanning, penetration testing, and compliance audits without having to download and install software.

71.5 History

The SAINT (Security Administrator's Integrated Network Tool) network vulnerability scanner was based on SATAN (Security Administrators Tool for Analyzing Networks) which was developed by Dan Farmer and Wietse Venema and released in 1995. SAINT Corporation (formerly World Wide Digital Security, Inc. (WWDSI)) continued development and released SAINT in July 1998. WWDSI changed its name to SAINT Corporation in January 2002.

SAINT products are developed by SAINT Corporation, headquartered in Bethesda, Maryland.

71.6 References

[1] http://www.scmagazineus.com/ saint-integrated-vulnerability-scanner/review/3087/

[2] http://nvd.nist.gov/scapproducts.cfm

[3] https://www.pcisecuritystandards.org/approved_ companies_providers/approved_scanning_vendors.php

[4] http://www.saintcorporation.com/products/ productsOverview.html

[5] http://www.saintcorporation.com/company/press/SAINT_ SCinnovator.pdf

71.7 External links

• SAINT home page

Chapter 72

ScienceLogic

ScienceLogic is a software and service vendor. It produces information technology (IT) management and monitoring solutions for IT Operations and Cloud computing.[2]

The company's product is a monitoring and management system that performs discovery, dependency mapping, monitoring, alerting, ticketing, runbook automation, dashboarding and reporting for networks, compute, storage and applications.[3]

The ScienceLogic platform monitors both on-premises and cloud-based IT assets, enabling customers who use public cloud services, such as Amazon Web Services (AWS), to migrate workloads to the cloud.[4]

72.1 History

ScienceLogic was founded in Reston, Virginia, in 2003.

By 2005, the company tripled its revenue growth year-over year,[5] and had triple digit growth from 2005-2007.[6]

In 2008, ScienceLogic posted $5.9M in revenue.[7] Also in 2008, Inc. Magazine placed ScienceLogic on its annual list of America's 500 Fastest Growing Private Companies at #350, also including it as #42 in the Top 100 IT Services Companies the same year.[8] In 2009, the position on the list was #490.[9] ScienceLogic also was ranked #59 in the Deloitte's 2009 Technology Fast 500 Ranking.[10] From 2003 to 2009, ScienceLogic had overall sales growth of more than 70%, without outside investment.

In 2010, ScienceLogic received $15 million in Series A funding from New Enterprise Associates.[11] In 2012, ScienceLogic raised an additional $15 million in funding from Intel Capital.[12]

In 2013, ScienceLogic's IT monitoring software was chosen and deployed by Whoa Networks Inc.[13] Mark Amarant, CEO of Whoa Networks Inc, chose the ScienceLogic platform because of its customizable dashboards and real-time visibility and analysis, and ticketing system.[14]

Since the second round of funding, ScienceLogic has received a number of prestigious awards, including:

- MSPmentor 250[15]
- Red Herring Global 100[16]
- InfoWorld 2013 Technology of the Year[17]

Along with the 2013 Technology of the Year award from InfoWorld, ScienceLogic's product review written by Brian Chee, names ScienceLogic as "the best network monitoring system on earth".[18]

In 2014, ScienceLogic introduced CloudMapper[19] which automatically discovers and maps the relationships between IT assets in public cloud services, such as AWS, as well as on the customers own premises in a hybrid IT environment. This dependency mapping enables customers to identify non-performing assets in both environments.

72.2 References

[1] Leadership http://www.sciencelogic.com/company/leadership

[2] MarketWatch "ScienceLogic Expands Management Team to Propel Corporate Growth." June 21, 2011.

[3] ScienceLogic.com "http://www.sciencelogic.com/product" IT Monitoring Software

[4] ScienceLogic.com "http://www.sciencelogic.com/product/cloudmapper"

[5] ScienceLogic Press Release "http://ww2.sciencelogic.com/news-events/press-releases/2006/ScienceLogic-More-Than-Triples-Its-Growth-in-2005/999" ScienceLogic More Than Triples Its Growth in 2005

[6] ScienceLogic Press Release "http://ww2.sciencelogic.com/news-events/press-releases/2007/ScienceLogic-Announces-Third-Straight-Year-of-TripleDigit-Growth/990" ScienceLogic Announces Third Straight Year of Triple-Digit Growth

[7] TechCrunch "http://techcrunch.com/2010/04/06/ sciencelogic-raises-15-million-for-cloud-and-data-center-monitoring-services/" ScienceLogic Raises $15 Million for Cloud And Data Center Monitoring Services

[8] http://www.inc.com "http://www.inc.com/inc5000/2008/ company-profile.html?id=200803500" Company Profile: ScienceLogic

[9] http://www.inc.com "http://www.inc.com/inc5000/2009/ company-profile.html?id=200904900" Company Profile: ScienceLogic

[10] http://www.deloitte.com "http://www.deloitte.com/assets/ Dcom-UnitedStates/Local%20Assets/Documents/TMT_ us_tmt/us_tmt_Fast500winnersbyrank_101509.pdf" Deloitte's 2009 Technology Fast 500 Ranking

[11] TechCrunch "http://techcrunch.com/2010/04/06/ sciencelogic-raises-15-million-for-cloud-and-data-center-monitoring-services/" ScienceLogic Raises $15 Million for Cloud And Data Center Monitoring Services

[12] ScienceLogic Press release "http://www. sciencelogic.com/news-and-events/press-releases/ sciencelogic-raises-15-million-led-intel-capital-names-technology" ScienceLogic Raises $15 Million Led by Intel Capital

[13] http://www.sciencelogic.com/company/press-releases/ whoa-deploys-sciencelogic. Missing or empty |title= (help)

[14] Kusnetsky, Dan. "WHOA.com selects ScienceLogic, here's Why". Retrieved 25 June 2014.

[15] ScienceLogic Press Release "http://www. sciencelogic.com/news-and-events/press-releases/ sciencelogic-honored-fifth-annual-mspmentor-250" ScienceLogic Honored in Fifth Annual MSPmentor 250

[16] ScienceLogic Press Release "http://www. sciencelogic.com/news-and-events/press-releases/ sciencelogic-named-red-herring-global-100-award-winner" ScienceLogic Named Red Herring Global 100 Award Winner

[17] InfoWorld "http://www.infoworld.com/slideshow/80986/ infoworlds-2013-technology-of-the-year-award-winners-210419# slide35" Network Management Tool Award

[18] InfoWorld "http://www.infoworld.com/d/data-center/ review-the-best-network-monitoring-system-earth-212335" Best Network Monitoring System on Earth

[19] ScienceLogic.com CloudMapper http://www. sciencelogic.com/company/press-releases/ sciencelogic-debuts-cloudmapper

- ScienceLogic EM7 Overview
- ScienceLogic Blog
- CrunchBase Profile
- "Managing the Chaos of Cloud Computing." IT Business Edge, May 12, 2011
- "ScienceLogic's EM7 Manages Apps in the Cloud." InformationWeek, May 13, 2011
- "Best Network Monitoring System on Earth" InfoWorld, February 6, 2013
- ScienceLogic on IT Central Station

72.3 External links

- ScienceLogic Web site

Chapter 73

Security Administrator Tool for Analyzing Networks

"SATAN" redirects here. For other uses, see Satan (disambiguation).

Security Administrator Tool for Analyzing Networks (**SATAN**) was a free software vulnerability scanner for analyzing networked computers. SATAN captured the attention of a broad technical audience, appearing in PC Magazine[1] and drawing threats from the United States Department of Justice.[1] It featured a web interface, complete with forms to enter targets, tables to display results, and context-sensitive tutorials that appeared when a vulnerability had been found.

73.1 Naming

For those offended by the name SATAN, the software contained a special command called *repent*, which rearranged the letters in the program's acronym from "SATAN" to "SANTA".

73.2 Description

The tool was developed by Dan Farmer and Wietse Venema. Neil Gaiman drew the artwork for the SATAN documentation.

SATAN was designed to help systems administrators automate the process of testing their systems for known vulnerabilities that can be exploited via the network. This was particularly useful for networked systems with multiple hosts. Like most security tools, it was useful for good or malicious purposes – it was also useful to would-be intruders looking for systems with security holes.

SATAN was written mostly in Perl and utilized a web browser such as Netscape, Mosaic or Lynx to provide the user interface. This easy to use interface drove the scanning process and presents the results in summary format. As well as reporting the presence of vulnerabilities, SATAN also gathered large amounts of general network information, such as which hosts are connected to subnets, what types of machines they are and which services they offered.[2]

73.3 Status

SATAN has fallen from popularity after the height of its popularity in the 1990s. SATAN was released in 1995 and development has ceased. In 2006, SecTools.Org conducted a security popularity poll and developed a list of 100 network security analysis tools in order of popularity based on the responses of 3,243 people. Results suggest[3] that SATAN has been replaced by nmap, Nessus and to a lesser degree SARA (Security Auditor's Research Assistant; discontinued September 1, 2009), and SAINT.

73.4 References

[1] Tabibian, O. Ryan (April 23, 1996). "Internet Scanner Finds Security Holes". *PC Magazine*. Retrieved 30 May 2014.

[2] Farmer, Dan; Wietse Venema (1993). "Improving the Security of Your Site by Breaking Into it". *Sun Microsystems*. Eindhoven University of Technology. Retrieved 30 May 2014.

[3] Heiser & Kruse (2002). *Computer Forensics: Incident Response Essentials*. Lucent Technologies. ISBN 0201707195.

73.5 External links

- Official home page

- History of SATAN

Chapter 74

Shinken (software)

Shinken is an open source computer system and network monitoring software application compatible with Nagios. It watches hosts and services, gathers performance data and alerts users when error conditions occur and again when the conditions clear.

Shinken's architecture aims to offer easier load balancing and high availability. The administrator manages a single configuration, the system automatically "cuts" it into parts and dispatches it to worker nodes. It takes its name from this functionality: a Shinken is a Japanese sword.

Shinken was written by Jean Gabès as a proof of concept for a new Nagios architecture. Believing the new implementation was faster and more flexible than the old C code, he proposed it as the new development branch of Nagios 4.[3] This proposal was turned down by the Nagios authors, so Shinken became an independent network monitoring software application compatible with Nagios.[4]

Shinken is designed to run under all operating systems where Python runs. The development environment is under Linux, but also runs well on other Unix variants and Windows. The reactionner process (responsible for sending notifications) can also be run under the Android OS. It is free software, licensed under the terms of the Affero General Public License as published by the Free Software Foundation.

74.1 Overview

- Design

  - Monitoring system written in Python

  - Distributed architecture using Pyro remote objects

- Active and Passive monitoring methods

  - Monitoring of network services (SMTP, POP3, HTTP, NNTP, ICMP, SNMP, FTP, SSH)

- Monitoring of host resources (processor load, disk usage, system logs) on a majority of network operating systems, including Microsoft Windows

  - Using agents such as NSClient++, send_nsca, Check MK, Thrift TSCA

  - Using agents permitting remotely run scripts via Nagios Remote Plugin Executor (An embedded pure-Python implementation is included with Shinken)

  - Using agent-less methods such as SNMP, WMI, scripted SSH or HTTP(SSL)

  - Send check results directly from programs using Apache Thrift (Java, Python, Ruby)

- Monitoring of systems which have the ability to send collected data via a network to specifically written plugins (Ex. VMWare ESX3/4/5, Collectd)

- Remote monitoring supported through SSH or SSL encrypted tunnels.

- Simple plugin design that allows users to easily develop their own service checks depending on needs, by using the tools of choice (shell scripts, C++, Perl, Ruby, Python, PHP, C#, etc.)

- Ability to calculate KPIs from State and performance data in the Shinken core to create new services and performance data

- System external interfaces

  - Livestatus compatible API that exposes state, configuration and performance information

  - Exports data to graphing modules (PNP4Nagios, Graphite, and others available)

  - Support for native messaging API of Android

  - Export event data to logging systems using syslog and RabbitMQ

  - Modules can be attached to any Shinken process to extend its capabilities in very efficient ways

- Performance

  - Parallelized service and host checks available

  - Ability to distribute poller processes on multiple servers

  - Support for implementing easily redundant and load balanced monitoring hosts

  - Support for multiple redundant external interfaces

  - Ability to route checks to dedicated pollers (processes specialized in executing plugins)

- Correlation and business intelligence

  - Parent child relations

    - Ability to define network host hierarchy using "parent" hosts, allowing detection of and distinction between hosts that are down and those that are unreachable

    - 1 to 1, 1 to N

  - Free form dependency trees between any service and host

    - 1 to 1, 1 to N

  - Support for integrated business rules

    - Calculated hosts or services representing the state of a business service

    - Support assigning a business impact to each service, host or business process

  - Ability to show only root problems

  - Automatically changes child states to unknown when parent is unavailable

- Other features

  - Contact notifications when service or host problems occur and get resolved (via e-mail, pager, SMS, or any user-defined method through plugin system)

  - Ability to define event handlers to be run during service or host events for proactive problem resolution

  - Ability to redefine the severity of an alert based on regular expression rules

  - Support for UTF-8 objects names

  - Support for monitoring multiple customers with one administration point

  - Support for recurring downtimes through the maintenance_period attribute

  - Advanced template system with inheritance and overloading

74.2   Architecture

A Shinken installation consists of several processes, each optimized for a specific task.

- Arbiter

  - Loads the configuration files and dispatches the host and service objects to the scheduler(s)

  - Watchdog for all other processes and responsible for initiating failovers if an error is detected

  - Can route check result events from a Receiver to its associated Scheduler

  - Arbiter modules

    - There is a variety of modules to manipulate configuration data

- Scheduler

  - Plans the next run of host and service checks

  - Dispatches checks to the poller(s)

  - Calculates state and dependencies

  - Applies KPI triggers

  - Raises Notifications and dispatches them to the reactionner(s)

  - Updates the retention file (or other retention backends)

  - Sends broks (internal events of any kind) to the broker(s)

- Poller

  - Gets checks from the scheduler, execute plugins or integrated poller modules and send the results to the scheduler

  - Poller modules

    - NRPE - Executes active data acquisition for Nagios Remote Plugin Executor agents

    - SNMP - Executes active data acquisition for SNMP enabled agents (In beta stage using PySNMP)

    - CommandPipe - Receives passive status and performance data from check_mk script, will not process commands

- Reactionner

  - Gets notifications and eventhandlers from the scheduler, executes plugins/scripts and sends the results to the scheduler

- Broker

  - Has multiple modules (usually running in their own processes)

  - Gets broks from the scheduler and forwards them to the broker modules

  - Modules decide if they handle a brok depending on a brok's type (log, initial service/host status, check result, begin/end downtime, ...)

  - Modules process the broks in many different ways. Some of the modules are:

    - webui - updates in-memory objects and provides a webserver for the native Shinken GUI

    - livestatus - updates in-memory objects which can be queried using an API by GUIs like Thruk or Check_MK Multisite

    - graphite - exports data to a Graphite database

    - ndodb - updates an ndo database (MySQL or Oracle)

    - simple_log - centralize the logs of all the Shinken processes

    - status_dat - writes to a status.dat file which can be read by the classic cgi-based GUI

- Receiver (optional)

  - Receives data passively from local or remote protocols

  - Passive data reception that is buffered before forwarding to the appropriate Scheduler (or Arbiter for global commands)

  - Allows to set up a "farm" of Receivers to handle a high rate of incoming events

  - Modules for receivers

    - NSCA - NSCA protocol receiver

    - Collectd - Receive performance data from collectd via the network

    - CommandPipe - Receive commands, status updates and performance data

    - TSCA - Apache Thrift interface to send check results using a high rate buffered TCP connection directly from programs

    - Web Service - A web service that accepts http posts of check results (beta)

There can be multiple instances for each type of process, either on a single host or spread over many hosts. Adding more processes automatically distributes the load.

The Shinken WebUI is the builtin Web interface that provides near real time status information, configuration, interaction, a dashboard to visualize trending data from Graphite databases and the visualization of dependency tree graphs.

The Shinken skonfUI is an independent web front-end used to manage the discovery process and configuration tasks.

The shinken-admin CLI script is used to manage during runtime process level aspects of the system, such as changing logging levels and getting health reports.

The install.sh CLI script is the main management script to install, remove or update Shinken and its associated software.

74.3 Development

Shinken has an open and test-driven development approach, with contributors to the project providing new features, code refactoring, code quality and bug fixing.[5]

The source code is hosted on GitHub.[6] An integration server runs tests at each commit and in depth tests at regular intervals.

The Shinken documentation is hosted on a wiki.

74.4 See also

- Comparison of network monitoring systems
- NRPE
- Icinga
- Nagios
- Collectd

74.5 References

[1] Official release in the Nagios mailing list at http://sourceforge.net/p/nagios/mailman/message/24087464/

[2] http://shinkenlab.io/release-2-4/

[3] Gabès, Jean (2009-12-01). "Shinken : a new implementation proposal". GitHub. Retrieved 2014-03-04. I would like to have your feed back about a (unfinished) reimplementation of Nagios named "Shinken" I wrote in Python that is faster and more modular than the current Nagios implementation in C

[4] Gabès, Jean (2010-06-01). "Shinken : a mix with Nagios is not possible". Shinken team. Retrieved 2010-06-01. We never got an answer for the initial Shinken proposal because we are seen as a renegade project. In fact, now we can say that we are a fork.

[5] Shinken contributors on Ohloh

[6] source code on GitHub

74.6   External links

- Official website

- Monitoring Plugins the home of the official plugins

- (German) Linux Magazin article about Shinken in the German Linux Magazin 04/2010

Chapter 75

SNMPTT

SNMPTT is an SNMP trap handler written in Perl for use with the NET-SNMP/UCD-SNMP snmptrapd program. Received traps are translated into user friendly messages using variable substitution. Output can be to STDOUT, text log file, syslog, NT Event Log, MySQL (Linux/Windows), PostgreSQL, or an ODBC database. User defined programs can also be executed.

75.1 Distribution

SNMPTT can be downloaded from the SourceForge project page or the project web page.

75.2 Books

Information on SNMPTT is available in the following books:

- Turnbull, James; (2006) *Pro Nagios 2.0* - San Francisco: Apress ISBN 1-59059-609-9

- Schubert, Max et al.; (2008) *Nagios 3 Enterprise Network Monitoring* - Syngress ISBN 978-1-59749-267-6

- Barth, Wolfgang; (2008) "Nagios: System And Network Monitoring, 2nd edition - *No Starch Press ISBN 1-59327-179-4*

Chapter 76

snoop (software)

snoop is a very flexible command line packet analyzer included as part of Sun Microsystems' Solaris operating system. Its source code is available via the OpenSolaris project.

For command line arguments see the **snoop** manpage.

76.1 See also

- Comparison of packet analyzers
- Network tap

76.2 References

76.3 External links

- TCP/IP and Data Communications Administration Guide
- docs.sun.com: man snoop(1M)
- OpenSolaris: snoop source code

Chapter 77

SolarWinds

This article is about the IT company. For the astronomical phenomenon, see solar wind. For other uses, see Solar wind (disambiguation).

SolarWinds Inc. develops enterprise information technology (IT) infrastructure management software for IT professionals.[1] SolarWinds is headquartered in Austin, Texas, with sales and product development offices in Lehi, Utah, Boulder, Colorado, Cork, Ireland, Brno, Czech Republic, Singapore, Chennai, India, and Sydney, Australia.[2] The company hosts an online community called thwack.[3]

77.1 History

In 2007, SolarWinds raised funding from Austin Ventures, Bain Capital and Insight Venture Partners.[4][5] Following the funding, SolarWinds acquired several companies including Neon Software and ipMonitor Corp. and opened a European sales office in Ireland.[6]

SolarWinds completed its initial public offering of $112.5 million in 2009.[7] The company introduced the Solar-Winds Certified Professional Program (SCP) for network management, to test professionals in five areas: network management fundamentals, network management planning, network management operation, network performance troubleshooting and Orion Network Performance Monitor (NPM) administration and service.[8]

In 2012, SolarWinds' total revenue reached $269 million.[9] In 2013, SolarWinds announced plans to invest $50 million on an operations hub in Salt Lake City.[10]

In June 2014, the company purchased the Swedish web-monitoring company Pingdom.[11]

In August 2014, SolarWinds announced the launch of its deep packet inspection (DPI) free tool SolarWinds Response Time Viewer for Wireshark. It is the latest to join more than 30 free tools from SolarWinds' IT management product family.[12]

In October 2014, SolarWinds is among Forbes' Best Small Companies of 2014, and the company was ranked 11th overall.

In January 2015, SolarWinds acquired the San Francisco based metrics and monitoring company Librato, for $40 million.[13]

In April 2015, SolarWinds acquired Seattle based log management service Papertrail, for $41 million.[14]

In October 2015, SolarWinds announced it will be acquired by private equity technology investment firms Silver Lake Partners and Thoma Bravo, LLC., effectively becoming a private company.

77.2 Acquisitions

- Papertrail (2015)
- Librato (2015)
- Pingdom (2014)
- Confio Software (2013) for $103 million in cash.
- N-able Technologies (2013)[15]
- RhinoSoft (2012)[16]
- EminentWare (2012)[17]
- RoveIT (2012)[18]
- Hyper9, Inc. (2011)[19]
- TriGeo Network Security (2011)[20]

77.3 References

[1] Darryl K. Taft, eWeek. "IT Management: IT Admin's 'Summer Suitcase': 11 Helpful Tech Tools for Vacation." July 3, 2012. Retrieved Nov. 1, 2012.

[2] Kurt Badenhausen, Forbes. "SolarWinds Tops List Of America's Best Small Companies." Nov. 17, 2012. Retrieved June 17, 2013.

[3] http://www.networkworld.com/article/2344656/data-breach/solarwinds-marks--thwack--anniversary-with-free-tool-release.html

[4] Austin Business Journal. "SolarWinds Raises $7.5M." Feb. 5, 2007. Retrieved on June 17, 2013.

[5] Chris Morrison, VentureBeat. "Is Network Management Growing? SolarWinds Picks up Kiwi Enterprises." Jan. 6, 2009. Retrieved on June 17, 2013.

[6] Maxwell Cooter, TechWorld. "SolarWinds Finally Blows into Europe." October 9, 2007. Retrieved on January 6, 2009.

[7] Lori Hawkins, Austin American-Statesman. "SolarWinds keeps on growing." Nov. 20, 2011. Retrieved June 17, 2013.

[8] Ted Stevenson, EnterpriseNetworkingPlanet. "SolarWinds Inaugurates Network Management Certification." Aug. 14, 2009. Retrieved Aug. 20, 2009.

[9] SolarWinds Website. "SolarWinds Company News." Feb. 4, 2013. Retrieved June 17, 2013.

[10] Utah Business. "SolarWinds To Begin Presence in Utah." May 10, 2013. Retrieved June 17, 2013.

[11] http://mspmentor.net/acquisitions/062014/solarwinds-adds-pingdom-its-performance-management-portfolio

[12] MarketWatch. "." August 20, 2014. August 20, 2014.

[13] http://www.marketwatch.com/story/solarwinds-expands-its-cloud-monitoring-and-management-footprint-with-acquisition-of-librato-2015-01-29?reflink=MW_news_stmp

[14] "SolarWinds Acquires Log Management Service Papertrail For $41M"

[15] Wall Street Journal. "SolarWinds to Buy N-able Technologies for $120 Million." May 21, 2013. Retrieved June 20, 2013.

[16] Richard Hay, Windows Observer. "RhinoSoft Acquired by SolarWinds – FTP Voyager Now Offered as Free Tool." Dec. 18, 2012. Retrieved June 20, 2013.

[17] Bloomberg Business Week. "Company Overview of EminentWare LLC." June 23, 2013. Retrieved June 23, 2013.

[18] BlackBerry Cool. "Publicly Traded SolarWinds Acquires Rove Mobile Admin Technology." April 10, 2012. Retrieved June 23, 2013.

[19] Austin Business Journal. "SolarWinds acquires Hyper9." July 19, 2011. Retrieved June 23, 2013.

[20] Robin Wauters, TechCrunch. "SolarWinds Buys Network Security Company TriGeo For $35 Million In Cash." June 23, 2011. Retrieved June 22, 2013.

77.4 External links

- Official website

SolarWinds Subsidiaries:

- Papertrail
- Librato
- Pingdom
- Confio
- Serv-U
- Web Help Desk
- DameWare
- SolarWinds Federal
- N-able

Chapter 78

Sparrowiq

SparrowIQ is a packet-based traffic analysis and network performance monitoring solution that provides network managers with near real-time traffic visibility into network usage based on conversations, applications, users and class of service.[1][2]

The product was developed by Solana Networks (Ottawa, Canada) to allow smaller businesses to gain access to flow-based network traffic monitoring solutions - normally too complex or unaffordable. [3] [4] [5]

78.1 Features

SparrowIQ key features [6]

- Traffic Forensics for identifying business-relevant versus recreational and unauthorized traffic

- Real-time Traffic Alerting for instant notification when bandwidth crosses preset thresholds

- Automatic Report Generation and Distribution

78.2 References

[1] SparrowIQ- Cost Effective Network Performance Management for SMBs, EMA Analyst Product Brief, February 2013

[2] Sparrowiq Website

[3] Rajani Baburajan, Solana Networks Unveils Network Monitoring Solution for SMBs, March 21, 2013

[4] Product Brief Corbo, Tracy, EMA Product Brief, January 2013

[5] Solana Networks Product Specifications

[6] Softpedia Product Review

Chapter 79

SQLFilter

SQLFilter is a plugin for OmniPeek that indexes packets and trace files into an SQLite database. The packets can then be searched using SQL queries. The matching packets are loaded directly into OmniPeek and analyzed. The packet database can also be used to build multi-tier data mining and network forensics systems.

As more companies save large quantities of network traffic to disk, tools like the WildPackets SQLFilter make it possible to search through packet data more efficiently. For network trouble shooters, this revolutionizes the job of finding packets. Not only does the SQLFilter allow users to search for packets across thousands of trace files, it also loads the resulting packets directly into OmniPeek or Ether-Peek. This cuts out many of the steps usually involved in this process and dramatically shortens time to knowledge, and time to fix.

For a more indepth discussion of the SQLFilter read Packet Data Mining and Network Forensics.

Chapter 80

Subterfuge

For the concept of subterfuge, see Deception and Military deception. For the 1968 British film, see Subterfuge (film).

For the 1912 film, see Subterfuge (1912 film).

Subterfuge is a free and open source network security framework to demonstrate man-in-the-middle attacks and make it as simple as point and shoot.[1] Subterfuge demonstrates vulnerabilities in the Address Resolution Protocol by harvesting credentials that go across the LAN, and even exploiting machines through client-side browser injection. It is capable of running on all distributions of Linux, but developer support is limited to Kali Linux. It is capable of leveraging multiple man-in-the-middle attacks against target networks.

80.1   Features

Subterfuge Features include:

- ARP Cache Poisoning
- Credential Harvester
- Http Code Injection
- Wireless AP Generation
- WPAD Hijacking
- Rogue DHCP

80.2   Graphical interface

Subterfuge is known for its extremely modern web-based interface. The interface includes alternate perspectives for man-in-the-middle attacks through its unique network view. Subterfuge and its GUI's purpose are primarily to demonstrate the dangers of man-in-the-middle attacks through their ease of employment with the framework itself.

80.3   References

[1] "Subterfuge (Man-in-the-Middle Attack Framework)". Raj Chandler. 12 December 2012. Retrieved 18 November 2013.

80.4   External links

- Official website
- Project Page

141

Chapter 81

TCP Gender Changer

TCP Gender Changer is a method in computer networking for making an internal TCP/IP based network server accessible beyond its protective firewall.

81.1 Mechanism

It consists of two nodes, one resides on the internal the local area network where it can access the desired server, and the other node runs outside of the local area network, where the client can access it. These nodes are respectively called CC (Connect-Connect) and LL (Listen-Listen).

The reason behind naming the nodes are the fact that Connect-Connect node initiates two connections one to the Listen-Listen node and one to the actual server. The Listen-Listen node, however, passively Listens on two TCP/IP ports, one to receive a connection from CC and the other one for an incoming connection from the client.

The CC node, which runs inside the network will establish a control connection to the LL, and waiting for LL's signal to open a connection to the internal server. Upon receiving a client connection LL will signal the CC node to connect the server, once done CC will let LL know of the result and if successful LL will keep the client connection and thus the client and server can communicate while CC and LL both relay the data back and forth.

81.2 Use cases

One of the cases where it can be very useful is to connect to a desktop machine behind a firewall running VNC, which would make the desktop remotely accessible over the network and beyond the firewall. Another useful scenario would be to create a VPN using PPP over SSH, or even simply using SSH to connect to an internal Unix based server.

81.3 See also

- Firewall (computing)
- LAN
- Network Security
- VPN
- VNC

81.4 References

81.5 External links

- A more complete explanation of the working mechanism
- An article explaining the idea

81.5.1 Implementations

- tgcd, TCP Gender Changer Daemon is a Unix daemon implementation of TCP Gender Changer method (GNU GPL 2+)
- revinetd is an implementation of the TCP gender changer (GNU GPL 2)
- An implementation using socat utility (GNU GPL with OpenSSL linking exception)
- Firewall Tunnel is a Firewall Tunnel based on the TCP Gender Changer method (GNU GPL 2)

Chapter 82

tcpdump

tcpdump is a common packet analyzer that runs under the command line. It allows the user to display TCP/IP and other packets being transmitted or received over a network to which the computer is attached. Distributed under the BSD license,[3] tcpdump is free software.

Tcpdump works on most Unix-like operating systems: Linux, Solaris, BSD, OS X, HP-UX, Android and AIX among others. In those systems, tcpdump uses the libpcap library to capture packets. The port of tcpdump for Windows is called WinDump; it uses WinPcap, the Windows port of libpcap.

82.1 History

It was originally written in 1987 by Van Jacobson, Craig Leres and Steven McCanne who were, at the time, working in the Lawrence Berkeley Laboratory Network Research Group. By the late 1990s there were numerous versions of tcpdump distributed as part of various operating systems, and numerous patches that were not well coordinated. Michael Richardson (mcr) and Bill Fenner created www.tcpdump.org in 1999.

82.2 Common uses

Tcpdump prints the contents of network packets. It can read packets from a network interface card or from a previously created saved packet file. Tcpdump can write packets to standard output or a file.

It is also possible to use tcpdump for the specific purpose of intercepting and displaying the communications of another user or computer. A user with the necessary privileges on a system acting as a router or gateway through which unencrypted traffic such as Telnet or HTTP passes can use tcpdump to view login IDs, passwords, the URLs and content of websites being viewed, or any other unencrypted information.

The user may optionally apply a BPF-based filter to limit the number of packets seen by tcpdump; this renders the output more usable on networks with a high volume of traffic.

82.3 Privileges required

In some Unix-like operating systems, a user must have superuser privileges to use tcpdump because the packet capturing mechanisms on those systems require elevated privileges. However, the -Z option may be used to drop privileges to a specific unprivileged user after capturing has been set up. In other Unix-like operating systems, the packet capturing mechanism can be configured to allow non-privileged users to use it; if that is done, superuser privileges are not required.

82.4 See also

- Packetsquare, a protocol field (pcap) editor and replay tool

- Tcptrace, a tool for analyzing the logs produced by tcpdump

- EtherApe, a network mapping tool that relies on sniffing traffic

- Ngrep, a tool that can match regular expressions within the network packet payloads

- netsniff-ng, a free Linux networking toolkit

- Wireshark, a GUI based alternative to tcpdump

82.5 References

[1] "tcpdump and libpcap latest release". tcpdump & libpcap. Retrieved 2015-05-31.

[2] "tcpdump and libpcap license". tcpdump & libpcap. Retrieved 2012-04-13.

[3] "LICENSE file from source code (public GIT repository)".

82.6   External links

- Official site for tcpdump (and libpcap)

- Official site for WinDump

- A tcpdump Tutorial and Primer

- ngrep, a tcpdump-like tool

- Portable version of tcpdump for Windows

- Official site for tcpdump for Android devices

- Tutorial video for tcpdump in Linux

- WinDump Color Highlighting

- Fast path based tcpdump for 10 Gbps traffic

Chapter 83

Tcptrace

tcptrace is a tool written by Shawn Ostermann at Ohio University, for analysis of TCP dump files. It can take as input the files produced by several popular packet-capture programs, including tcpdump/WinDump/Wireshark, snoop, EtherPeek, and Agilent NetMetrix.

tcptrace can produce several different types of output containing information on each connection seen, such as elapsed time, bytes and segments sent and received, retransmissions, round trip times, window advertisements, throughput, and more. It can also produce a number of graphs for further analysis. As of version five, minimal UDP processing has been implemented in addition to the TCP capabilities.

Tcptrace is released under GNU GPL 2+.[1]

83.1 See also

- tcpdump, a packet analyzer

- Packetsquare, a protocol field (pcap) editor and replay tool

- EtherApe, a network mapping tool that relies on sniffing traffic

- Ngrep, a tool that can match regular expressions within the network packet payloads

- dsniff, a packet sniffer and set of traffic analysis tools

- netsniff-ng, a free Linux networking toolkit

- Wireshark, a GUI based alternative to tcpdump

83.2 References

[1] COPYRIGHT file in the tarball

83.3 External links

- tcptrace website

- parsercap website

Chapter 84

Telecom network protocol analyzer

Telecom Network Protocol Analyzer is a Protocol analyzer to analyze a switching and signaling telecommunication protocol between different nodes in PSTN or Mobile telephone networks, such as 2G or 3G GSM networks, CDMA networks, WiMAX and so on.

In a mobile telecommunication network it can analyze the traffic between MSC and BSC, BSC and BTS, MSC and HLR, MSC and VLR, VLR and HLR, and so on.

Protocol analyzers are mainly used for performance measurement and troubleshooting. These devices connect to the network to calculate key performance indicators to monitor the network and speed-up troubleshooting activities.

84.1   External links

- GL Communications GSM Protocol Analyzer Overview

- Tektronix Protocol Analyzer Overview

- Utel Systems - Network Monitoring

Chapter 85

Traceroute

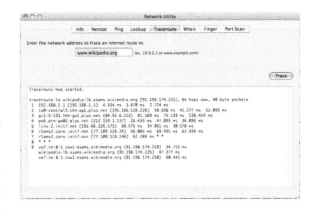

When run, traceroute outputs the list of traversed routers in a simple text format, together with timing information.

In computing, **traceroute** is a computer network diagnostic tool for displaying the route (path) and measuring transit delays of packets across an Internet Protocol (IP) network. The history of the route is recorded as the round-trip times of the packets received from each successive host (remote node) in the route (path); the sum of the mean times in each hop indicates the total time spent to establish the connection. Traceroute proceeds unless all (three) sent packets are lost more than twice, then the connection is lost and the route cannot be evaluated. Ping, on the other hand, only computes the final round-trip times from the destination point.

The traceroute command is available on a number of modern operating systems. On Apple Mac OS, it is available by opening "Network Utilities" and selecting "Traceroute" tab, as well as by typing the "traceroute" command in the terminal. On other Unix systems, such as FreeBSD or Linux, it is available as a traceroute(8) command in a terminal. On Microsoft Windows, it is named tracert. Windows NT-based operating systems also provide PathPing, with similar functionality. For Internet Protocol Version 6 (IPv6) the tool sometimes has the name traceroute6 or tracert6.

85.1 Implementation

Traceroute, by default, sends a sequence of User Datagram Protocol (UDP) packets addressed to a destination host; ICMP Echo Request or TCP SYN packets can also be used.[1] The time-to-live (TTL) value, also known as *hop limit*, is used in determining the intermediate routers being

Traceroute running on OS X Snow Leopard

traversed towards the destination. Routers decrement TTL values of packets by one when routing and discard packets whose TTL value has reached zero, returning the ICMP error message ICMP Time Exceeded.[2] Common default values for TTL are 128 (Windows OS) and 64 (Unix-based OS).

Traceroute works by sending packets with gradually increasing TTL value, starting with TTL value of one. The first router receives the packet, decrements the TTL value and drops the packet because it then has TTL value zero. The router sends an ICMP Time Exceeded message back to the source. The next set of packets are given a TTL value of two, so the first router forwards the packets, but the second router drops them and replies with ICMP Time Exceeded. Proceeding in this way, traceroute uses the returned ICMP Time Exceeded messages to build a list of routers that packets traverse, until the destination is reached and returns an ICMP Echo Reply message.[2]

The timestamp values returned for each router along the path are the delay (latency) values, typically measured in milliseconds for each packet.

Hop 192.168.1.2 Depth 1 Probe status: unsuccessful Parent: () Return code: Label-switched at stack-depth 1 **Sender timestamp:** 2008-04-17 09:35:27 EDT 400.88

msec **Receiver timestamp:** 2008-04-17 09:35:27 EDT 427.87 msec **Response time:** 26.92 msec MTU: Unknown Multipath type: IP Address Range 1: 127.0.0.64 ~ 127.0.0.127 Label Stack: Label 1 Value 299792 Protocol RSVP-TE

The sender expects a reply within a specified number of seconds. If a packet is not acknowledged within the expected interval, an asterisk is displayed. The Internet Protocol does not require packets to take the same route towards a particular destination, thus hosts listed might be hosts that other packets have traversed. If the host at hop #N does not reply, the hop is skipped in the output.

On Unix-like operating systems, the traceroute utility uses User Datagram Protocol (UDP) datagrams by default, with destination port numbers ranging from 33434 to 33534. The traceroute utility usually has an option to instead use ICMP Echo Request (type 8) packets, like the Windows tracert utility does, or to use TCP SYN packets.[1][2] If a network has a firewall and operates both Windows and Unix-like systems, more than one protocol must be enabled inbound through the firewall for traceroute to work and receive replies.

Some traceroute implementations use TCP packets, such as tcptraceroute or layer four traceroute. PathPing is a utility introduced with Windows NT that combines ping and traceroute functionality. MTR is an enhanced version of ICMP traceroute available for Unix-like and Windows systems. The various implementations of traceroute all rely on ICMP Time Exceeded (type 11) packets being sent to the source.

The implementations of traceroute shipped with Linux, FreeBSD, NetBSD, OpenBSD, DragonFly BSD, and OS X include an option to use ICMP Echo packets (-I), or any arbitrary protocol (-P) such as UDP, TCP or ICMP. On Linux, tracepath is a utility similar to traceroute, with the primary difference of not requiring superuser privileges.[3]

Cisco's implementation of traceroute also uses a sequence of UDP datagrams, each with incrementing TTL values, to an invalid port number at the remote host; by default, UDP port 33434 is used. Extended version of this command (known as the *extended traceroute* command) can change the destination port number used by the UDP probe messages.[4]

85.2   Usage

Most implementations include at least options to specify the number of queries to send per hop, time to wait for a response, the **hop limit** and port to use. Invoking traceroute with no specified options displays the list of available op-

tions, while man traceroute presents more details, including the displayed error flags. Simple example on Linux:

$ traceroute -w 3 -q 1 -m 16 example.com

In the example above, selected options are to wait for three seconds (instead of five), send out only one query to each hop (instead of three), limit the maximum number of hops to 16 before giving up (instead of 30), with example.com as the final host.

This can help identify incorrect routing table definitions or firewalls that may be blocking ICMP traffic, or high port UDP in Unix ping, to a site. Note that a firewall may permit ICMP packets but not permit packets of other protocols.

Traceroute is also used by penetration testers to gather information about network infrastructure and IP ranges around a given host.

It can also be used when downloading data, and if there are multiple mirrors available for the same piece of data, one can trace each mirror to get a good idea of which mirror would be the fastest to use.

85.3   Origins

The traceroute manual page states that the original traceroute program was written by Van Jacobson in 1987 from a suggestion by Steve Deering, with particularly cogent suggestions or fixes from C. Philip Wood, Tim Seaver and Ken Adelman. Also, the inventor of the ping program, Mike Muuss, states on his website that traceroute was written using kernel ICMP support that he had earlier coded to enable raw ICMP sockets when he first wrote the ping program.[5]

85.4   See also

• Looking Glass server

• MTR (software) – computer software which combines the functionality of the traceroute and ping programs in a single network diagnostic tool

• netsniff-ng – a Linux networking toolkit with an autonomous system traceroute utility

• PathPing – a Windows NT network utility that combines the functionality of ping with that of traceroute (or tracert)

85.5 References

[1] "traceroute(8) - Linux man page". linux.die.net. Retrieved 2014-02-26.

[2] Comer, Douglas (2004). *Computer Network and Internets with Internet Applications*. Pearson Education, Inc. pp. 360–362. ISBN 0131433512.

[3] "tracepath(8) – Linux man page". *linux.die.net*. Retrieved 2015-06-21.

[4] "Understanding the Ping and Traceroute Commands". *Cisco IOS Software Releases 12.1 Mainline*. cisco.com. 2006-11-29. Retrieved 2013-12-08.

[5] The Story of the PING Program

This article is based on material taken from the Free On-line Dictionary of Computing prior to 1 November 2008 and incorporated under the "relicensing" terms of the GFDL, version 1.3 or later.

85.6 External links

- RFC 1393: Traceroute using an IP Option Internet RFC

- How traceroute works – InetDaemon

- Tracert – Windows XP Command-line reference

Chapter 86

University Toolkit

University Toolkit is a software package developed by the MPAA for University system administrators to track and log what types of, and how much, traffic goes through their network, and over the internet provided by the University. The toolkit was available for free at www.universitytoolkit. org until a developer for Ubuntu (the operating system which the toolkit is based on) contacted the MPAA and requested that it be taken down,[1] citing GPL violations, stating that under the GPL, any software must have its source code released under the GPL as well. The MPAA has not released the source code to University Toolkit, despite it being supposedly based entirely on open-source software, specifically snort and ntop.

86.1 References

[1] mjg59: Spot the difference

86.2 External links

- http://blog.washingtonpost.com/securityfix/2007/11/ mpaa_university_toolkit_opens_1.html

Chapter 87

URL Snooper

URL Snooper is a program to find URLs of streaming media and data. This allows streamed files download through any download manager. Its scope is the same as that of a stream recorder. It usually uses library such as pcap/Winpcap for packet capturing.

87.1 See also

- Comparison of download managers

87.2 External links

- Official website

- All streaming media recording software

- PyURLSnooper is OS independent and open source (uses pcapy for packet capturing)

Chapter 88

w3af

w3af (*web application attack and audit framework*) is an open-source web application security scanner. The project provides a vulnerability scanner and exploitation tool for Web applications.[1] It provides information about security vulnerabilities and aids in penetration testing efforts. Users have the choice between a graphic user interface and a command-line interface.[2]

w3af identifies most web application vulnerabilities using more than 130 plug-ins. After identification, vulnerabilities like (blind) SQL injections, OS commanding, remote file inclusions (PHP), cross-site scripting (XSS), and unsafe file uploads, can be exploited in order to gain different types of access to the remote system.

88.1   w3af Architecture

w3af is divided into two main parts, the **core** and the **plug-ins**.[3] The core coordinates the process and provides features that are consumed by the plug-ins, which find the vulnerabilities and exploit them. The plug-ins are connected and share information with each other using a knowledge base.

Plug-ins are categorized in the following types:

- Discovery

- Audit

- Grep

- Attack

- Output

- Mangle

- Evasion

- Bruteforce

88.2   w3af History

w3af was started by Andres Riancho in March 2007, after many years of development by the community. In July 2010, w3af announced its sponsorship and partnership with Rapid7. With Rapid7's sponsorship the project will be able to increase its development speed and keep growing in terms of users and contributors.

88.3   See also

- Metasploit Project

- Low Orbit Ion Cannon (LOIC)

- Web application security

- OWASP Open Web Application Security Project

88.4   References

[1] www.w3af.org

[2] w3af documentation

[3] Part 1 of Andres Riancho's presentation "w3af - A framework to 0wn the Web "at Sector 2009, Download PDF

88.5   External links

- Official website

- w3af documentation

Chapter 89

WarVOX

WarVOX is a free, open-source VOIP-based war dialing tool for exploring, classifying, and auditing phone systems. WarVOX processes audio from each call by using signal processing techniques and without the need of modems.[1] WarVOX uses VoIP providers over the Internet instead of modems used by other war dialers.[2] It compares the pauses between words to identify numbers using particular voice-mail systems.[3]

WarVox was merged into the Metasploit Project in August 2011. [4]

89.1 See also

- H. D. Moore

- Metasploit

- Rapid7

- ToneLoc, a war dialer for DOS.

- War dialing

- w3af

89.2 References

[1] ZDnet: Metasploit's HD Moore releases 'war dialing' tools

[2] Dark Reading: Next Generation 'War-Dialing' Tool On Tap

[3] Security Focus: War dialing gets an upgrade

[4] Dark Reading: WarVOX Gets An Overhaul; Wardialing Added To Metasploit

89.3 External links

- WarVOX official website

- The Metasploit Project Metasploit Project website, which hosts the WarVOX code

Chapter 90

Weplab

Weplab is a tool designed to teach how the Wired Equivalent Privacy (WEP) wireless encryption protocol works, explain the security vulnerabilities in the protocol, and demonstrate attacks that can be used to compromise a WEP protected wireless network. Weplab is designed not only to crack WEP keys but to analyze the wireless security of a network from an educational point of view. The author has attempted to make the source code as clear as possible, instead of implementing optimizations that would obfuscate it.

Weplab works on Unix-like systems like GNU/Linux, *BSD or Mac OS X and with Cygwin layer on Windows.

90.1 Features

Weplab tries to break the WEP key using several known attacks:

- attempting to brute force the key

- loading a list of words or passphrases and trying each one in plain or MD5 form. Weplab relies on John the Ripper to generate the word list.

- using the FMS attack, but with some differences. Unlike traditional implementations of the FMS attack, Weplab tests all initialization vectors to determine whether they are weak, and it attacks both the first and the second bytes. More recent versions of Weplab also include the newer Korek's attacks; with these attacks it is possible to crack a 64-bit key after collecting only 100,000 packets, or crack a 128-bit key after collecting 300,000 packets.

90.2 External links

- Official webpage

154

Chapter 91

Wireshark

Wireshark is a free and open-source packet analyzer. It is used for network troubleshooting, analysis, software and communications protocol development, and education. Originally named **Ethereal**, the project was renamed Wireshark in May 2006 due to trademark issues.[5]

Wireshark is cross-platform, using the GTK+ widget toolkit in current releases, and Qt in the development version, to implement its user interface, and using pcap to capture packets; it runs on Linux, OS X, BSD, Solaris, some other Unix-like operating systems, and Microsoft Windows. There is also a terminal-based (non-GUI) version called TShark. Wireshark, and the other programs distributed with it such as TShark, are free software, released under the terms of the GNU General Public License.

91.1 Functionality

Wireshark is very similar to tcpdump, but has a graphical front-end, plus some integrated sorting and filtering options.

Wireshark lets the user put network interface controllers that support promiscuous mode into that mode, so they can see all traffic visible on that interface, not just traffic addressed to one of the interface's configured addresses and broadcast/multicast traffic. However, when capturing with a packet analyzer in promiscuous mode on a port on a network switch, not all traffic through the switch is necessarily sent to the port where the capture is done, so capturing in promiscuous mode is not necessarily sufficient to see all network traffic. Port mirroring or various network taps extend capture to any point on the network. Simple passive taps are extremely resistant to tampering.

On Linux, BSD, and OS X, with libpcap 1.0.0 or later, Wireshark 1.4 and later can also put wireless network interface controllers into monitor mode.

If a remote machine captures packets and sends the captured packets to a machine running Wireshark using the TZSP protocol or the protocol used by OmniPeek, Wireshark dissects those packets, so it can analyze packets captured on a remote machine at the time that they are captured.

91.2 History

In the late 1990s, Gerald Combs, a computer science graduate of the University of Missouri–Kansas City, was working for a small Internet service provider. The commercial protocol analysis products at the time were priced around $1500[6] and did not run on the company's primary platforms (Solaris and Linux), so Gerald began writing Ethereal and released the first version around 1998.[1] The Ethereal trademark is owned by Network Integration Services.

In May 2006, Combs accepted a job with CACE Technologies. Combs still held copyright on most of Ethereal's source code (and the rest was re-distributable under the GNU GPL), so he used the contents of the Ethereal Subversion repository as the basis for the Wireshark repository. However, he did not own the Ethereal trademark, so he changed the name to Wireshark.[7] In 2010 Riverbed Technology purchased CACE[8] and took over as the primary sponsor of Wireshark. Ethereal development has ceased, and an Ethereal security advisory recommended switching to Wireshark.[9]

Wireshark has won several industry awards over the years,[10] including *eWeek*,[11] *InfoWorld*,[12][13][14][15][16] and *PC Magazine*.[17] It is also the top-rated packet sniffer in the Insecure.Org network security tools survey[18] and was the SourceForge Project of the Month in August 2010.[19]

Combs continues to maintain the overall code of Wireshark and issue releases of new versions of the software. The product website lists over 600 additional contributing authors.

91.3 Features

Wireshark is software that "understands" the structure (encapsulation) of different networking protocols. It can parse and display the fields, along with their meanings as specified by different networking protocols. Wireshark uses pcap to capture packets, so it can only capture packets on the types of networks that pcap supports.

- Data can be captured "from the wire" from a live network connection or read from a file of already-captured packets.

- Live data can be read from a number of types of networks, including Ethernet, IEEE 802.11, PPP, and loopback.

- Captured network data can be browsed via a GUI, or via the terminal (command line) version of the utility, TShark.

- Captured files can be programmatically edited or converted via command-line switches to the "editcap" program.

- Data display can be refined using a display filter.

- Plug-ins can be created for dissecting new protocols.[20]

- VoIP calls in the captured traffic can be detected. If encoded in a compatible encoding, the media flow can even be played.

- Raw USB traffic can be captured.[21]

- Wireless connections can also be filtered as long as they transverse the monitored Ethernet.

- Various settings, timers, and filters can be set that ensure only triggered traffic appear.

Wireshark's native network trace file format is the libpcap format supported by libpcap and WinPcap, so it can exchange captured network traces with other applications that use the same format, including tcpdump and CA NetMaster. It can also read captures from other network analyzers, such as snoop, Network General's Sniffer, and Microsoft Network Monitor.

91.4 Security

Capturing raw network traffic from an interface requires elevated privileges on some platforms. For this reason, older versions of Ethereal/Wireshark and tethereal/TShark often ran with superuser privileges. Taking into account the huge number of protocol dissectors that are called when traffic is captured, this can pose a serious security risk given the possibility of a bug in a dissector. Due to the rather large number of vulnerabilities in the past (of which many have allowed remote code execution) and developers' doubts for better future development, OpenBSD removed Ethereal from its ports tree prior to OpenBSD 3.6.[22]

Elevated privileges are not needed for all operations. For example, an alternative is to run tcpdump or the *dumpcap* utility that comes with Wireshark with superuser privileges to capture packets into a file, and later analyze the packets by running Wireshark with restricted privileges. To emulate near realtime analysis, each captured file may be merged by *mergecap* into growing file processed by Wireshark. On wireless networks, it is possible to use the Aircrack wireless security tools to capture IEEE 802.11 frames and read the resulting dump files with Wireshark.

As of Wireshark 0.99.7, Wireshark and TShark run dumpcap to perform traffic capture. Platforms that require special privileges to capture traffic need only dumpcap run with those privileges. Neither Wireshark nor TShark need to or should be run with special privileges.

91.5 Color coding

The user typically sees packets highlighted in green, blue, and black. Wireshark uses colors to help the user identify the types of traffic at a glance. By default, green is TCP traffic, dark blue is DNS traffic, light blue is UDP traffic, and black identifies TCP packets with problems — for example, they could have been delivered out-of-order. Users can change existing rules for coloring packets, add new rules, or remove rules.

91.6 See also

- Comparison of packet analyzers

- Capsa

- Fiddler (software)

- EtherApe

- netsniff-ng

- Ngrep

- Omnipeek

- Packetsquare

- pcap

- tcpdump

- Tcptrace

91.7 Notes

[1] "Q&A with the founder of Wireshark and Ethereal". *Interview with Gerald Combs*. protocolTesting.com. Retrieved 2010-07-24.

[2] "Wireshark 1.12.8 Released". October 14, 2015.

[3] "Wireshark 2.0.0rc1 Released". October 14, 2015.

[4] "Wireshark FAQ License".

[5] "Wireshark FAQ". Retrieved 31 December 2011.

[6] InfoWorld Nov 17, 1997

[7] "What's up with the name change? Is Wireshark a fork?". *Wireshark: Frequently Asked Questions*. Retrieved 2007-11-09.

[8] "Riverbed Expands Further Into The Application-Aware Network Performance Management Market with the Acquisition of CACE Technologies". Riverbed Technology. 2010-10-21. Retrieved 2010-10-21.

[9] "enpa-sa-00024". Ethereal. 2006-11-10. Retrieved 2010-06-08.

[10] "Awards and Accolades". *Wireshark: About*. Retrieved 2010-09-20.

[11] eWEEK Labs (2012-05-28). "Wireshark". *The Most Important Open-Source Apps of All Time*. eWEEK. Retrieved 2012-08-12.

[12] Yager, Tom (2007-09-10). "Best of open source in networking". *InfoWorld*. Retrieved 2014-12-01.

[13] "Wireshark". *VoIP monitoring*. InfoWorld. Retrieved 2015-04-28.

[14] Mobley, High (2012-09-18). "Bossie Awards 2012: The best open source networking and security software". *InfoWorld*. Retrieved 2015-04-28.

[15] Ferrill, Paul (2013-09-17). "Bossie Awards 2013: The best open source networking and security software". *InfoWorld*. Retrieved 2015-04-28.

[16] Garza, Victor R. (2014-09-29). "Bossie Awards 2014: The best open source networking and security software". *InfoWorld*. Retrieved 2015-04-28.

[17] Lynn, Samara. "Wireshark 1.2.6". *Wireshark 1.2.6 Review & Rating* (PC Magazine). Retrieved 2010-09-20.

[18] "Wireshark is No. 1 of Top 14 Packet Sniffers". Insecure.Org. Retrieved 2012-08-12.

[19] "Wireshark, SourceForge Project of the Month, August 2010". SourceForge. Retrieved 2012-08-12.

[20] "Dissector compilation example". *OmniIDL*. Retrieved 18 April 2013.

[21] "USB capture setup". *Wireshark Wiki*. Retrieved 31 December 2011.

[22] "CVS log for ports/net/ethereal/Attic/Makefile". Openbsd.org. Retrieved 2010-06-08.

91.8 References

- Orebaugh, Angela; Ramirez, Gilbert; Beale, Jay (February 14, 2007). "Wireshark & Ethereal Network Protocol Analyzer Toolkit". Syngress. p. 448. ISBN 1-59749-073-3.

- Sanders, Chris (May 23, 2007). "Practical Packet Analysis: Using Wireshark to Solve Real-World Network Problems". No Starch Press. p. 192. ISBN 1-59327-149-2.

- Chappell, Laura (March 31, 2010). "Wireshark Network Analysis: The Official Wireshark Certified Network Analyst Study Guide". Protocol Analysis Institute, dba "Chappell University". p. 800. ISBN 1-893939-99-5.

- Cheok, Roy (July 1, 2014). "Wireshark: A Guide to Color My Packets". SANS Institute.

91.9 External links

- Official website

- Wireshark on SourceForge.net

Chapter 92

Xplico

Xplico is a network forensics analysis tool (NFAT), which is a software that reconstructs the contents of acquisitions performed with a packet sniffer (e.g. Wireshark, tcpdump, Netsniff-ng).

Unlike the protocol analyzer, whose main characteristic is not the reconstruction of the data carried by the protocols, Xplico born expressly with the aim to reconstruct the protocols's application data and it is able to recognize the protocols with a technique named Port Independent Protocol Identification (PIPI).[2]

The name "xplico" refers to the latin verb explico and its significance.

Xplico is free and open-source software, subject to the requirements of the GNU General Public License (GPL), version 2.[3]

92.1 Overview

To clarify what Xplico does we can imagine to have the raw data (Ethernet or PPP) of a web navigation (HTTP protocol), in this case Xplico is able to extract and reconstruct all the Web pages and contents (images, files, cookies, and so on). Similarly Xplico is able to reconstruct the e-mail exchanged with the IMAP, POP and SMTP protocols.

Among the protocols that Xplico identifies and reconstructs there are VoIP, MSN, IRC, HTTP, IMAP, POP, SMTP and FTP.

92.2 Features

92.2.1 Software architecture

The Xplico's software architecture provides:

- an *input module* to handle data input (from probes or packet sniffer)

- an *output module* to organize the decoded data and presenting them to the end user

- a set of *decoding modules*, called *protocol dissector* for the decoding of the individual network protocol

With the *output module* Xplico can have different user interfaces, in fact it can be used from command line and from a web user interface called "Xplico Interface". The *protocol dissector* is the modules for the decoding of the individual protocol, each *protocol dissector* can reconstruct and extract the data of the protocol.

All modules are plug-in and, through the configuration file, they can be loaded or not during execution of the program. This allows to focus the decoding, that is, if you want to decode only VoIP calls but not the Web traffic then you configure Xplico to load only the RTP and SIP modules excluding the HTTP module.[4]

92.2.2 Large scale pcap data analysis

Another feature of Xplico is its ability to process (reconstruct) huge amounts of data, it is able to manage pcap files of many Gbyte and also Tbyte and from multiple capture probes simultaneously, this thanks to the use of various types of "input modules". The pcap files can be uploaded in many way, directly from the Xplico Web user interface or with a SFTP or with a transmission channel called PCAP-over-IP.

For this features Xplico is used the in contexts of Lawful interception [5][6] and in Network Forensics.[7]

92.2.3 VoIP calls

Xplico and also its specific version called pcap2wav is able to decode VoIP calls based on the RTP protocol (SIP, H323, MGCP, SKINNY) and supports the decodidica of audio codecs G711ulaw, G711alaw, G722, G729, G723, G726 and MSRTA (Microsoft's Real-time audio).[8]

92.3 Basic commands working from command line

In these examples, it is assumed that *eth0* is the used network interface.

- real-time acquisition and decoding:

xplico -m rltm -i eth0

- decoding of a single pcap file:

xplico -m pcap -f example.pcap

- decoding a directory which contains many files pcap

xplico -m pcap -d /path/dir/

in all cases the data decoded are stored in the a directory named *xdecode*. With the parameter *-m* we can select the "*input module*" type. The input module named *rltm* acquires the data directly from the network interface, vice versa the input module named *pcap* acquires data form pcap files or directory.

92.4 Distributions

Xplico is installed by default in the major distributions of digital forensics and penetration testing:

- Kali Linux,[9]
- BackTrack,[10]
- DEFT,[11]
- Security Onion
- Matriux
- BackBox
- CERT Linux Forensics Tools Repository.[12]

92.5 See also

- Comparison of packet analyzers
- tcpdump, a packet analyzer
- pcap, an application programming interface (API) for capturing network traffic

- snoop, a command line packet analyzer included with Solaris
- wireshark, a network packet analyzer
- dsniff, a packet sniffer and set of traffic analysis tools
- netsniff-ng, a free Linux networking toolkit
- ngrep, a tool that can match regular expressions within the network packet payloads
- etherape, a network mapping tool that relies on sniffing traffic
- tcptrace, a tool for analyzing the logs produced by tcpdump

92.6 References

[1] http://www.xplico.org/archives/1367

[2] "ISSA Journal" (PDF). Retrieved June 2012.

[3] "Xplico License".

[4] Gabriele Faggioli, Andrea Ghirardini (2009). *Computer Forensics*. Italy: Apogeo. pp. 5, 227, 278, 369–370. ISBN 978-88-503-2816-1.

[5] "On detecting Internet-based criminal threats (European FP7-SEC Project INDECT)" (PDF). Retrieved 2010.

[6] "Sistema de interceptación y análisis de comunicaciones) I".

[7] Cameron H. Malin, Eoghan Casey BS MA (2012). *Malware Forensics Field Guide for Windows Systems: Digital Forensics Field Guides*. ISBN 978-1597494724.

[8] pcap2wav Xplico interface http://www.xplico.org/archives/1287

[9] Kali, Xplico as a package.

[10] "Backtrack 5".

[11] "Projects DEFT Linux".

[12] "Linux Forensics Tools Repository".

92.7 External links

- (English) Xplico Demo Cloud
- (English) PCAP2WAV and RTP2WAV Demo Cloud

Chapter 93

Xymon

Xymon, a network monitoring application using free software, operates under the GNU General Public License; its central server runs on Unix and Linux hosts.

93.1 History

The application was inspired by the open-source version of Big Brother, a network monitoring application, and maintains backward compatibility with it. Between 2002 and 2004 Henrik Storner wrote an open-source software add-on called **bbgen toolkit**, then in March 2005 a stand-alone version was released called **Hobbit**. Versions of this were released between 2005 and 2008, but since a prior user of the trademark "Hobbit" existed, the tool was finally renamed Xymon.[3] In January 2012, Quest Software discontinued development of Big Brother.[4] In September 2014 a branch of Xymon authored by Storner included an upcoming version which among other bug-fixes features protection against the "Shellshock" vulnerability. "Xymon Branch...". Retrieved 2014-10-11.

93.2 Functionality

Xymon offers graphical monitoring, listing the various services of each machine, as well as listing the number of mail messages queued after a defined level of downtime. Statistics are shown graphically for all monitored services.

Monitored hosts require installation of a client, which is also free software, and which forwards monitoring information to a Xymon server. Clients are available for Unix and Linux (in formats including source tarball, RPM and Debian package) from the Xymon download site at Sourceforge.[2] Windows hosts can use the Big Brother and Xymon-compatible BBWin client.[5] Plugins extend monitoring to new types of applications and services,[6] and many extension scripts for Big Brother will run unchanged on Xymon.[7]

93.3 See also

- Big Brother
- MRTG
- Nagios

93.4 References

[1] "About the Xymon". Xymon.com. Retrieved 2012-02-16.

[2] "Xymon systems and network monitor - Browse /Xymon at". Sourceforge.net. Retrieved 2015-04-17.

[3] "About the Xymon". Xymon.com. Retrieved 2012-02-16.

[4] "We sold out...". blog.maclawran.ca. 2012-02-05. Retrieved 2012-09-26.

[5] "BBWin WebPage". Bbwin.sourceforge.net. Retrieved 2012-02-16.

[6] "Xymonton [about]". Xymonton.org. 2009-11-23. Retrieved 2012-02-16.

[7] "Xymonton [tutorials:devel]". Xymonton.org. 2009-01-31. Retrieved 2012-02-16.

93.5 External links

- http://www.xymon.com/

Chapter 94

Zx Sniffer

Zx Sniffer is a freeware packet analyzer for Microsoft Windows used for network troubleshooting and analysis.

Zx Sniffer's main function is to passively collect packets sent across a computer network by putting the network card into promiscuous mode. It's also capable of decoding plaintext passwords from packets, unlike the low-level packet analyzer tcpdump. Later releases included a basic packet capture utility making it also a protocol analyzer, such as Wireshark.

Zx Sniffer is no longer maintained and its website is currently down.

94.1 Features

- Graphical user interface

- Supports packet sniffing and capture of: TCP, UDP, ICMP and IGMP protocols.

- Data can be captured "off the wire" from a live network connection and saved to either a .txt or .html format.

- Password decoding including: POP, FTP, ICQ, and HTTP.

- Data display can be refined using a display filter.

- Includes a Whois, Host Lookup, and Port Lookup tool, which resolves a port to a protocol.

94.2 Text and image sources, contributors, and licenses

94.2.1 Text

- **Accelops** *Source:* https://en.wikipedia.org/wiki/Accelops?oldid=681042419 *Contributors:* Sadads, BoKu, Airinpeterandrews, Shashibg, Jojalozzo, Enjaysea, Auntof6, DanielPharos, W Nowicki, Scottgwikip, John of Reading, Timtempleton, Iqlas, Alpha Quadrant, Bomazi, Kbentaieb and Anonymous: 5

- **Aircrack-ng** *Source:* https://en.wikipedia.org/wiki/Aircrack-ng?oldid=689607276 *Contributors:* ChangChienFu, Ixfd64, LMB, Chealer, Lzur, David Gerard, Zigger, Bumm13, Guy Harris, Mindmatrix, Pol098, Marudubshinki, FayssalF, Dialectric, BOT-Superzerocool, Rwalker, Ms2ger, XAVeRY, NetRolller 3D, SmackBot, Reedy, Bluebot, Frap, Addshore, Diemunkiesdie, Mespinola, Dave420, Fabian.a, RLE64, X-Destruction, Widefox, HyperDrive, Dustin gayler, Peachey88, MastCell, Rob356, S.borchers, Letisgo, Huisho, T sasahara, Nikitakit, AlexStanev, Le Piedbot~enwiki, Scouten, ClueBot, DJ Jeri, SF007, Dsync0, Fathing112, Addbot, Mortense, QwertyFP, Maslen, Aunva6, 5 albert square, Zorrobot, Luckas-bot, Youngchildren, Kyfoo, Ubergeekguy, Obersachsebot, Xqbot, Blenheimears, Bloodmage2, Dinamik-bot, Auscompgeek, Yuanli.H, Edwin.wei, Born2bgratis, EmausBot, Tuankiet65, Werieth, Yashartha Chaturvedi, EdoBot, Failerrrrr, Matthiaspaul, CocuBot, Kooshagpl, M0rphzone, Exercisephys, Dreamteamone, WiFiEngineer, Amovitz, Rudloff, Semsi Paco Virchow, KaosMuppet, Kib0rg1337 and Anonymous: 90

- **AirSnort** *Source:* https://en.wikipedia.org/wiki/AirSnort?oldid=625890626 *Contributors:* Pnm, Somercet, Moxfyre, Gronky, Guy Harris, Mceder, Rcbarnes, Fritz Saalfeld, Tas50, Dialectric, Icelight, SmackBot, Ohnoitsjamie, Morte, Ryan Roos, Brainix, Cheezerman, Jessecollins, Morgabra, SHARU(ja), T sasahara, EmxBot, Casablanca2000in, DanielPharos, Addbot, AnomieBOT, Blenheimears, Full-date unlinking bot, BattyBot and Anonymous: 20

- **Argus - Audit Record Generation and Utilization System** *Source:* https://en.wikipedia.org/wiki/Argus_-_Audit_Record_Generation_and_Utilization_System?oldid=689389389 *Contributors:* Michael Hardy, CatherineMunro, Robbot, TheParanoidOne, BD2412, Dialectric, Cydebot, Postcard Cathy, R'n'B, Niceguyedc, SchreiberBike, Addbot, Yobot, AnomieBOT, Chellyaz, Mogism and Anonymous: 3

- **ArpON** *Source:* https://en.wikipedia.org/wiki/ArpON?oldid=681112417 *Contributors:* Smyth, Tabletop, BD2412, Khazar, Kvng, Andyjsmith, Nick Number, Widefox, Natg 19, Pjoef, Gene93k, Boleyn, MystBot, Ashpilkin, W Nowicki, Spikeyrock, BattyBot, Cyberbot I, Monkbot and Anonymous: 9

- **Burp suite** *Source:* https://en.wikipedia.org/wiki/Burp_suite?oldid=677154015 *Contributors:* C Fenijn, Bearcat, Velella, Gpvos, Dialectric, Frap, Magioladitis, Ccyber5, Boleyn, Addbot, Mortense, Yobot, AnomieBOT, A Quest For Knowledge, Smile4ever, Benzband, John from Idegon, Dr Dinosaur IV, Dodi 8238, Scottiwkt and Anonymous: 11

- **Cain and Abel (software)** *Source:* https://en.wikipedia.org/wiki/Cain_and_Abel_(software)?oldid=686833720 *Contributors:* Haakon, AlistairMcMillan, ArnoldReinhold, RichardJFoster, Sole Soul, Sverde1, Mac Davis, Danhash, Eztli, Sandover, Tizio, Nneonneo, Nigosh, Alvin-cs, Diwen, Renamed user gQYDM0WJs1, Bachrach44, Kingpomba, Ospalh, Paste120, Rurik, JLaTondre, SmackBot, Faisal.akeel, Jacek Kendysz, Commander Keane bot, Bluebot, Emurphy42, MichaelBillington, Shadow1, Aboutblank, Kvng, Hu12, Vinnie1337, Phatom87, Alaibot, Underpants, DewiMorgan, RobotG, Popcorn2008, TARBOT, Speck-Made, R'n'B, Fishyghost, Xeysz, Natg 19, Sephiroth storm, Thewalrus0034, AngelOfSadness, Casablanca2000in, ImageRemovalBot, Martarius, J3r0, DanielPharos, Vanished user uih38riiw4hjlsd, Mitch Ames, Addbot, Ronhjones, Isderion, AnomieBOT, Aleph Infinity, GrouchoBot, Happykaka, I dream of horses, LlamaLlamaLamp, Florian.silbereis, Christoph hausner, EmausBot, K6ka, ZéroBot, Maggiechen88, Ernstkm, General.TerroR!, ClueBot NG, Bobcool11121314, Patrias, WikiTryHardDieHard, Tiscando, Freepassword, BattyBot, Dexbot, Epicgenius, Patrios, Swizyy0, Edmeme, Crashplays and Anonymous: 67

- **Capsa** *Source:* https://en.wikipedia.org/wiki/Capsa?oldid=675622730 *Contributors:* Jmabel, Guy Harris, RHaworth, BD2412, Bgwhite, Robertcornell68, SmackBot, CanyonMan, Freedomelf, Dawnseeker2000, CommonsDelinker, VQuakr, Download, Yobot, Yandri, FrescoBot, Networked, Yuanli.H, EmausBot, John of Reading, Werieth, No1Jenny, ClamDip, Frietjes, Steven.dai, Stevendaijun, Cpartsenidis, Dave Braunschweig, Lotfi Ehsan, Nancy.liu611 and Anonymous: 9

- **Carnivore (software)** *Source:* https://en.wikipedia.org/wiki/Carnivore_(software)?oldid=684005509 *Contributors:* AxelBoldt, Bewildebeast, Arpingstone, DJ Clayworth, Everyking, Jacob1207, Beland, StephanDoerner, Gazpacho, Mike Rosoft, Shiftchange, Vsmith, Gronky, Bender235, ZeroOne, Sydneyw, Mwanner, Aude, Shanes, ZayZayEM, Sade, MoraSique, Dismas, Richard Arthur Norton (1958-), Ilario, Rchamberlain, Wayward, Dysepsion, Elvey, Josh Parris, Ronocdh, FlaBot, Gywst, Jrtayloriv, Adoniscik, YurikBot, Retired username, Armadni-General, Arthur Rubin, Petri Krohn, Tom Morris, Mhardcastle, SmackBot, Mmernex, Clpo13, Ccscott, SmartGuy Old, Rearden Metal, Lazyquasar~enwiki, MK8, HoodedMan, Frap, JonHarder, Mistress Selina Kyle, Gbinal, ArglebargleIV, Xandi, Disavian, Aarktica, Rnb, CapitalR, IronChris, CieloEstrellado, Dimligt, Hires an editor, Fayenatic london, Gwern, CliffC, Kyle the bot, Aymatth2, Mwilso24, Brianbuck, SieBot, Smitherfield, BotMultichill, ClueBot, Richrakh, Pacificus, John Nevard, Niteshift36, Pee Tern, Addbot, Xp54321, Download, Lightbot, Jarble, Yobot, RevZoe, Jim1138, Commander Shepard, Aneah, LilHelpa, Surv1v4l1st, Comet Tuttle, ZéroBot, Wingman4l7, ClueBot NG, SunCountryGuy01, Mesoderm, Sowsnek, Chmarkine, P2Peter, Someone not using his real name and Anonymous: 69

- **Clarified Networks** *Source:* https://en.wikipedia.org/wiki/Clarified_Networks?oldid=596529758 *Contributors:* Hmains, Mblumber, Leolaursen, Fabrictramp, Funandtrvl, Tiptoety, JL-Bot, Ari.takanen, Mild Bill Hiccup, UnCatBot, AnomieBOT, Chazz08, Mesoderm, ChrisGualtieri, Hmainsbot1 and Anonymous: 3

- **CommView** *Source:* https://en.wikipedia.org/wiki/CommView?oldid=607407823 *Contributors:* Chris the speller, Dsimic, Yobot, RjwilmsiBot, Helpful Pixie Bot, Millertime246, WiFiEngineer, Monkbot and Anonymous: 1

- **Comparison of packet analyzers** *Source:* https://en.wikipedia.org/wiki/Comparison_of_packet_analyzers?oldid=661280378 *Contributors:* Guy Harris, GregorB, Bgwhite, Steppres, Jokes Free4Me, Connor Behan, Roshanpinto007, Jerryobject, Justin Piper, Akshaygs, Addbot, AnomieBOT, Amaury, WaldirBot, Yuanli.H, Bdijkstra, No1Jenny, WiFiEngineer, Jose Manuel Caballero, Captain Conundrum, ScotXW, Nancy.liu611, Sduffy34 and Anonymous: 24

- **Debookee** *Source:* https://en.wikipedia.org/wiki/Debookee?oldid=680776362 *Contributors:* Varnent, Yobot, WMartin74, Henrick63504 and Anonymous: 1

- **DRDO NETRA** *Source:* https://en.wikipedia.org/wiki/DRDO_NETRA?oldid=675945001 *Contributors:* Bearcat, Vsmith, Arthur Rubin, JohnInDC, Katharineamy, Trivialist, Mar4d, Anir1uph, GermanJoe, A1candidate, Batard0, BattyBot, Mrt3366, WBRSin, Lemnaminor, Wikiuser13, SkateTier and Anonymous: 8

- **DSniff** *Source:* https://en.wikipedia.org/wiki/DSniff?oldid=687656965 *Contributors:* Modster, Slusk, Joy, JosephBarillari, Hapsiainen, TheParanoidOne, Guy Harris, FlaBot, Shaddack, Ytcracker, JLaTondre, SmackBot, KVDP, Chris the speller, Nintendude, JonHarder, SMasters, Hu12, Sdistefano, Phatom87, Cydebot, Gabriel Lein, Jm3, Jdm64, Druiloor, Escarbot, Storkk, Cadsuane Melaidhrin, Asymmetric, Halofan.3, Muro Bot, 7, SF007, Mikeloco14, Addbot, Tothwolf, Yobot, Gladysv, Jfmantis, HiW-Bot, Palosirkka, Gnutoolbox, EdoBot, Richardo42, Snotbot, Rgelpke, Theopolisme, Nikolas342, ChrisGualtieri, TwoMartiniTuesday, Kmerk, Remietaccad and Anonymous: 22

- **Ettercap (software)** *Source:* https://en.wikipedia.org/wiki/Ettercap_(software)?oldid=670343676 *Contributors:* Glenn, Nikai, Rockear, Joy, Jonathan Drain, John Vandenberg, Acjelen, Wrs1864, Aero Leviathan, Woohookitty, FlaBot, IanManka, Voidxor, Kjak, Abune, SmackBot, Faisal.akeel, Gilliam, Frap, Mwtoews, KurtRaschke, Ergy, Unixguy, Thijs!bot, Krpors, FlamingSilmaril, Kl4m-AWB, M4gnum0n, SF007, Addbot, PlankBot, Axonizer, FrescoBot, Jfmantis, Sandharb, Hammadi2100, Spikeyrock, Klilidiplomus, BattyBot, Eduardofeld, LocutusOfBorg1, Idavmat, ScotXW and Anonymous: 33

- **Fiddler (software)** *Source:* https://en.wikipedia.org/wiki/Fiddler_(software)?oldid=682831345 *Contributors:* Nurg, Aledeniz, TonyW, John Vandenberg, Polluks, Mysdaao, Typhoonhurricane, Dialectric, NeilN, AndrewWTaylor, SmackBot, Xaosflux, Toddintr, Frap, OranL, Soumyasch, Dl2000, FleetCommand, Cayuga, Zian, Nick Number, Remember the dot, Jcislowski, Starofale, FindWindow, DaveNorthrup, Mortense, AnomieBOT, Friederbluemle, Iggymwangi, Lilydjwg, Hoo man, Anir1uph, +⬜⬜+⬜⬜, Chmarkine, 13375up4h4x0r, ChrisGualtieri, Monkbot, Mfnpka, Jaysonharris445, The Quixotic Potato and Anonymous: 33

- **FlowMon** *Source:* https://en.wikipedia.org/wiki/FlowMon?oldid=607213894 *Contributors:* RHaworth, Calaka, Xe7al, Download, Ondra.lengal, Springl and Filedelinkerbot

- **Glasswire** *Source:* https://en.wikipedia.org/wiki/Glasswire?oldid=675600062 *Contributors:* JL-Bot, Orenburg1, Zollerriia, Josve05a, 13375up4h4x0r, BattyBot, LowLevel73, NancyWazHere, Snaptabulous, Animal Triste and Anonymous: 3

- **Hping** *Source:* https://en.wikipedia.org/wiki/Hping?oldid=613412616 *Contributors:* Michael Hardy, Den fjättrade ankan~enwiki, Glenn, Joy, .mau., Mendaliv, HopeSeekr of xMule, Chris Chittleborough, SmackBot, Pegua, Frap, JonHarder, Neelix, Isilanes, JAnDbot, Kr4d, JonWinge, McM.bot, Wowbagger42, COBot, Kl4m-AWB, Addbot, DutchDevil, GrouchoBot, Jfmantis, Volker Siegel, The2014wiki and Anonymous: 10

- **HTTP Debugger** *Source:* https://en.wikipedia.org/wiki/HTTP_Debugger?oldid=671832514 *Contributors:* Guy Harris, Dsimic, Gorobay, BattyBot and Mfnpka

- **Ipsectrace** *Source:* https://en.wikipedia.org/wiki/Ipsectrace?oldid=674695253 *Contributors:* Woohookitty, SmackBot, Cydebot, Bunnyhop11, SDPatrolBot, RjwilmsiBot, Sross (Public Policy), Lsukari, Crazymonkey1123, Helpful Pixie Bot, BG19bot, Squishy Crayons, BattyBot and ChrisGualtieri

- **Ipswitch, Inc.** *Source:* https://en.wikipedia.org/wiki/Ipswitch%2C_Inc.?oldid=675951407 *Contributors:* Blaxthos, BD2412, Qwertyus, Rjwilmsi, SmackBot, Vajrang, Manorainjan, Tgeairn, Evanthx, De728631, Plasticspork, RjwilmsiBot, Faolin42, Alpha Quadrant, Vishsuri, Wbm1058, BG19bot, Kidneysrus and Anonymous: 6

- **Isyvmon** *Source:* https://en.wikipedia.org/wiki/Isyvmon?oldid=591710955 *Contributors:* Woohookitty, The Rambling Man, Cydebot, Wilhelmina Will, MrOllie, Palosirkka, Katicub, Helpful Pixie Bot, ChrisGualtieri, Captain Conundrum and Anonymous: 3

- **Justniffer** *Source:* https://en.wikipedia.org/wiki/Justniffer?oldid=687732057 *Contributors:* Guy Harris, Khazar, Cydebot, Nikthestunned, Reaper Eternal, GoingBatty, Alex6273 and Anonymous: 6

- **KisMAC** *Source:* https://en.wikipedia.org/wiki/KisMAC?oldid=627953515 *Contributors:* Glenn, K1Bond007, Centrx, AlistairMcMillan, D6, Twinxor, Gronky, Sandymac, Kiand, Apyule, Guy Harris, CyberSkull, BD2412, Trivial, Brianreading, Tas50, YurikBot, Brandon, Swanduck, SmackBot, Fulldecent, Ohnoitsjamie, Duozmo, Midnightcomm, T3h, Sigma 7, Arto B, Hamish2k, Otsego, Phatom87, Cydebot, Adriangm20, Dawnseeker2000, IlliterateSage, CommonsDelinker, Doggkruse, Antimatter666, Wondercow, DumZiBoT, MystBot, Addbot, AnomieBOT, Photographerguy, Nameless23, PigFlu Oink, DrilBot, Aoidh, Giannisf, ZéroBot, Sgrsudo, Netspotone, Dreamteamone, RogersDA 76 and Anonymous: 34

- **Kismet (software)** *Source:* https://en.wikipedia.org/wiki/Kismet_(software)?oldid=653044802 *Contributors:* Bdesham, Fvw, Garo, Matt Crypto, Godsmoke, Sam Hocevar, Boism, Gronky, Kb, Anthony Appleyard, Guy Harris, Alan Canon, Marudubshinki, Mysekurity, Dadu~enwiki, YurikBot, Ravedave, Sneftel, Siigna, Yvwv, SmackBot, Faisal.akeel, Whollabilla, Key134, Ohnoitsjamie, Mgeorg~enwiki, Frap, JonHarder, Midnightcomm, Jec, Hu12, Pmyteh, Remyrb, Jdm64, Siokaos, Dawnseeker2000, Lovibond, Foxb, Kerr avon, VolkovBot, WarddrBOT, NPrice, Martarius, Kl4m-AWB, DumZiBoT, MystBot, Addbot, Knowhands enjoykeep, Zorrobot, Luckas-bot, AnomieBOT, FrescoBot, SwineFlew?, Mpe3k, Aoidh, Wjlafrance, Giannisf, Widr, Dreamteamone and Anonymous: 42

- **Layer four traceroute** *Source:* https://en.wikipedia.org/wiki/Layer_four_traceroute?oldid=582374426 *Contributors:* RedWolf, Guy Harris, Essjay, Spasemunki, Hm2k, SmackBot, Bluebot, JonHarder, AnK, Gahs, Phatom87, DGG, R'n'B, MKoltnow, Wvonbraun, StaceyGrove, Addbot, Yobot, NJITgeek, BenzolBot, Vwvonbraun, Helpful Pixie Bot and Anonymous: 7

- **Lorcon** *Source:* https://en.wikipedia.org/wiki/Lorcon?oldid=659368456 *Contributors:* Glenn, Altenmann, Levin, Evert, MZMcBride, Vegaswikian, Tom5760, Damsleth, Teancum, Cydebot, Reedy Bot, Jaizovic, Dawynn, Hiihammuk, Erik9, EdoBot, Mark viking, Semsi Paco Virchow and Anonymous: 2

- **Microsoft Network Monitor** *Source:* https://en.wikipedia.org/wiki/Microsoft_Network_Monitor?oldid=677011037 *Contributors:* Xezbeth, Guy Harris, Riana, Ksnow, Geoff Wing, SmackBot, Chris the speller, Frap, OrphanBot, Ckatz, Alaibot, Faust.ua, CommonsDelinker, OsamaK, ImageRemovalBot, PaulELong, Steven.dai, BG19bot, Zeary and Anonymous: 20

- **Monitor mode** *Source:* https://en.wikipedia.org/wiki/Monitor_mode?oldid=687604166 *Contributors:* Spoon!, Guy Harris, Tabletop, Nagytibi, Dotancohen, Tony1, NetRolller 3D, SmackBot, Bluebot, Frap, Christan80, JonHarder, A5b, Jdm64, Dawnseeker2000, R'n'B, Le Piedbot~enwiki, Dsimic, Addbot, AnomieBOT, FrescoBot, Yuanli.H, ZéroBot, ClueBot NG, Sharino12345, WiFiEngineer, AlbusShin, Lesser Cartographies, Andres.tarasco and Anonymous: 26

- **MTR (software)** *Source:* https://en.wikipedia.org/wiki/MTR_(software)?oldid=687869386 *Contributors:* Htaccess, Joy, Isidore, Rich Farmbrough, Ynhockey, Blaxthos, Woohookitty, Dionyziz, Karam.Anthony.K, AlisonW, Quuxplusone, Intgr, Hm2k, SmackBot, Frap, JonHarder, Kvng, Playphil, Widefox, Storkk, Redrock5432, Tavix, Prolixium, Jerryobject, Niceguyedc, Muhandes, Miami33139, Addbot, Favonian, Luckas-bot, Natano, Cybjit, Marchash, ZéroBot, Romacities, SteveAyre, Beradsd, Ulf.renman, Epicgenius and Anonymous: 23
- **Multi Router Traffic Grapher** *Source:* https://en.wikipedia.org/wiki/Multi_Router_Traffic_Grapher?oldid=661021798 *Contributors:* Yaronf, Roadmr, Joy, Greudin, Nurg, EagleOne, Random contributor, Fleung, SniperBeamer~enwiki, Pforret, Blaxthos, Ott, Woohookitty, Broquaint, Саша Стефановић, FlaBot, YurikBot, Brookshawn, Hyphen1, Sandstein, KnightRider~enwiki, SmackBot, Reedy, Thumperward, Rene Mas, Frap, Shadow1, Mleinart, Hdkiller, Ksn, Roeme, Cydebot, Cmw1, Thijs!bot, Bobblehead, Druiloor, Lumbercutter, Progdev, Resonte, Stolsvik, Motley Fool, Reliablehosting, Schmiditwo~enwiki, VolkovBot, MenasimBot, Cjlittle, OKBot, Qji, Barkjon, PipepBot, Cambrasa, Kl4m-AWB, Fr3d org, 718 Bot, Three-quarter-ten, Addbot, Klaber, Tothwolf, Adamathefrog, SpBot, Sshipway, Geppa dee, Yakinew, KarikaSlayer and Anonymous: 42
- **Naemon** *Source:* https://en.wikipedia.org/wiki/Naemon?oldid=680848018 *Contributors:* PamD, Llorenzi, SwisterTwister, Strugee and BattyBot
- **Nagios** *Source:* https://en.wikipedia.org/wiki/Nagios?oldid=689592161 *Contributors:* Yaronf, Glenn, Daniel Quinlan, Andrewman327, Joy, RedWolf, Nurg, TMLutas, JesseW, Wereon, Pengo, Rick Block, AlistairMcMillan, Gadfium, Two Bananas, Elwell, Corti, D6, NightMonkey, Noisy, RossPatterson, Evert, Klykken, Samboy, Lucious, Asl, CanisRufus, Kop, Kwamikagami, Sietse Snel, Polluks, Maebmij, Pearle, Hooperbloob, Tookr, Mikeshk, Lystrata, Mrzaius, Demi, Forderud, SET, Bellenion, Deeahbz, Pol098, Bluemoose, Mayz, LimoWreck, Graham87, FlaBot, Ysangkok, Jrtayloriv, Costas Skarlatos, Tas50, Hm2k, NetVicious, Boinger, Brandon, Alpha 4615, Nachoman-au, Nagios~enwiki, Leuk he, Tom Morris, SmackBot, Reedy, Chutz, Chairman S., Eskimbot, Chris the speller, Thumperward, Sloanr, ADobkin, JGXenite, Frap, SQB, Kuru, Robofish, DynamicBits, Beefyt, Raysonho, Frederik Holden, Cydebot, Corpx, DumbBOT, Thijs!bot, Cain Mosni, Reswobslc, Dawnseeker2000, Bliksim, Glasnt, Vernetto, Deflective, Julio123, KagamiNoMiko, Srice13, Upholder, Japo, Vssun, Filik, Gwern, R'n'B, Jcalcote, NerdyNSK, Pshankland, Woudenberg, Brvman, Llorenzi, Ckoniecny, Stompersly, T sasahara, Cuddlyable3, Blurpeace, AbelChiaro, Ronmore, SieBot, TJRC, Netdiva, Rkarlsba, Treekids, Kl4m-AWB, Niceguyedc, Skittels, Plaes, DeltaQuad, KmiZole, SoxBot III, DumZiBoT, XLinkBot, Frood, Kirilln, Addbot, Jncraton, MrOllie, Jhein, Mro, Luckas-bot, AnomieBOT, Silvioricardoc, KingJ, Steavor, Pereant antiburchius, Craig.trader, Mark Renier, Uncopy, JayMGoldberg, Jandalhandler, Al3ph, Tbhotch, Olafski, Bento00, EmausBot, Naparuba, Lausser, Slightsmile, Socketubs, KuduIO, Emerime, Teh klev, Nagiosinc, Mstarr4, Widr, Dguenault, Tevkar, Helpful Pixie Bot, HMSSolent, Gsinghglakes, JohnChrysostom, MrOllie2, Scenebad, Msruzicka, Ph156, Dropnagios, Fheigl, Rahgu, AutomaticStrikeout, SoledadKabocha, ABC123twytom, Milesandkilometrestogo, Keepcalmangela, Captain Conundrum, Iamthemcmaster, Xuigh, Sabflik, 19kate96, ScotXW, Filedelinkerbot, Scarlettail, Dai Pritchard, KH-1, Netidy, KasparBot and Anonymous: 218
- **NeDi** *Source:* https://en.wikipedia.org/wiki/NeDi?oldid=588682770 *Contributors:* Bearcat, ErikHaugen, Blurpeace, Tide rolls, ArticlesForCreationBot, BattyBot, ChrisGualtieri, Rfkrishnan, Lovegagan, Unifiedgroup and Dawill2233
- **Nessus (software)** *Source:* https://en.wikipedia.org/wiki/Nessus_(software)?oldid=685728284 *Contributors:* Ixfd64, Pagingmrherman, Den fjättrade ankan~enwiki, Glenn, Nikai, Schneelocke, Nv8200pa, Joy, Yuenkitmun, Popebrak, Everyking, Sunny256, Finn-Zoltan, Neilc, Hgfernan, Bluefoxicy, ArnoldReinhold, Bishonen, Tr606~enwiki, Spearhead, Spoon!, Pearle, Hooperbloob, Guy Harris, H2g2bob, Deeahbz, Andymadigan, Who, AJR, Tas50, RussBot, Bachrach44, Fang Aili, Dveeden, DonutLover, Mike Gale, SmackBot, Pgk, Vm666~enwiki, Thumperward, JonHarder, Short Circuit, Mion, Ben Moore, Ehheh, Peyre, Hu12, Nczempin, Mblumber, A876, Kubanczyk, Thedarxide, 64bitz, RebelRobot, PhilKnight, Toutoune25, Magioladitis, Kr4d, Felipe1982, Captain panda, KylieTastic, VolkovBot, PaulKillingley, Sephiroth storm, Jericho347, Niceguyedc, Fossguy, Socrates2008, XLinkBot, Fkargl, Addbot, LaaknorBot, Peti610botH, OlEnglish, BaldPark, Yobot, Legobot II, AnomieBOT, Xqbot, Pradameinhoff, Locobot, Erik9, Jonesey95, Speakeasy2, JohnBBrookes, Super48paul, Oxeleo, Bomazi, Martin Dimitrov, Shajgs, ClueBot NG, Kasunchathuranga, Helpful Pixie Bot, Silverwindx, Calabe1992, Mariosegafreak, ChrisGualtieri, Hmainsbot1, Heavyglory2012, Krazy alice, Amitkankar, Monkbot, 69W2u8CnM6HPx4p6 and Anonymous: 82
- **Netcat** *Source:* https://en.wikipedia.org/wiki/Netcat?oldid=685209385 *Contributors:* Ellmist, Jimfbleak, Glenn, Joy, Chealer, Sverdrup, Techtonik, Tobias Bergemann, Qartis, Smurfix, Frencheigh, Rchandra, Vadmium, ThG, EagleOne, Thorwald, Antaeus Feldspar, Byrial, Lorn, CanisRufus, Sietse Snel, John Vandenberg, Polluks, Kundor, Furrybeagle, Wrs1864, SPUI, TheParanoidOne, Guy Harris, Interiot, Jesset77, Stephan Leeds, H2g2bob, KTC, Feezo, Mindmatrix, Myleslong, Rjwilmsi, Wiebel~enwiki, Gareth McCaughan, FlaBot, Family Guy Guy, Episiarch, Romanc19s, Welsh, HopeSeekr of xMule, The imp, `Orum, Cedar101, Xrblsnggt, Rurik, SmackBot, Incnis Mrsi, Bluebot, Thumperward, Carnesc, Frap, SmitherIsGod, Bauani, Sockseh, Netol, CmdrObot, PuerExMachina, Cydebot, Khatru2, Amists, SymlynX, Akb4, Druiloor, Calaka, Widefox, Prolog, Isilanes, JAnDbot, Magioladitis, Schily, Andreas Bischoff, Crh0872, Bamed, Gnot, IttanZ, Priyeshgpatel, Remember the dot, Bonadea, Scwerllguy, VolkovBot, Claym001, Inductiveload, Djmckee1, Tomalak geretkal, Nnkx00, Johnanth, Svick, ClueBot, Kl4m-AWB, Diegocr, XLinkBot, MystBot, Kace7, Addbot, Oracle Techie, Mortense, CL, LaaknorBot, P4p4 n0eL~enwiki, Pmj005, Luckas-bot, Bruceblacklaws, Efa, Apnicsolutions, Redraiment, Twindruff~enwiki, Pradameinhoff, Draganglumac, Axonizer, Samermaz, FrescoBot, Zero Thrust, Qbeep, I dream of horses, Hoo man, Diblidabliduu, Itu, Jesse V., DARTH SIDIOUS 2, Vadim s. sabinich~enwiki, Saifikhan, John of Reading, WikitanvirBot, Dewritech, Pavlixnet, Wikipiero, Mamaoyot, Voomoo, ClueBot NG, Kasirbot, BG19bot, Félix Wolf, Rousselmanu, Nohus, Rosslagerwall, Geir3542, Myconix, Kalsira, The2014wiki, Amortias, $n13lyWh1pl4zh, Jtbeckha and Anonymous: 170
- **NetCrunch** *Source:* https://en.wikipedia.org/wiki/NetCrunch?oldid=688855954 *Contributors:* Causa sui, Woohookitty, Absurdist, FlaBot, RussBot, Dialectric, JLaTondre, SmackBot, WilyD, EdGl, Mwtoews, Robofish, Cydebot, Rwiggum, CommonsDelinker, Pdeitiker, TXiKiBoT, Mild Bill Hiccup, Sun Creator, Carriearchdale, MystBot, Addbot, Yobot, Bunnyhop11, Glizza, GrouchoBot, Pasta party, FrescoBot, Ani2009, Captain Conundrum, Mrojek and Anonymous: 5
- **Netsniff-ng** *Source:* https://en.wikipedia.org/wiki/Netsniff-ng?oldid=667904691 *Contributors:* Guy Harris, Daniel.Cardenas, Phatom87, Cydebot, Mild Bill Hiccup, Trivialist, Yobot, Heddmj, BG19bot, Foob44r, Tklauser, ScotXW and Anonymous: 11
- **Network intelligence** *Source:* https://en.wikipedia.org/wiki/Network_intelligence?oldid=675890681 *Contributors:* Cydebot, TerrierHockey, Melcombe, Alexanderrock, OlEnglish, AnomieBOT, FrescoBot, Langloisgroup, Erik.larsson, Jessica Schieve, BG19bot, MichaelT.Culver and Anonymous: 6
- **Network Security Toolkit** *Source:* https://en.wikipedia.org/wiki/Network_Security_Toolkit?oldid=688239303 *Contributors:* Pnm, Glenn, Chealer, Brookie, Where next Columbus?, JLaTondre, SmackBot, E smith2000, Cydebot, R'n'B, Nemo bis, Technopat, RwhAlbany, ImageRemovalBot, Excirial, Arjayay, XLinkBot, Legobot, Yobot, Fraggle81, AnomieBOT, Rwhalb, Erik9, Zero Thrust, Skyerise, Paule1s, Tijfo098, Frietjes, Widr, Arunraj704, Loganathan Algoritz and Anonymous: 8

- **Network weathermap** *Source:* https://en.wikipedia.org/wiki/Network_weathermap?oldid=604844373 *Contributors:* Discospinster, Magioladitis, Palosirkka, BattyBot and Nsb83

- **Ngrep** *Source:* https://en.wikipedia.org/wiki/Ngrep?oldid=689387780 *Contributors:* Glenn, ZZyXx, OoberMick, Hns~enwiki, Woohookitty, IanManka, Gaius Cornelius, Kimchi.sg, SmackBot, Thornrag, Phatom87, Cydebot, JNW, R'n'B, FrescoBot, Jesse V., Jfmantis, Slon02, Palosirkka, Wikiax4, Excitator, Wbm1058, Hmcaun and Anonymous: 21

- **Nimsoft** *Source:* https://en.wikipedia.org/wiki/Nimsoft?oldid=689446504 *Contributors:* Rich Farmbrough, Alansohn, JLaTondre, Skysurfer, Kuru, Nick Number, Magioladitis, Jojalozzo, Wilhelmina Will, Beeblebrox, Niceguyedc, Aleksd, Rbudde, Qthrul, Addbot, Thaejas, LaaknorBot, Luckas-bot, Bunnyhop11, RevelationDirect, W Nowicki, EmausBot, WikitanvirBot, SkNs, Matthiaspaul, HDReport, Lockwoodl, Basway2005, Plrowe, UmairMKhan and Anonymous: 12

- **Nmap** *Source:* https://en.wikipedia.org/wiki/Nmap?oldid=688923328 *Contributors:* AxelBoldt, Michael Hardy, Ixfd64, Egil, Glenn, Marteau, Slusk, Nikai, Evercat, Dysprosia, Enigmasoldier, Joy, Secretlondon, Robbot, Chealer, Carnildo, Honta, Fennec, Taviso, Frencheigh, Finn-Zoltan, Eequor, Madcow, Thomas Springer, Am088, Ojw, Cky, M1ss1ontomars2k4, Thorwald, Porges, Hinrik, Bender235, Spoon!, .:Ajvol:., Kappa, Csabo, Computerjoe, Martian, Njk, Woohookitty, Mindmatrix, Apokrif, Easyas12c, Hbdragon88, Mandarax, BD2412, Jclemens, Ketiltrout, Bratch, FlaBot, Mister Matt, Nihiltres, Maustrauser, GreyCat, Kedadi, Ahunt, Jmorgan, Chobot, DVdm, YurikBot, Borgx, RussBot, Bachrach44, Gadget850, Kjak, HopeSeekr of xMule, Walterk29, SmackBot, Faisal.akeel, Gilliam, Korvar, Bluebot, Thumperward, Pegua, Frap, NoExec, BWDuncan, Marc-André Aßbrock, Ktdreyer, Jay.slovak, Bilboq, Ryanjunk, Hu12, Ojan, JoeBot, Requestion, Arrenlex, Equendil, Cydebot, Croikle, Gimmetrow, Thijs!bot, Druiloor, Dawnseeker2000, LachlanA, Gioto, Isilanes, Lfstevens, I80and, Magioladitis, Cadsuane Melaidhrin, GODhack~enwiki, Kr4d, JonWinge, Gwern, Blitzinteractive, Nunojpg, Felipe1982, Captain panda, Ian.thomson, Bektur, Goarany, Phsyc0recon, WOSlinker, Technopat, Felmon, Ziounclesi, Gillyweed, Falcon8765, Ulf Abrahamsson~enwiki, Daniel Roethlisberger, Ub3rst4r, Hestonk, PeterCanthropus, Zemoxian, Sephiroth storm, Wageslave, Ddxc, Janfri, Dp67, MrValdez, Kl4m-AWB, SF007, DumZiBoT, Bodhisattvabot, Addbot, Chakkalokesh, Mortense, Download, AndersBot, Favonian, Lightbot, Jack who built the house, Luckas-bot, Yobot, 4thotaku, AnomieBOT, Killiondude, Materialscientist, ArthurBot, Xqbot, Lookyboop4lyfe, S0aasdf2sf, Jspa, Pradameinhoff, Mark Renier, Citation bot 1, Deetah, LauraHale, Spidey104, Jacorream, Hoo man, Fluffy 543, McHildinger, DixonDBot, SubtractM, Jfmantis, RjwilmsiBot, Identime123, J36miles, EmausBot, WikitanvirBot, Ajraddatz, GoingBatty, Mo ainm, MikeyMouse10, 15turnsm, Yurisk, DoesNotFollow, Staszek Lem, Palosirkka, Bomazi, ChuispastonBot, Mark Martinec, Vineet2304, Star destroyer1960, Patrias, Widr, Helpful Pixie Bot, Tomko222, BG19bot, Bonsaiwiking, Mark Arsten, SmagR59R60R61, Lambda Magician, Rolve, Wj2dy, DarafshBot, Faisal ALbarrak, Jhouse36606, Hksamuello, Dr Dinosaur IV, Tilikammon, Bitobor, Ahtesham088, JaconaFrere, Trevelyn412, Mipiro and Anonymous: 130

- **Ntop** *Source:* https://en.wikipedia.org/wiki/Ntop?oldid=683776184 *Contributors:* Glenn, Steve Abrahall, Angelo.romano, JohnEnok, Oges007, Melancholie, SmackBot, BiT, Frap, OrphanBot, FlyHigh, Krishna.pothula, Underpants, Vernetto, Emeraude, PixelBot, SilvonenBot, Addbot, EjsBot, LarryJeff, Etrillaud, Jguarino, Encycloshave, BG19bot, BattyBot and Anonymous: 13

- **Ntopng** *Source:* https://en.wikipedia.org/wiki/Ntopng?oldid=587530972 *Contributors:* Technopat, James.tantalo, LittleWink and Anonymous: 2

- **OmniPeek** *Source:* https://en.wikipedia.org/wiki/OmniPeek?oldid=640745557 *Contributors:* Arpingstone, Peruvianllama, AlistairMcMillan, John Vandenberg, Guy Harris, Scoutersig, SmackBot, Roger Davies, Watson Ladd, Unixguy, Jokes Free4Me, Cydebot, Eastmain, SpacePacket, R'n'B, Skier Dude, Psmith811, TubularWorld, Niceguyedc, Jerrysmith222, W Nowicki, My007ms, RjwilmsiBot, GoingBatty, Fredeccles, Nancy.liu611 and Anonymous: 8

- **Openkore** *Source:* https://en.wikipedia.org/wiki/Openkore?oldid=662233514 *Contributors:* Dreamyshade, Woohookitty, Rjwilmsi, FlaBot, RussBot, Rwalker, JLaTondre, SmackBot, BullRangifer, Woodroar, Cydebot, R'n'B, ImageRemovalBot, 718 Bot, Rror, Addbot, Yobot, Evaders99, Yowuza, Holoc, LilHelpa, Ultrasux555, FrescoBot, LucienBOT, Citation bot 1, Diwas, DrilBot, John of Reading, GoingBatty, H3llBot, Palosirkka, Openkoreuser, BG19bot, Botfest, Sharewaredown, ScotXW, Monkbot, Prisencolin, DerryAdama and Anonymous: 18

- **OpenVAS** *Source:* https://en.wikipedia.org/wiki/OpenVAS?oldid=687793546 *Contributors:* Den fjättrade ankan~enwiki, Johnleach, Derobert, Marudubshinki, SmackBot, Bluebot, DStoykov, Snori, Frap, Mion, Evolutionaryit.com, Thijs!bot, LazyEditor, Sjwk, Paxcoder, TXiKiBoT, Mmairs, Dojcubic, Kl4m-AWB, Addbot, DantE Mike, Yobot, EmausBot, ZéroBot, ChuispastonBot, Zakiakhmad, Tababala and Anonymous: 32

- **PA Server Monitor** *Source:* https://en.wikipedia.org/wiki/PA_Server_Monitor?oldid=651786966 *Contributors:* BD2412, Johnbryanpeters, Drumlineramos, Drmies, Rankersbo, L235, BG19bot, Mdann52, Spencet, Dnebeker and Anonymous: 2

- **Packet analyzer** *Source:* https://en.wikipedia.org/wiki/Packet_analyzer?oldid=685180258 *Contributors:* AxelBoldt, Manaskb, B4hand, Edward, Ahoerstemeier, Glenn, Selket, Saltine, Omegatron, Joy, RedWolf, Moondyne, Nurg, JosephBarillari, Giftlite, Omegium, Idril, Paulfeakins, Frencheigh, Gracefool, AlistairMcMillan, Maximaximax, Lucanos, Lostchicken, Kate, Gazpacho, Discospinster, Rich Farmbrough, Rhobite, Ninjaktty, RJHall, Wipe, Hooperbloob, Dhar, Qwghlm, Guy Harris, Rick Sidwell, Paul1337, Faithtear, Kgrr, Btyner, Casey Abell, Jake Wartenberg, FlaBot, Jrtayloriv, Intgr, Chobot, YurikBot, Brookshawn, RobotE, Hairy Dude, CesarB's unpriviledged account, Jpbowen, Voidxor, Getcrunk, Abune, Neilbmartin, Mebden, Luk, Veinor, SmackBot, Haza-w, Hydrogen Iodide, Bjelleklang, Unyoyega, KVDP, Thumperward, Bradyok, DHN-bot~enwiki, Frap, NoExec, Addshore, Midnightcomm, UU, Wirbelwind, Jeffmcfarland, Ryan Roos, Drphilharmonic, Bogsat, Lambiam, Dirtydan667, Negrulio, Kvng, Newman9997, Hu12, Huntscorpio, Tawkerbot2, Wafulz, Imcdnzl, Pgr94, Brooks.filmond, Badseed, Cydebot, Trevor d, Gogo Dodo, Corpx, Thijs!bot, Jdm64, Paquitotrek, Dawnseeker2000, Malcolm, Gundark, Ioeth, NapoliRoma, Seddon, Gerald.combs, VoABot II, MartinBot, Anaxial, AlphaEta, J.delanoy, Mange01, MarkFrancisMullins, NI Team, FJPB, Ron shelf, Squids and Chips, VolkovBot, Kk2mkk, Mantipula, EGSchwartz, Kai, Netmoninc, Calmcz, Nmatpt, Smsarmad, Vidiii, Martyvis, Steven Crossin, Tmaufer, Justin Piper, ClueBot, PaulELong, Dgrahame, Ppike, Marksza, M4gnum0n, Colasoft capsa, Andponomarev, Johnuniq, XLinkBot, Gbelknap, MystBot, Mudalagi, Deineka, Addbot, Chakkalokesh, Djsuess, MrOllie, Dky89, Legobot, Luckas-bot, Ec2049, Jerrysmith222, Pcap, Nallimbot, Rogger.Ferguson, Diodime, AnomieBOT, Bobier, Rwhalb, Xqbot, GrouchoBot, Amaury, FrescoBot, Wheet, BayTech, Haeinous, Tammyzhou1983, Piandcompany, Banej, Networked, MarkmacVSS, Kthnxrick, Yuanli.H, Dalba, Netcrash87, EmausBot, Gfoley4, Nitiniit, ZéroBot, AManWithNoPlan, No1Jenny, Roy2009, Smithwillscott, Wpifer, ClueBot NG, Satellizer, Mesoderm, Bezzm, Helpful Pixie Bot, Christophernoland, Wbm1058, Alex6273, Nop1984, Guy.talbot, Comfr, WiFiEngineer, Bgibbs2, TimMouraveiko, Kn330wn, Jose Manuel Caballero, Dave Braunschweig, Bailey402, Nancy.liu611, Chrisliom, Mfnpka, Sduffy34, Lrobertshaw, KasparBot and Anonymous: 252

- **Packet crafting** *Source:* https://en.wikipedia.org/wiki/Packet_crafting?oldid=683451571 *Contributors:* Woohookitty, Spaceman85, DVdm, Frap, JonHarder, Macha, Prozhen, R'n'B, Annandale, Jeff G., VVVBot, Socrates2008, Johnuniq, Chakkalokesh, Yobot, FrescoBot, Leet Sher, Grahamca31 and Anonymous: 11

- **Packet generator** *Source:* https://en.wikipedia.org/wiki/Packet_generator?oldid=683604126 *Contributors:* Bearcat, Amorymeltzer, Pegship, SmackBot, Frap, Teancum, Cydebot, Thomas d stewart, Biscuittin, Jaizovic, XLinkBot, Addbot, Chakkalokesh, Luckas-bot, Yobot, Yuanli.H, GoingBatty, Shilpi2809, Let4time, Kasirbot, Cxxxap, WiFiEngineer, Simplepacket, Nancy.liu611, The2014wiki, KH-1 and Anonymous: 32

- **Packet Sender** *Source:* https://en.wikipedia.org/wiki/Packet_Sender?oldid=677579397 *Contributors:* DavidCary, Frap, Yobot, Tucoxn, LittleWink, BG19bot, Timothyjaden, The2014wiki, Q5W5 and Anonymous: 1

- **Packetsquare** *Source:* https://en.wikipedia.org/wiki/Packetsquare?oldid=687668005 *Contributors:* Rich Farmbrough, Bender235, Guy Harris, Woohookitty, Ber, Jerome Charles Potts, Frap, CBM, Cydebot, Trvth, AnomieBOT, FrescoBot, Shilpi2809, Vijaymohanb4u, BattyBot, ScotXW and Anonymous: 1

- **PacketTrap** *Source:* https://en.wikipedia.org/wiki/PacketTrap?oldid=683447972 *Contributors:* Sole Soul, Guy Harris, Mayz, DVdm, Gadget850, SmackBot, Xaosflux, Pierretapia, Stwalkerster, CmdrObot, Click23, Dawnseeker2000, Smartse, Magioladitis, Bonadea, Omniadeo, Npd2983, SummerWithMorons, Mild Bill Hiccup, 718 Bot, C628, XLinkBot, Networkengine, Chakkalokesh, Corporate4, Zulon, Yobot, Legobot II, Capricorn42, DrilBot, Ovenlight, ClueBot NG, Arg342, Smmgeek, MSPguy, 069952497a, ClydeWBennett, Thewikiguru1, Nicky mathew, Jphxm and Anonymous: 20

- **Paessler Router Traffic Grapher** *Source:* https://en.wikipedia.org/wiki/Paessler_Router_Traffic_Grapher?oldid=631329082 *Contributors:* Joy, Aledeniz, EagleOne, TheParanoidOne, Fritz Saalfeld, Brookshawn, Dpaessler, FF2010, SmackBot, A. B., JonHarder, David Legrand, Cmw1, Alaibot, Iam8up, Falcon8765, BDJason, Robbie098, Popperian, Addbot, Dinamik-bot, Anton555a and Anonymous: 12

- **Panorama9** *Source:* https://en.wikipedia.org/wiki/Panorama9?oldid=580104106 *Contributors:* Rich Farmbrough, Heywoodg, XLinkBot, Yobot, AnomieBOT, Ramblersen, Linguisticgeek, John of Reading, Allanthorvaldsen, ClueBot NG, Athorvaldsen, BattyBot, ChrisGualtieri, SFK2 and Anonymous: 3

- **Paping** *Source:* https://en.wikipedia.org/wiki/Paping?oldid=651804503 *Contributors:* Topbanana, MSGJ, Bender235, Cydebot, Magioladitis, Terrek, Someguy1221, Favonian, Yobot, FrescoBot, John of Reading, Codhubiv and Anonymous: 2

- **PathPing** *Source:* https://en.wikipedia.org/wiki/PathPing?oldid=655840063 *Contributors:* CesarB, Markhurd, HappyDog, Fuelbottle, AlistairMcMillan, Tagishsimon, Pt, HasharBot~enwiki, The RedBurn, DVdm, NymphadoraTonks, Hm2k, Xpclient, Cedar101, DoriSmith, SmackBot, Aaron of Mpls, Bluebot, Warren, Hu12, Mator, Cydebot, Playphil, A876, Detroit, Kozuch, Tedickey, N3ddy, Billinghurst, Rustic, Rainwulf, Addbot, Ghettoblaster, Austro, FrescoBot, Christoph hausner, Strcat, Frietjes, ChrisGualtieri, Bastianboss, Codename Lisa, Sriram872012 and Anonymous: 24

- **Pcap** *Source:* https://en.wikipedia.org/wiki/Pcap?oldid=689629328 *Contributors:* Glenn, Danhuby, Unfree, Joconnor, Gdt, Spoon!, Christian Kreibich, John Vandenberg, Helix84, Guy Harris, Feb30th1712, KJK::Hyperion, FvdM, Armando, NeoChaosX, Meneth, BD2412, Tizio, Intersofia, Jmorgan, Falcon9x5, Chrisholland, Raistolo, SmackBot, Od Mishehu, Twillgoo, Xaosflux, Thumperward, Frap, Pcharles, Errorx666, Arkrishna, Hu12, Cydebot, Thijs!bot, N5iln, Jdm64, Isilanes, .anacondabot, Think outside the box, Lukeaw, Gwern, Wstearns, SimonDoherty, PhilipMcGurk, Iida-yosiaki, VolkovBot, BlackVegetable, Iwantaceaseletter, Belamp, Frxstrem, Sephiroth storm, Tmaufer, Deflator, Mpeylo, PaulELong, Kl4m-AWB, M4gnum0n, NBPat, Johnuniq, XLinkBot, MystBot, Addbot, MissFluffyCat, Chakkalokesh, TheJH, Thierry-44, Millerlai, Luckas-bot, Ptbotgourou, Jerrysmith222, IRP, Cyril Wack, Marchash, Kkj11210, Informationh0b0, Trac3R, SwineFlew?, Cnwilliams, Ayeowch, Dc987, Jesse V., Jfmantis, EmausBot, ZéroBot, Shilpi2809, Aavindraa, DennisIsMe, Xeraph0, Jhpotter123, 4368a, Timlyo, BattyBot, Doors5678, Mattjonkman, Smitmartijn, Sanincredible and Anonymous: 96

- **Ping (networking utility)** *Source:* https://en.wikipedia.org/wiki/Ping_(networking_utility)?oldid=686700550 *Contributors:* WojPob, Tuxisuau, Zundark, Mark, Drj, Shii, Mbecker, Frecklefoot, JohnOwens, Liftarn, MartinHarper, Breakpoint, Ahoerstemeier, Haakon, Glenn, Netsnipe, Rotem Dan, Evercat, Htaccess, Dysprosia, Wik, Furrykef, Nv8200pa, SEWilco, Joy, Francs2000, JorgeGG, Paranoid, RedWolf, ZekeMacNeil, Auric, Bkell, Mdrejhon, Rsduhamel, Tobias Bergemann, Ancheta Wis, Connelly, DocWatson42, Jimjoe, Marcika, Raph, Malbear, Joconnor, Frencheigh, Robbrown, Tagishsimon, Neilc, Yath, Gordoni, Dnas, Robert Brockway, Taka, Sam Hocevar, Rgrg, Jcw69, EagleOne, Generica, Mike Rosoft, Mormegil, DanielCD, Swedophile, Discospinster, Twinxor, Pmsyyz, Vsmith, Max Terry, Bootedcat, Perfecto, Bobo192, Shnout, Toh, A Wikipedia user from Minnesota, Krellis, Alansohn, Gary, Mo0, Nealcardwell, Jeltz, Andrewpmk, Burn, Neilmckillop, Tribh, Szumyk, Cburnett, Danhash, RainbowOfLight, Dan100, Ceyockey, Japanese Searobin, Woohookitty, Mindmatrix, Scjessey, WadeSimMiser, Gniw, Tjbk tjb, Pete142, Ashmoo, Graham87, Magister Mathematicae, Tzadikv, JIP, JamesBurns, Mendaliv, Josh Parris, Sjö, Vary, Tangotango, Nneonneo, AlisonW, Nguyen Thanh Quang, Aegican~enwiki, Aveekbh, FlaBot, Pumeleon, Ewlyahoocom, Gurch, ElfQrin, Alvin-cs, Tnarb, SirGrant, Garas, Theymos, YurikBot, Calamari, NTBot~enwiki, Icarus3, Bhny, Stephenb, NawlinWiki, DragonHawk, Hm2k, Gzabers, Uni4dfx, Mortein, Dhollm, Larsinio, Vlad, DeadEyeArrow, ReneGarcia, Yudiweb, Ebarrett, Bdmcmahon, Graciella, Fie, JasonXV, Closedmouth, Arthur Rubin, Cedar101, Spliffy, Sneftel, Toniher, Mdwyer, Chris Chittleborough, MacsBug, Yakudza, DNSstuff, SmackBot, Gregory finster, Direvus, Reedy, Royalguard11, CrazyTerabyte, Btm, Anastrophe, VxP, Eskimbot, Vilerage, Nil Einne, Csab, Skizzik, KD5TVI, DanPope, Thumperward, Liamdaly620, SchfiftyThree, Robocoder, Titera, WeniWidiWiki, Octahedron80, Darth Panda, TheGerm, Frap, OrphanBot, Lantrix, JonHarder, DGerman, Radagast83, Nakon, Mistamagic28, Shadow1, Esb, Daniel.Cardenas, Mion, J.smith, Zac67, Autopilot, Kuzaar, Vanished user 9i39j3, Gingaman, This user has left wikipedia, Ninnnu~enwiki, Akhilsharma86, SunAdmin111, Ckatz, Beetstra, EdC~enwiki, Jpbisguier, Kvng, Dl2000, Hu12, Iridescent, ToastyMallows, Pimlottc, Daveyork, Tawkerbot2, Deathvader, StephenFalken, FatalError, CmdrObot, John Switzer, Rohan2kool, Cydebot, Karimarie, Mblumber, A876, Gogo Dodo, Tawkerbot4, Zzsql, Joseph.leahy@gmail.com, JoeMK, Papajohnin, JohnInDC, Thijs!bot, Mojo Hand, E. Ripley, Druiloor, Sam42, AntiVandalBot, Bradycardia, Prolog, Lugiadoom, Darklilac, Alphachimpbot, Dman727, JAnDbot, MER-C, LeedsKing, Jahoe, Toutoune25, Ideoplex, Bongwarrior, VoABot II, Cic, Schily, VegKilla, PaulDon, Vssun, Kgfleischmann, Einhov, UnfriendlyFire, Peros038, R'n'B, Mycroft7, Huzzlet the bot, J.delanoy, Tannerbrockwell, Amitlovestosurf, Dispenser, Silas S. Brown, FunnyMonkey101, Polnian, Ts1and2fanatic, Jrs363, Remember the dot, Er.punit, Halmstad, Inetpup, Tawlboy, Dwlegg, LeilaniLad, Chsandeep, TXiKiBoT, EvanCarroll, Dictouray, Jason C.K., Ziounclesi, ErikWarmelink, Jhawkinson, Spinningspark, Demize, Runewiki777, Kbrose, Tauriel-1, Technion, Weeliljimmy, Rockstone35, Adrian13, Yeohlee06, Tiptoety, Oxymoron83, Ddxc, MahoneyUK, Bluesonic43, HighInBC, Wiknerd, Jons63, ImageRemovalBot, WikiBotas, Elassint, ClueBot, Torchwood Four, Abaumgar, The Thing That

Should Not Be, Alksentrs, T3hBra1nWa5her, Rjd0060, Number774, Webmaster4india, Control-alt-delete, Trioculus, Boing! said Zebedee, Blanchardb, Jwz, Occamsrzr, Cillie, Daveisrategud, Timsdad, Fuzzymoochicken, Error49, Jotterbot, Cory Donnelly, Thingg, Aitias, Egmontaz, The Zig, Miami33139, XLinkBot, Spitfire, Yanksfanatic2000, A63falcon, C. A. Russell, NellieBly, Mifter, Khaleel 1345, MystBot, Dsimic, Addbot, Ghettoblaster, Mabdul, Ronhjones, HobbitAndy, Dov Jacobson, 0pen$0urce, LaaknorBot, Gxchaos, Favonian, Comphelper12, InvincibleMario, Тиверополник, Tide rolls, Lightbot, م,انی, Zorrobot, Luckas-bot, Yobot, Themfromspace, OrgasGirl, Ptbotgourou, GDI Commando, THEN WHO WAS PHONE?, KamikazeBot, TestEditBot, Thabonch, AnomieBOT, Vikasminda, Floquenbeam, Parinphoenix, Galoubet, Kingpin13, Flewis, Aneah, Tfewster, Tbvdm, LilHelpa, Andrewmc123, Xqbot, TheAMmollusc, 4twenty42o, Appy123, XAakashx, Lrdiver, Gnuish, FrescoBot, Dilic, Oldlaptop321, Qbeep, Chiranjiv wikian, Maher27777, Pinethicket, Todd Peng, MatthewGreber, RedBot, SpaceFlight89, Mr.opc, FoxBot, Lotje, Reaper Eternal, Jhenderson777, Prodeji, TheMesquito, Minimac, Deluxebgn, Ravinlv, WikitanvirBot, Immunize, Nevillespade, Tarayzaminpar, DiiCinta, Blin00, JosJuice, Donner60, Bgenzoli, Prudhvi09, Ebehn, Lilprincesskrishna, Voomoo, Shaynarsey, ClueBot NG, Nimiew, Yournansarm, Widr, Chint82, Helpful Pixie Bot, Tumicking, Epicping, PaganPanzerfaust, Benpul, Mihir6692, Andrewvlk88, Eidab, Billie usagi, Mdann52, Th4n3r, Cjhoare1, None but shining hours, Rds33, Patrickjonasfletcher, Faizann20, Rezonansowy, Webclient101, Hksamuello, FenixFeather, Jshjdcb, XDroubay, ZipperJam, Nancy.liu611, Aaniya B, Paravizal, Ajiratech, Vaibspider, Uwinsoftware and Anonymous: 569

- **Pirni** *Source:* https://en.wikipedia.org/wiki/Pirni?oldid=651803360 *Contributors:* Gadfium, Bender235, Guy Harris, RussBot, Dialectric, Jerryobject, Steamroller Assault, Tassedethe, AnomieBOT, Axel.moller, Phitantic, BattyBot and Anonymous: 1

- **Plink** *Source:* https://en.wikipedia.org/wiki/Plink?oldid=688656593 *Contributors:* Glenn, Bauani, Widefox, Magioladitis, Tedickey, Adrinolink, AnomieBOT, MenoBot II, Palosirkka, Jodosma, PerlMonk Athanasius and Anonymous: 1

- **Plixer International** *Source:* https://en.wikipedia.org/wiki/Plixer_International?oldid=653520836 *Contributors:* Chowbok, Ceyockey, Rsrikanth05, Ekjon Lok, Ken Gallager, Fences and windows, Ttonyb1, NuclearWarfare, XLinkBot, Materialscientist, Sammael 42, Lahnfeear, Fowartehlluz, Pw1208, SchreyP, Mean as custard, Alpha Quadrant, BG19bot, Laurasmith13 and Anonymous: 3

- **Prefix WhoIs** *Source:* https://en.wikipedia.org/wiki/Prefix_WhoIs?oldid=532137709 *Contributors:* Zundark, SmackBot, Cydebot, Auntof6, MuffledThud, HamburgerRadio, Vwvonbraun, Palosirkka, BG19bot and Anonymous: 1

- **Promiscuous mode** *Source:* https://en.wikipedia.org/wiki/Promiscuous_mode?oldid=679224792 *Contributors:* The Anome, B4hand, Shellreef, Dcoetzee, Saltine, Betterworld, Joy, Flockmeal, GPHemsley, Aenar, Chris 73, Drago9034, ElBenevolente, Tieno, Pgan002, John Vandenberg, Dreish, Cohesion, Blotwell, Jcsutton, Guy Harris, Cjcollier, Lightdarkness, Amelia Hunt, Woohookitty, Elvey, Flarn2006, Margosbot~enwiki, Brookshawn, Jeremy Visser, SmackBot, MalafayaBot, Frap, Christan80, JonHarder, T.J. Crowder, UU, Diman011, Jdm64, Gnitset, R'n'B, Felipe1982, Buhadram, VolkovBot, Tburket, Jon-emery, Jamelan, BryKKan, Poindexter Propellerhead, Qhalilipa, ClueBot, StenSoft, Excirial, Sun Creator, Mlaffs, Funtaff, XLinkBot, Addbot, Graham.Fountain, LaaknorBot, Legobot II, AnomieBOT, ArthurBot, Xqbot, Shadowjams, Erik9bot, TobeBot, Tbhotch, Yuanli.H, ZéroBot, AManWithNoPlan, Gz33, ClueBot NG, Jau53, Bezzm, Douglas Saraiva, TheyCallMeHeartbreaker, AvocatoBot, WiFiEngineer, Doors5678, SoledadKabocha, Dave Braunschweig, AbhishekGoel137, Subodhsaxena, Castlecorp and Anonymous: 81

- **PRTG Network Monitor** *Source:* https://en.wikipedia.org/wiki/PRTG_Network_Monitor?oldid=679247382 *Contributors:* Malcolma, SmackBot, PKT, Qji, Johnuniq, Anton555a, Liam McM, Makecat, Lengfelder, BattyBot, GreatMarkO, Muxorphos, Br4nislav, SKYFRAME and Anonymous: 16

- **SAINT (software)** *Source:* https://en.wikipedia.org/wiki/SAINT_(software)?oldid=636757831 *Contributors:* C Fenijn, Chowbok, Apotheon, Naraht, SmackBot, Gobonobo, Hroðulf, Cadsuane Melaidhrin, SkeletorUK, DanielPharos, Anon126, Addbot, Dawynn, Pradameinhoff, Erik9, Thecheesykid, CaroleinVirginia, Morphyis, ChrisGualtieri, Unician, Rlaudermilk and Anonymous: 8

- **ScienceLogic** *Source:* https://en.wikipedia.org/wiki/ScienceLogic?oldid=655079387 *Contributors:* Discospinster, LtNOWIS, Kintetsubuffalo, Manticore, MystBot, Addbot, Yobot, FrescoBot, Plasticspork, Brian Boyko, BG19bot, Cclowney, Cethomp6, Probablyyou, Adena613, Mcclntck and Anonymous: 3

- **Security Administrator Tool for Analyzing Networks** *Source:* https://en.wikipedia.org/wiki/Security_Administrator_Tool_for_Analyzing_Networks?oldid=689159489 *Contributors:* Chlor~enwiki, Wwwwolf, Sakshale, Glenn, Discospinster, Echuck215, Redfarmer, Kay Dekker, Graham87, Naraht, Marlow4, IanManka, Romal, The Halo, Twintop, SmackBot, Yuyudevil, JonHarder, Soap, Meco, Cydebot, Epbr123, Jm3, Dfrg.msc, Toutoune25, Magioladitis, JNW, Kr4d, MartinBot, Speck-Made, Sesshomaru, SieBot, AngelOfSadness, Excirial, Alexbot, Socrates2008, Addbot, Dawynn, Thierry-44, Teles, AnomieBOT, Jim1138, 9258fahsflkh917fas, Ctdisgay0, Enorelbot, WikitanvirBot, Starcheerspeaksnewslostwars, ZéroBot, Palosirkka, AaronBStephens, ClueBot NG, Aaronbob95, Pangean, Steven.dai, Morphyis, BG19bot, Imjesus09, Monkbot, Unician and Anonymous: 34

- **Shinken (software)** *Source:* https://en.wikipedia.org/wiki/Shinken_(software)?oldid=689592118 *Contributors:* Levin, Kenyon, Marasmusine, Skierpage, JLaTondre, SmackBot, Chris the speller, Thumperward, Cydebot, Ozzieboy, Xhienne, Llorenzi, Addbot, MrOllie, Luckas-bot, Yobot, AnomieBOT, LucienBOT, JnRouvignac, EmausBot, John of Reading, Naparuba, Lausser, Emerime, EdoBot, Delusion23, Nagiosinc, ChrisGualtieri, ITexp, ABC123twytom, Captain Conundrum, Wdv4758h, Helios crucible, Norvoid and Anonymous: 16

- **SNMPTT** *Source:* https://en.wikipedia.org/wiki/SNMPTT?oldid=689017189 *Contributors:* SmackBot, Cydebot, Xhienne, Sam Barsoom, Addbot, FrescoBot, Alex b99, Captain Conundrum and Anonymous: 1

- **Snoop (software)** *Source:* https://en.wikipedia.org/wiki/Snoop_(software)?oldid=603815954 *Contributors:* Boism, Pmsyyz, Guy Harris, Frap, Kukini, Raysonho, Cydebot, NapoliRoma, Glastation, VolkovBot, Addbot, Canberranone, Yutsi, Full-date unlinking bot and Anonymous: 8

- **SolarWinds** *Source:* https://en.wikipedia.org/wiki/SolarWinds?oldid=687783690 *Contributors:* Ronz, Pmsyyz, Jeffkramer, Bgwhite, TexasAndroid, Malcolma, SmackBot, Takamaxa, FleetCommand, CmdrObot, Ken Gallager, PKT, Tony in Devon, FisherQueen, Shortride, Truthanado, Pjoef, ClueBot, Niceguyedc, Alexbot, Svgalbertian, Lefton4ya, Addbot, Corporate4, Jaromir Adamek, AnomieBOT, J04n, Lahnfeear, Fowartehlluz, Mario777Zelda, Kparsons08, Jinxynix, CorporateM, Erik9bot, FrescoBot, Mdelavina, Karebear 1022, John of Reading, Alpha Quadrant, AndyAgr, Smmgeek, BG19bot, Lcn0015, Lifeboatvad, Beto1010, Mrojek, Maryrose 92354, Scarlettail, BryanCoggins, JP1453, IdlePlayground, PardonTheComma and Anonymous: 32

- **Sparrowiq** *Source:* https://en.wikipedia.org/wiki/Sparrowiq?oldid=683447968 *Contributors:* DVdm, Hebrides, R'n'B, Squids and Chips, Chakkalokesh, Hads1, Palosirkka, Sosthenes12, Bangalore-chennai and Anonymous: 1

- **SQLFilter** *Source:* https://en.wikipedia.org/wiki/SQLFilter?oldid=421971650 *Contributors:* Rholton, Bluebot, Ryan Roos, Cydebot, Invitatious, SpacePacket, R'n'B and Anonymous: 1

- **Subterfuge** *Source:* https://en.wikipedia.org/wiki/Subterfuge?oldid=688985755 *Contributors:* Ncox, Rich Farmbrough, Tabletop, Neelix, Gioto, KConWiki, Corrector of Spelling, AnomieBOT, RowanQuigley, ClueBot NG, Wgolf, WikiTryHardDieHard, BattyBot, 0sm0s1z and Anonymous: 1

- **TCP Gender Changer** *Source:* https://en.wikipedia.org/wiki/TCP_Gender_Changer?oldid=685684667 *Contributors:* Glenn, Rich Farmbrough, YUL89YYZ, SmackBot, Cydebot, R'n'B, DanielPharos, Erik9bot, Farazv, Palosirkka, Norvoid and Anonymous: 1

- **Tcpdump** *Source:* https://en.wikipedia.org/wiki/Tcpdump?oldid=674322030 *Contributors:* Derek Ross, Aldie, SimonP, B4hand, Edward, Kwertii, CesarB, CatherineMunro, Glenn, Nikai, Joy, Honta, ZZyXx, Pmsyyz, Gronky, Mcr314, Hooperbloob, A Karley, Guy Harris, Jeltz, Evil Monkey, Woohookitty, Brighterorange, FlaBot, Margosbot~enwiki, Mipadi, Voidxor, Gronau~enwiki, Jef poskanzer, SmackBot, Fidocancan~enwiki, Gilliam, Drewnoakes, Frap, Daniel.Cardenas, Beetstra, Kvng, Hu12, Unixguy, Raysonho, Cydebot, Thijs!bot, Jdm64, SpacePacket, Druiloor, Isilanes, NapoliRoma, Rich257, Nevit, VasilievVV, Prolixium, VVVBot, Enigmatarius, Vjardin, Pxma, Ngriffeth, Kl4m-AWB, M4gnum0n, SF007, Legatofdarkness, Deineka, Addbot, Mortense, V-Teq~enwiki, AgadaUrbanit, Luckas-bot, Materialscientist, Sharhalakis, GrouchoBot, My007ms, MastiBot, Jesse V., Jfmantis, Shilpi2809, Staszek Lem, ChuispastonBot, ClueBot NG, Timothyjaden, BattyBot, Never.min, Doors5678, Frosty, P aria2006, Ofp1979 and Anonymous: 53

- **Tcptrace** *Source:* https://en.wikipedia.org/wiki/Tcptrace?oldid=687730021 *Contributors:* Joy, Lvl, Guy Harris, Rwendland, RJFJR, SteinbDJ, Josh Parris, Intgr, SmackBot, Bluebot, Jgrahn, Cydebot, Alaibot, Jdm64, MarshBot, Goldenrowley, NapoliRoma, Swaq, M4gnum0n, Alemayehu Mekuria, Palosirkka, ChrisGualtieri, Workforit, Ofp1979 and Anonymous: 8

- **Telecom network protocol analyzer** *Source:* https://en.wikipedia.org/wiki/Telecom_network_protocol_analyzer?oldid=535320743 *Contributors:* Glenn, RHaworth, RussBot, Irnavash, Peter Chastain, Cab.jones, Addbot, Alvin Seville, Erik9bot, AdventurousSquirrel and Anonymous: 1

- **Traceroute** *Source:* https://en.wikipedia.org/wiki/Traceroute?oldid=679113719 *Contributors:* PierreAbbat, Shii, Ixfd64, Zeno Gantner, Haakon, Snoyes, PeterBrooks, Nikai, Cherkash, [212], Htaccess, Dysprosia, ErikStewart, Joy, Finlay McWalter, Denelson83, RedWolf, Jrash, Massysett, Peruvianllama, Digital infinity, Sdfisher, MJaap~enwiki, AlistairMcMillan, Khalid hassani, Tagishsimon, MSTCrow, Pgan002, Yath, Thomas Springer, Beland, Dnas, Kooo, Kbh3rd, Janaagaard, Nabber00, CanisRufus, Sietse Snel, Femto, Mooses, Wrs1864, JohnyDog, Gary, Guy Harris, Kotasik, Burn, Wtmitchell, Blaxthos, Ott, Weyes, Briansp~enwiki, Cbustapeck, Dionyziz, LimoWreck, Bilbo1507, AlisonW, Aapo Laitinen, Aegicen~enwiki, FlaBot, Gurch, Quuxplusone, Intgr, Fresheneesz, Ramorum, Spasemunki, Shaggyjacobs, YurikBot, Borgx, Rowan Moore, Ibc111, Hm2k, Mortein, Larsinio, Calvin08, Mdwyer, GrinBot~enwiki, SmackBot, Lcarsdata, Samdutton, Anastrophe, Mauls, Xaosflux, Gilliam, Oli Filth, Robocoder, JonHarder, Wes!, DGerman, Krich, Rajrajmarley, Martijn Hoekstra, Warren, Mion, Zac67, Mike the k, Harryboyles, Erwin, Meco, Sreeji~enwiki, Pwforaker, Mylogon, StephenFalken, JForget, Anon user, T23c, Equendil, Cydebot, Playphil, A876, Fl, DumbBOT, Cosmonaut3030, Ryanmshea, Ebrahim, Thijs!bot, Electron9, Druiloor, Dawnseeker2000, Northumbrian, AntiVandalBot, Widefox, Nikolas Karalis, AndreasWittenstein, Dman727, JAnDbot, Jahoe, Salinix, Freshacconci, JamesBWatson, Kgfleischmann, RockMFR, Rotationx, CFCF, Slogsweep, TimurFriedman, MKoltnow, Bonadea, Tasior~enwiki, Er.punit, Trismegister, Akrycek, CardinalDan, Breante, Philip Trueman, Jmath666, Billinghurst, Jhawkinson, Kbrose, Dusti, VVVBot, Adrian13, Lightmouse, HighInBC, Kathleen.wright5, Stepshep, Eeekster, Jotterbot, Versus22, Johnuniq, Jovianeye, Skarebo, Dsimic, Addbot, Mortense, Ghettoblaster, D0762, Favonian, HerculeBot, GDR!, Matt.T, Legobot, Luckas-bot, Themfromspace, THEN WHO WAS PHONE?, AnomieBOT, Vikasminda, Materialscientist, Xqbot, Cybjit, White rotten rabbit, FrescoBot, Dilic, Josefnpat, I dream of horses, Todd Peng, Viritrudis, Ayeowch, Yappy2bhere, EmausBot, GoingBatty, Weylin.piegorsch, ZéroBot, MessiFCB, ClueBot NG, Nimiew, Strcat, BG19bot, Pine, Mark Arsten, Chmarkine, Thenor, MrBill3, GoShow, TheJJJunk, Codename Lisa, Shierro, Rlcw0630, Richman35, TheoryCloud, Abhisatya, Ciscozine, WikiJackool, Vieque, Moltonlava, Tacmamaeujnayn, Batmanaz23, Ajiratech, Uwinsoftware and Anonymous: 203

- **University Toolkit** *Source:* https://en.wikipedia.org/wiki/University_Toolkit?oldid=538546877 *Contributors:* Samsara, Klemen Kocjancic, Rich Farmbrough, Phuzion, SF007, DumZiBoT, Addbot, Dawynn, Yobot and Shire Reeve

- **URL Snooper** *Source:* https://en.wikipedia.org/wiki/URL_Snooper?oldid=681050275 *Contributors:* Scott, Polluks, Armando, SmackBot, Xaosflux, Inukjuak, Cydebot, Addbot, KaiKemmann, DrTrigon, Deleteduser2015, WikiU2013 and Anonymous: 3

- **W3af** *Source:* https://en.wikipedia.org/wiki/W3af?oldid=675145518 *Contributors:* Edward, Jwbrown77, Thorwald, Danhash, Moe Epsilon, JLaTondre, Cydebot, LittleBenW, Jojalozzo, DanielPharos, Mortense, Yobot, LilHelpa, Pradameinhoff, Nameless23, FrescoBot, Andres.riancho, ClueBot NG, WhitehatGuru, Dexbot, Rezonansowy, Codename Lisa and Anonymous: 9

- **WarVOX** *Source:* https://en.wikipedia.org/wiki/WarVOX?oldid=683199475 *Contributors:* Cydebot, DanielPharos, Yobot, Pradameinhoff, Nameless23, VernoWhitney, VWBot and Anonymous: 1

- **Weplab** *Source:* https://en.wikipedia.org/wiki/Weplab?oldid=607071351 *Contributors:* Marudubshinki, Dialectric, Letsmakemybed, SmackBot, CBRQ, Gmags2003, JohnCD, Jesse Viviano, Fabian.a, Bubba hotep, AnomieBOT, Dvaer, BattyBot and Anonymous: 1

- **Wireshark** *Source:* https://en.wikipedia.org/wiki/Wireshark?oldid=688981844 *Contributors:* Caltrop, Ixfd64, Julesd, Glenn, Jonik, Schneelocke, Bevo, Garo, Nurg, Mattflaschen, Pabouk, Rich Farmbrough, Plugwash, Sole Soul, Tmh, Richi, Wrs1864, Guy Harris, Diego Moya, Hohum, H2g2bob, Kenyon, Mindmatrix, Kgrr, GregorB, Macaddct1984, 74s181, Mandarax, Reisio, Casey Abell, FlaBot, Intgr, Ahunt, Windharp, Sceptre, PS2pcGAMER, Jeremy Visser, Wknight94, SmackBot, John Lunney, Imz, Faisal.akeel, Bjelleklang, Eskimbot, Thumperward, Sloanr, Jerome Charles Potts, ADobkin, Frap, Max David, Chlewbot, Ortzinator, DylanW, Xlaran, Harryboyles, Guyjohnston, Ktdreyer, Peyre, Courcelles, Ozzy 98, Kaze0010, HDCase, Mtthshe, Cydebot, Croikle, UncleBubba, BillWeiss, After Midnight, Thijs!bot, Jdm64, Druiloor, Escarbot, Gioto, Isilanes, Spencer, Alphachimpbot, Dreaded Walrus, JAnDbot, NapoliRoma, Gerald.combs, Flameass, .anacondabot, Eus Kevin, Cic, Japo, Edward321, CommonsDelinker, Davy p, Chevalier de la charrette, Lear's Fool, TheOtherJesse, TXiKiBoT, Jdpal, MusicScience, Mezzaluna, JoshuaGrainger, Michael Frind, EmxBot, Bentogoa, Flyer22 Reborn, Wabbit98, Kl4m-AWB, Zarkthehackeralliance, Tomwas54, Alexbot, Willyowiki, Johnuniq, SF007, DumZiBoT, Jovianeye, Deineka, Bazj, Addbot, MissFluffyCat, Mortense, Grandscribe, MrOllie, Snaily,

Legobot, Luckas-bot, DisillusionedBitterAndKnackered, Msgersch, Baron1984, 4th-otaku, AnomieBOT, Jim1138, JackieBot, Aneah, Lkt1126, Jaap Keuter, XPhenomen, GrouchoBot, Pradameinhoff, TheSameGuy, Daniel Hen, Citation bot 1, Skyerise, RedBot, MastiBot, Ivan sus77, Xadhix, McHildinger, Exarion1, Jamietw, Yuanli.H, Jesse V., Minimac, Jfmantis, Mean as custard, RjwilmsiBot, DEagleBot, RA0808, Giannisf, TuHan-Bot, Blin00, ZéroBot, GeorgeBarnick, Just4justice, L2d4y3, Senator2029, Wireshark2010, Gmt2001, ClueBot NG, Smtchahal, Star destroyer1960, Flashgordon1960, Gareth Griffith-Jones, Yourmomblah, Millermk, Fp.kumar2, Patrias, Helpful Pixie Bot, Iitywybmad, Nishant dhokte, Chmarkine, 13375up4h4x0r, Lekensteyn, Popescualin, Doors5678, Dexbot, Rezonansowy, Bgibbs2, Bdimcheff, Ginsuloft, Spyderbro, Titokhanmod, ScotXW, Ethereal Static, Nancy.liu611, Ofp1979, Mfnpka, Sahu987456321, ITguyABC, Sdxu, Nathandelhaye, Grzaks, Jdc5394, KasparBot, Gomes151992 and Anonymous: 174

- **Xplico** *Source:* https://en.wikipedia.org/wiki/Xplico?oldid=687730819 *Contributors:* Bearcat, Rwalker, PKT, Addbot, Citation bot, Cnwilliams, John of Reading, SporkBot, BG19bot, ArticlesForCreationBot, BattyBot, TheCascadian, Baummc88, Captain Conundrum, ScotXW and Anonymous: 8

- **Xymon** *Source:* https://en.wikipedia.org/wiki/Xymon?oldid=689694597 *Contributors:* Stephen, Goldfndr, Jccleaver, Xaosflux, FalconZero, Derek R Bullamore, Cydebot, Widefox, Leftcase, Seb7, JackPotte, Winterst, LittleWink, John of Reading, Palosirkka, Rsercher, BG19bot, Ramesh Ramaiah, BattyBot, Waffle Runoff and Anonymous: 8

- **Zx Sniffer** *Source:* https://en.wikipedia.org/wiki/Zx_Sniffer?oldid=607071414 *Contributors:* Orzetto, TheParanoidOne, Guy Harris, Oleg Alexandrov, Melancholie, Dialectic, Druid of nature, Frap, Hteen, 16@r, Cydebot, Jdm64, ImageRemovalBot, Addbot, AnomieBOT, BattyBot and Anonymous: 1

94.2.2 Images

- **File:AdRem_Software_2015_Logo.png** *Source:* https://upload.wikimedia.org/wikipedia/en/1/15/AdRem_Software_2015_Logo.png *License:* Fair use *Contributors:* https://www.facebook.com/AdRemSoftware *Original artist:* ?

- **File:AirSnortScreenshot.JPG** *Source:* https://upload.wikimedia.org/wikipedia/commons/8/81/AirSnortScreenshot.JPG *License:* Public domain *Contributors:* Transferred from en.wikipedia to Commons. *Original artist:* Morgabra at English Wikipedia

- **File:Aircrack-ng-new-logo.jpg** *Source:* https://upload.wikimedia.org/wikipedia/en/c/c3/Aircrack-ng-new-logo.jpg *License:* Fair use *Contributors:*
http://www.aircrack-ng.org/resources/aircrack-ng-new-logo.jpg *Original artist:* ?

- **File:Ambox_important.svg** *Source:* https://upload.wikimedia.org/wikipedia/commons/b/b4/Ambox_important.svg *License:* Public domain *Contributors:* Own work, based off of Image:Ambox scales.svg *Original artist:* Dsmurat (talk · contribs)

- **File:Ambox_wikify.svg** *Source:* https://upload.wikimedia.org/wikipedia/commons/e/e1/Ambox_wikify.svg *License:* Public domain *Contributors:* Own work *Original artist:* penubag

- **File:Ao-logo-whitebg.jpg** *Source:* https://upload.wikimedia.org/wikipedia/en/f/f5/Ao-logo-whitebg.jpg *License:* Fair use *Contributors:*
The logo is from the accelops.net website.
Original artist: ?

- **File:ArpON_logo.png** *Source:* https://upload.wikimedia.org/wikipedia/commons/8/8b/ArpON_logo.png *License:* CC BY-SA 3.0 *Contributors:* Own work *Original artist:* Spikeyrock

- **File:Ashunt.png** *Source:* https://upload.wikimedia.org/wikipedia/commons/5/5b/Ashunt.png *License:* CC BY 3.0 *Contributors:* Foob44r (talk) (Uploads) *Original artist:* Foob44r at en.wikipedia

- **File:Bus_icon.svg** *Source:* https://upload.wikimedia.org/wikipedia/commons/c/ca/Bus_icon.svg *License:* Public domain *Contributors:* No machine-readable source provided. Own work assumed (based on copyright claims). *Original artist:* No machine-readable author provided. Booyabazooka assumed (based on copyright claims).

- **File:Clarified-Logo.png** *Source:* https://upload.wikimedia.org/wikipedia/en/5/54/Clarified-Logo.png *License:* Fair use *Contributors:*
https://www.clarifiednetworks.com/Logos *Original artist:* ?

- **File:Cmd-ping.png** *Source:* https://upload.wikimedia.org/wikipedia/commons/c/cf/Cmd-ping.png *License:* Public domain *Contributors:* Own work *Original artist:* Cristianzambrano

- **File:Commons-logo.svg** *Source:* https://upload.wikimedia.org/wikipedia/en/4/4a/Commons-logo.svg *License:* ? *Contributors:* ? *Original artist:* ?

- **File:Computer-aj_aj_ashton_01.svg** *Source:* https://upload.wikimedia.org/wikipedia/commons/d/d7/Desktop_computer_clipart_-_Yellow_theme.svg *License:* CC0 *Contributors:* https://openclipart.org/detail/105871/computeraj-aj-ashton-01 *Original artist:* AJ from openclipart.org

- **File:Edit-clear.svg** *Source:* https://upload.wikimedia.org/wikipedia/en/f/f2/Edit-clear.svg *License:* Public domain *Contributors:* The *Tango! Desktop Project*. *Original artist:*
The people from the Tango! project. And according to the meta-data in the file, specifically: "Andreas Nilsson, and Jakub Steiner (although minimally)."

- **File:Fiddler_after_loading_Wikipedia.png** *Source:* https://upload.wikimedia.org/wikipedia/en/7/79/Fiddler_after_loading_Wikipedia.png *License:* ? *Contributors:*
This screenshot is taken and uploaded by Remember the dot (talk · contribs) on 16 January 2007. *Original artist:* ?

- **File:Fiddler_logo.png** *Source:* https://upload.wikimedia.org/wikipedia/en/b/b7/Fiddler_logo.png *License:* Fair use *Contributors:*
http://www.fiddlertool.com/fiddler/ *Original artist:* ?

- **File:SubterfugeLogo.png** *Source:* https://upload.wikimedia.org/wikipedia/en/e/e3/SubterfugeLogo.png *License:* Fair use *Contributors:* https://code.google.com/p/subterfuge/logo?cct=1331828244 *Original artist:* ?

- **File:Symbol_list_class.svg** *Source:* https://upload.wikimedia.org/wikipedia/en/d/db/Symbol_list_class.svg *License:* Public domain *Contributors:* ? *Original artist:* ?

- **File:Symbol_neutral_vote.svg** *Source:* https://upload.wikimedia.org/wikipedia/en/8/89/Symbol_neutral_vote.svg *License:* Public domain *Contributors:* ? *Original artist:* ?

- **File:System-installer.svg** *Source:* https://upload.wikimedia.org/wikipedia/commons/d/db/System-installer.svg *License:* Public domain *Contributors:* The Tango! Desktop Project *Original artist:* The people from the Tango! project

- **File:Tcpdump.png** *Source:* https://upload.wikimedia.org/wikipedia/commons/6/6f/Tcpdump.png *License:* CC-BY-SA-3.0 *Contributors:* Free software snapshot. Own work. *Original artist:* Nevit Dilmen (<a href='//commons.wikimedia.org/wiki/User_talk:Nevit' title='User talk: Nevit'>talk</a>)

- **File:Text_document_with_red_question_mark.svg** *Source:* https://upload.wikimedia.org/wikipedia/commons/a/a4/Text_document_with_red_question_mark.svg *License:* Public domain *Contributors:* Created by bdesham with Inkscape; based upon Text-x-generic.svg from the Tango project. *Original artist:* Benjamin D. Esham (bdesham)

- **File:Traceroute.png** *Source:* https://upload.wikimedia.org/wikipedia/commons/6/66/Traceroute.png *License:* Public domain *Contributors:* Transferred from en.wikipedia to Commons. *Original artist:* Jaho at English Wikipedia

- **File:US-FBI-ShadedSeal.svg** *Source:* https://upload.wikimedia.org/wikipedia/commons/7/70/US-FBI-ShadedSeal.svg *License:* Public domain *Contributors:* Extracted from PDF version of a DNI 100-day plan followup report (direct PDF URL here). *Original artist:* Federal Bureau of Investigation

- **File:Unbalanced_scales.svg** *Source:* https://upload.wikimedia.org/wikipedia/commons/f/fe/Unbalanced_scales.svg *License:* Public domain *Contributors:* ? *Original artist:* ?

- **File:W3af-screenshot.png** *Source:* https://upload.wikimedia.org/wikipedia/commons/1/1e/W3af-screenshot.png *License:* GPL *Contributors:* Own work *Original artist:* ?

- **File:W3af_project_logo.png** *Source:* https://upload.wikimedia.org/wikipedia/en/0/0d/W3af_project_logo.png *License:* Fair use *Contributors:* http://w3af.org *Original artist:* ?

- **File:WepLab-01.jpg** *Source:* https://upload.wikimedia.org/wikipedia/commons/b/bd/WepLab-01.jpg *License:* GPL *Contributors:* Transferred from en.wikipedia; transferred to Commons by User:IngerAlHaosului using CommonsHelper. *Original artist:* Original uploader was Fabian.a at en.wikipedia

- **File:Wiki_letter_w.svg** *Source:* https://upload.wikimedia.org/wikipedia/en/6/6c/Wiki_letter_w.svg *License:* Cc-by-sa-3.0 *Contributors:* ? *Original artist:* ?

- **File:Wikibooks-logo-en-noslogan.svg** *Source:* https://upload.wikimedia.org/wikipedia/commons/d/df/Wikibooks-logo-en-noslogan.svg *License:* CC BY-SA 3.0 *Contributors:* Own work *Original artist:* User:Bastique, User:Ramac et al.

- **File:Wikiversity-logo.svg** *Source:* https://upload.wikimedia.org/wikipedia/commons/9/91/Wikiversity-logo.svg *License:* CC BY-SA 3.0 *Contributors:* Snorky (optimized and cleaned up by verdy_p) *Original artist:* Snorky (optimized and cleaned up by verdy_p)

- **File:Wireshark_icon.svg** *Source:* https://upload.wikimedia.org/wikipedia/commons/d/df/Wireshark_icon.svg *License:* GPL *Contributors:* Transferred from en.wikipedia to Commons. *Original artist:* The original uploader was Ktdreyer at English Wikipedia

- **File:Wireshark_screenshot.png** *Source:* https://upload.wikimedia.org/wikipedia/commons/0/03/Wireshark_screenshot.png *License:* GPL *Contributors:* self-taken screenshot *Original artist:* uploader

- **File:Xymon.png** *Source:* https://upload.wikimedia.org/wikipedia/commons/0/0c/Xymon.png *License:* CC BY-SA 3.0 *Contributors:* Own work *Original artist:* JackPotte

94.2.3 Content license

- Creative Commons Attribution-Share Alike 3.0